Clements R. Markham (ed.)

The Voyages of William Baffin

weitsuechtig

Clements R. Markham (ed.)

The Voyages of William Baffin

ISBN/EAN: 9783943850796

Auflage: 1

Erscheinungsjahr: 2013

Erscheinungsort: Bremen, Deutschland

@ weitsuechtig in Access Verlag GmbH, Fahrenheitstr. 1, 28359 Bremen. Alle Rechte beim Verlag und bei den jeweiligen Lizenzgebern.

weitsuechtig

WORKS ISSUED BY

𝕮𝖍𝖊 𝕳𝖆𝖐𝖑𝖚𝖞𝖙 𝕾𝖔𝖈𝖎𝖊𝖙𝖞.

THE
VOYAGES OF WILLIAM BAFFIN.

FIRST SERIES. NO. LXIII-MDCCCLXXXI

The Honourable Sr Thomas Smith Knight, late Embassador from his Maᵗⁱᵉ to yͤ great Emperour of Russie, Gouernour of yͤ Honble and famous Societyes of Marchants tradinge to yͤ East-Indies, Muscovy; the French and Somer Ilands Company; Treasurer for Virginia: etc.

Simon Passæus sculp. Lond: Aº 1616. Jo: Woodall excu

Dawsons Photo. Sc

THE VOYAGES

OF

WILLIAM BAFFIN,

1612–1622.

EDITED,

With Notes and an Introduction,

BY

CLEMENTS R. MARKHAM, C.B., F.R.S.

BURT FRANKLIN, PUBLISHER
NEW YORK, NEW YORK

CONTENTS.

	PAGE
INTRODUCTION	i

THE FIRST RECORDED VOYAGE OF WILLIAM BAFFIN :—

Part I.—Written by John Gatonbe . . .	1
„ II.—Fragment written by Baffin himself . .	20

THE SECOND RECORDED VOYAGE OF WILLIAM BAFFIN :—

I.—A Journal written by Baffin . . .	38
II.—A Journal probably by Fotherby . . .	54
III.—A Brief Description of King James his New Land .	69
IV.—The manner of killing the Whale and the whole proceedings for performing of the Voyage . .	72

THE THIRD RECORDED VOYAGE OF WILLIAM BAFFIN :—

Narrative by Robert Fotherby . . .	80

THE FOURTH RECORDED VOYAGE OF WILLIAM BAFFIN :—

I.—Letter from Baffin to his Employers . .	103
II.—The Breefe Journall	106
III.—" A Tru Relation" by Baffin . . .	111

THE FIFTH RECORDED VOYAGE OF WILLIAM BAFFIN :—

I.—A Briefe and True Relation or Journal by Baffin .	138
II.—Baffin's Letter to Sir John Wolstenholme . .	149
III.—Baffin's Instructions	174

DISCOURSE AS TO A NORTH-WEST PASSAGE :—

Briefe Discourse of the Probabilitie of a Passage . .	155
Story of Thomas Cowles as to what he heard at Lisbon .	160
Note by Michael Lok on Discoveries of Juan de Fuca .	161
Treatise by Henry Briggs	169

INDEX	176

ILLUSTRATIONS.

Portrait of Sir Thomas Smith . . . *Frontispiece*

Map of the Coast of Arabia, and entrance to the Persian Gulf . xliii

Series of Five Maps to Illustrate the History of the Delineation of Baffin's Bay :—

> I.—From the Circumpolar Chart of Luke Fox, 1635 .
> II.—From Hexham's Edition of Hondius, 1636 .
> III.—From Moll's Atlas, 1720 lvi
> IV.—From Daines Barrington, 1818 . .
> V.—Baffin's Bay, according to Modern Charts .

Part of the West Coast of Greenland . . . 1

West Coast of Spitzbergen 21

Facsimile of Baffin's Chart of Hudson's Strait . . 103

INTRODUCTION.

WILLIAM BAFFIN, the narratives of whose voyages are now for the first time collected in a single volume, occupies a deservedly high place in the list of our early navigators. Although he is only known to us during the last twelve years of his life, and his previous history is an absolute blank, yet the record of those later achievements secures for him an honourable niche in England's temple of fame. He was a daring seaman, a scientific observer, and a great discoverer.

I propose, in this Introduction, to consider Baffin's position successively in those three capacities. But it will, I believe, be alike an act of justice to those who enabled Baffin to perform his work, and conducive to a more thorough appreciation of that work, if I devote my opening pages to a notice of the grand old Merchant Adventurers, who were the munificent patrons of discovery during the Elizabethan age.

Baffin gratefully immortalised the names of the generous patrons who set forth the voyages in which he served; of Sir Thomas Smith, Sir Francis Jones, Sir Dudley Digges, Sir John Wolstenholme, and Sir James Lancaster; and among these pillars of

England's commercial greatness, Sir Thomas Smith takes the foremost rank. To his wisdom and patriotism, to his disinterested zeal for discovery, and adventurous boldness, the marvellous extension of our trade, and the honour of many of our maritime exploits, are mainly due.

Thomas Smith of Westenhanger, in Kent, better known as "Customer Smith", was the son of a yeoman, of long descent in Wiltshire, and was for many years one of the Farmers of the Queen's Customs. By his wife Alice, daughter of the Lord Mayor, Sir Andrew Judd, he had four sons who survived him, and three daughters. Alice Judd was descended from Sir Robert Chicheley, through whom her children were Founder's Kin of All Souls, and she was a first cousin of Sir Henry Cromwell, grandfather of the great Protector.[1] Customer Smith died in 1591, and was buried at Ashford. Of his four sons, the eldest, Sir John of Westenhanger and Ashford, was father of Thomas Smythe, first Viscount Strangford. His line became extinct with that accomplished geographer, the eighth Viscount, who was Vice-President of the Royal Geographical Society, and died in 1869. Sir Thomas, the second son, was the Merchant Adventurer. Simon, the third, was slain at Cadiz in 1597. The fourth, Sir

---

[1] Sir Thomas Murfin, Lord Mayor, had a daughter Alice, wife of Sir Andrew Judd and mother of Alice, who married "Customer" Smith; and another daughter, Frances, who married Sir Richard Williams, alias Cromwell, and was mother of Sir Henry Cromwell of Hinchinbrook, and great grandmother of Oliver Cromwell.

Richard Smythe, was of Leeds Castle, which his daughter sold to Sir Thomas Colepepper of Hollingbourne. Of the three daughters, Catharine married Sir Rowland Hayward, Lord Mayor of London; Elizabeth married Sir Henry Fanshaw, and Jane was wife of J. Fanshaw, of Ware Park.

Thomas Smith,[1] the second son, succeeded his father as Customer to Queen Elizabeth, and became a successful London Merchant. He inherited, from his father, the manor of Bidborough, and an estate in the parish of Sutton-at-Hone, in Kent, called Brooke Place, where he built a large house. He also had another house at Deptford, and town houses in Philpot Lane, and in Gracechurch Street. He became wealthy and influential, and it was his great merit to have encouraged maritime enterprise and discovery throughout a long life, not mainly for the sake of gain, but for the honour of his country.

Sir Thomas Smith was an active Member of the Muscovy Company, and was among those adventurers who despatched the first voyages to Spitzbergen. He also took a leading part in the found-

---

[1] He must not be confused with his contemporary, the learned Sir Thomas Smith, who was born at Saffron Walden in 1514, and whose life was written by Strype. This Sir Thomas Smith was of Queen's College, Cambridge. In conjunction with Cheke he brought in a new way of pronouncing Greek, and was University Orator. He was Secretary of State in the reign of Edward VI, sent ambassador to France by Queen Elizabeth, again Secretary of State in 1572, and died in 1577. He must have been many years the senior of his namesake the Merchant Adventurer. His descendant is Sir W. Bowyer Smijth, Bart., of Hill Hall, in Essex.

ation of the East India Company, and was elected its first Governor in 1600. He was Sheriff of London in the same year, and was knighted by James I, at the Tower, on May 13th, 1603. In 1604, he was sent Ambassador to Muscovy, sailing in June, and arriving at Archangel on the 22nd of July. Thence he proceeded to Moscow, and succeeded in obtaining privileges for English merchants from Boris Godunof.[1] He returned in the following year, and was afterwards employed, on several occasions, in affairs of State connected with commerce.

Sir Thomas Smith was re-elected Governor of the East India Company in 1607, and again in 1609; when, for his great services, and for having procured the first and second charters, a sum of £500 was voted for his acceptance. But he refused to take the oath of Governor until the Company took back £250. "The residue his Worship kindly yielded to take." The East India Company flourished mightily under his wise and energetic administration; and in 1610, the largest merchant vessel that had ever been built, was launched in presence of the King. She was named by James I, the "Trade's Increase", and at the same time his Majesty, with his own hands, placed a gold chain, worth £200, with his portrait hanging to it, round the neck of Sir Thomas Smith.

[1] The narrative of the Embassy was published unknown to Sir Thomas Smith and without his consent. "*Sir Thomas Smith's Voyage and Entertainment in Russia, with the Tragical Ends of Two Emperors and One Empress within one month of his being there*," London, 1605. See also *Purchas*, iii, 747.

The great Merchant Adventurer, while thus developing the trade with India, was ever mindful of Arctic discovery. As a manager of the Muscovy Company, he despatched Jonas Poole to Spitzbergen, in 1609; and he had previously induced the East India Company to send Captain Weymouth in search of a North-West Passage, in 1602. But there were men of less patriotic aims in the direction; and when Weymouth returned unsuccessful, it was resolved that the attempt should utterly be left off. Sir Thomas Smith was, however, a true friend to Arctic discovery, through good report and evil report. He resolutely and persistently advocated the glorious cause, and at length, in 1611, he once more induced the East India Company to adventure £300 towards the discovery of the North-West Passage. Again, "the business did not succeed according to desire". Still, Sir Thomas remained true. In 1614, he urged the Company "not to refuse to adventure again, somewhat more, considering it were dishonourable to withdraw from so worthy a work". Grudgingly it was resolved to adventure £200, "so that there may be no expectation of any further supply".

But, in the meanwhile, a new Company had been formed in 1612, with the special object of Arctic discovery, and Sir Thomas Smith became its first Governor. It was called "the Company of Merchants of London, Discoverers of the North-West Passage", and Sir Thomas gathered round him, as colleagues, Sir James Lancaster, Sir Dudley Digges,

Sir William Cockayne, Sir Francis Jones, Sir John Wolstenholme, Richard Wyche, Ralph Freeman, and William Stone, all names well known in Arctic geography. They had already, before they were actually formed into a Company, despatched Henry Hudson, in 1610, on his last fatal voyage; and in 1612, Sir Thomas Button's expedition started, under the special patronage of Henry, Prince of Wales. The voyages of Bylot and Baffin followed.

Both Arctic discovery and Indian trading ventures received the unceasing and laborious attention of Sir Thomas Smith during many years, and he wore himself out by his incessant work in the service of the great trading Companies. In 1615, he was again re-elected Governor of the East India Company; again, in 1618, though old, and wishing to retire; and again, in 1620, by special wish of the King. His house at Deptford was accidentally burnt to the ground in 1619, nothing being saved, except the people, who escaped narrowly. He was at the very time engaged, with Sir Dudley Carleton, in negotiating with Commissioners from the States General, on matters relating to trade. He feasted them in his house in London, in July 1619.

At length, in July 1621, Sir Thomas Smith was allowed to retire from the Governorship of the East India Company, after serving for upwards of twenty years. He resigned from weakness and old age; after having created and fully established the prosperity of a famous body which, in after years, was destined to found a great Empire. Sir Thomas had himself adventured £20,000; he had closely attended to details respecting the equipment of ships, training of officers, and regulation of trade; and had instilled his own enthusiasm, and desire to advance the honour as well as the wealth of his country, into the Company's servants. He encouraged the scientific branches of a seaman's profession, and lectures on navigation were delivered at his house by Dr. Hood,[1] and Edward Wright. At the same time, he was careful to ensure the permanent record of the voyages sent out under his auspices, by furnishing historical materials to Hakluyt, and afterwards to Purchas. He was the perfect model of an enlightened and patriotic Merchant Adventurer, a type which has now, alas! disappeared from this country.

Sir Thomas Smith died on the 4th of September 1625, and was buried in the church of Sutton-at-Hone, in Kent. A monument to his memory may still be seen in the south aisle, with the following inscription :—

M. S.

To the glorie of God and to ye pious
Memorie of the ho^{nble} Sr *Thomas Smith* Kt.

(late *Gouernour* of ye East-Indian Muscovia French and Sommer-Island *Companies: Treasvrer* for the Virginian Plantations : Prime Vndertaker in the year 1612 for that noble Designe the Discouerie of the *North-West Passage:* Principall *Comissioner* for the London-expedition against y^e *Pirates*: and for a Voiage to ye Ryver *Senega* upon ye Coast of *Africa*: one of ye cheefe Comis-

---

[1] The speech made by Dr. Hood in the house of Sir Thomas Smith in Gracechurch Street, in November 1588, was published in the same year. There is a copy in the British Museum.

sioners for y͏e Nauie-Roial and sometime *Ambassadour* from y͏e Matie of Gr. *Brit.* to y͏e Emperour and great Duke of *Russia* and Moscovia etc.) who hauinge iudiciously, conscionably, and with admirable facility managed many difficult and weighty affairs to y͏e honour and profit of this *Nation* rested from his labours the 4th day of Septem. 1625, and his soul returning to Him that gaue it, his body was here laid vp in y͏e hope of a blessed Resurrection.

> " From those large *Kingdomes* where the Svn doth rise;
> From that rich newefound-world that westward lies;
> From *Volga* to the floud of *Amazons;*
> From vnder both the *Poles,* and all the *Zones;*
> From all the famous *Ryuers, Landes,* and *Seas,*
> Betwixt this *Place* and our *Anti-Podes;*
> He gott intelligence, what might be found
> To giue contentment, through this massie *Round.*
> But finding earthly things did rather tire
> His longing *Soul,* then answer her desire;
> To this obscured Village he withdrewe :
> From hence his Heauenlie *Voiage* did pursue.
> Here, sum'd vp all, and when his *Gale* of Breath,
> Had left becalmed in the *Port of Death,*
> The soules fraile *Barke* (and safe had landed her
> Where *Faith* his *Factor,* and his *Harbinger*
> Made place before), he did (no doubt) obtaine
> That wealth wch here on Earth wee seek in vain."

There was a portrait of Sir Thomas Smith, engraved by Simon Passe.[1] The original print is very

---

[1] Simon Passe, the son of another famous engraver, Nicholas Passe, a native of Utrecht, was employed by Hilliard, and was ten years in England. His father, whose works are numerous, was in England for several years, and drew many of his portraits from life. This was also the practice of Simon Passe, whose earliest works were James I and his Queen, Prince Henry with a lance, Raleigh, Buck, Gondomar, Archbishop Abbot. He also engraved the Earl and Countess of Somerset, the Earls of Arundel, Dorset, and Pembroke, Sir E. Cecil and Sir T. Smith.

rare. Its date is 1617. It is bound up in the Grenville copy of the embassy to Russia, and in some copies of the *Surgeon's Mate*, a book dedicated to Sir Thomas Smith, and published in 1617. It is a half length figure, in hat, ruff, and furred robe, holding a map in the left hand, with the words— "Russia" and "Oceanus" on it. A second, and very inferior edition, appeared in 1707. The portrait which forms the frontispiece of the present volume is taken from the copy in the Grenville library.

Sir Thomas Smith was married three times. His first wife was Judith, daughter of Richard Culverwell. I have not been able to ascertain the name of the second; but the third was Sarah, daughter of William Blunt. She was the mother of his children, and she married secondly Robert Sydney, Earl of Leicester. There were two sons born to Sir Thomas Smith and Sarah Blunt. The eldest, Sir John Smyth, succeeded to Brooke Place, in the parish of Sutton-at-Hone, and married Isabella Rich, a daughter of Sir Philip Sydney's "Stella". The second son married another daughter of "Stella" by the Lord Mountjoy, in November 1618, but he left England in the following year, under some cloud. The male descendants of Sir Thomas Smith became extinct, on the death of the Chief Baron, Sir Sydney Stafford Smythe, in 1778.[1]

[1] The eldest son of Sir Thomas Smith, Sir John Smyth of Brooke Place, had, by Isabella Rich, a son, Robert, and a daughter, Isabella, married to John, Lord Robartes of Truro, in 1646. Robert Smythe (for he adopted this way of spelling the name) of Brooke

One of the most active among Sir Thomas Smith's colleagues, in the encouragement of maritime enterprise, was Alderman Francis Jones. This Merchant Adventurer was of a Shropshire family, citizen and haberdasher of London, Alderman of Aldgate Ward, and Lord Mayor. He was also one of the Farmers of Customs, and was knighted on March 12th 1617. He resided at Welford, and had a town house in the city, in the parish of St. Andrew Undershaft. Sir Francis died at Welford, in 1622.

A still more eminent encourager of Arctic enterprise, and one who should take rank next to Sir Thomas Smith, although he was a much younger man, was Sir Dudley Digges. He came of an eminently learned and accomplished family. Roger Digge was living at Mildenhall, in Suffolk, in the reign of Henry III, and his descendant, James Digges, came to Kent, and settled at Digges Court, in Barham. Here his son Leonard, the grandfather of Sir Dudley Digges, was born. Educated at Uni-

Place, married in 1652 the Lady Dorothy Sydney, widow of that Earl of Sunderland who was slain at the battle of Newbury in 1643. She was born in 1620, and was the "Saccharissa" of the poet Waller. By this marriage there was one son, Robert Smythe, Governor of Dover Castle, who died in 1698. By Catherine, daughter of William Stafford of Blatherwicke, he had a son, Henry Smythe, married to Elizabeth, daughter of Dr. Lloyd, Canon of Windsor. Henry sold Brooke Place in 1699 to Sir John le Thuillier, who pulled down the old house built by Sir Thomas Smith. Dying in 1706, Henry Smythe left an only child, Sydney Stafford Smythe, who was called to the bar in 1728, was Chief Baron in 1772, and died childless in 1778. Thus the male line of Sir Thomas Smith became extinct.

versity College, Oxford, Leonard became an accomplished mathematician, architect, and surveyor. He was the author of several learned works,[1] some of which were edited by his son. Leonard Digges, who was of Wootton Court, in Kent, married Bridget, sister of those two gallant soldiers, James and Thomas Wilford, by whom he had a son Thomas. He died in 1574. This Thomas Digges inherited his father's tastes, and was one of the most eminent mathematicians of his time. He was Muster Master to the Queen's Army in the Netherlands from 1585, and prepared exhaustive reports on several important military positions, and on their fortification, with plans. Thomas Digges was as remarkable for his piety as for his learning.[2] He married Agnes, daughter of Sir William St. Leger, by Ursula, daughter of George Neville, Lord Abergavenny, by whom he had a son Dudley, and a daughter Margaret, married to Sir Anthony Palmer. The

[1] He wrote *Tectonicum*, a book on land surveying, 4to., 1556; second edition, edited by his son, 1592; third edition, 1597. Also, *Pantometria*, a geometrical treatise, published by his son, folio, 1591; and *Prognostication*, rules to judge the weather by sun, moon, and stars, 1555; new edition by his son, 1592.

[2] His works were, *Alae sive Scalae Mathematicae*, 4to., 1573; *Arithmetical Military Treatise*, 4to., 1579; "*Stratioticos*, a geometrical treatise requisite for the practice of soldiers", begun by his father. At the end there is a report of the proceedings of the Earl of Leicester for the relief of Sluys, from his arrival at Flushing in June 1587, proving that his Excellency was not in fault for the loss of the town, 4to., 1579, second edition, 1590; *Perfect Description of the Celestial Orbs*, 4to., 1599; *England's Defence*, a treatise concerning invasion, written 1589, published 1686, folio.

great mathematician died on August 24th, 1595, and was buried in the church of St. Mary's, Aldermanbury. His monument was destroyed in the great fire of London, but the inscription is preserved in Strype's edition of Stowe.

Dudley Digges was born in 1583, and was educated at his grandfather's old college at Oxford, under Dr. Abbot, afterwards Archbishop of Canterbury. He took his degree in 1601, studied at the Inns of Court, travelled on the Continent, and was knighted on his return. In 1615, Sir Dudley Digges published a reply to an attack on the East India Company,[1] in which he gave an interesting account of their ships, and of the progress of their trade; and from this time he appears to have been intimately connected with Sir Thomas Smith's projects, and to have been his friend and worthy disciple. Sir Dudley was sent on an Embassy to Russia, in 1618, and an account of his voyage to Archangel is preserved in manuscript at Oxford.[2]

---

[1] *The Defence of Trade, in a Letter to Sir Thomas Smith, Knight, Governor of the East India Company, from one of that Societie*, London, 1615, pp. 50; signed "Dudley Digges". It is a reply to a pamphlet entitled, *Increase of Trade*.

[2] *MS. Ashmole*, vol. 824, xvi, p. 175. "A Viag of Ambasad undertaken by the Right Honnorable Sr Dudlie Diggs in the year 1618." The narrative commences with the embassy leaving the Thames in June 1618. The ship reached Archangel on July 14th, sailed for England again on August 5th, and reached St. Katherine's, near London, on the 22nd. The manuscript ends with notes on "Things by me observed", describing the Samoyeds, the houses, carts, farms, and vegetation round Archangel, and the Russian boats and sailing vessels. Pp. 22.

Next he was employed, in 1620, at the Hague, to obtain restitution of goods taken by the Dutch from English merchants in the East Indies. In the following year he entered Parliament, but he was so little compliant with Court measures, that he was sent to Ireland on a commission, but really as a punishment. He was again returned to Parliament, for the county of Kent, in 1626, and was one of the eight chief managers of the charges against the Duke of Buckingham, the others being Sir John Eliot, Pym, Selden, Wandesford, Glanvile, Sherland, and Herbert. Sir Dudley Digges, by way of prologue, made a short and eloquent speech, and read the preamble of the charges, while Sir John Eliot's speech concluded the impeachment. For these bold measures, both Sir Dudley Digges and Sir John Eliot were committed to the Tower, by command of Charles I. Buckingham accused Archbishop Abbot of instigating Sir Dudley and, in reply, the good old man spoke manfully in favour of his former pupil. "Ever since the days of Queen Elizabeth", he said, "I have been nearly acquainted with him. He was my pupil at Oxford, and a very towardly one. He calleth me father, and I call his wife my daughter, his eldest son is my godson, and their children are, in love, accounted my children." Digges continued to uphold the rights of the people. In 1627, he was appointed by the Commons to manage a conference with the Lords respecting the resolutions touching the liberty of the subject, and the right of every man to a writ of Habeas Corpus.

He opened the proceedings with an introductory historical speech of great ability, and was followed by Selden, Littleton, and Cook. In 1628 he was a member of another conference respecting the Petition of Right, and he boldly protested against the King's command to the Speaker, that no member should speak against the Government.[1] In April 1636, Sir Dudley Digges succeeded Sir Julius Cæsar as Master of the Rolls, and he died on March 18th, 1639.[2]

Sir Dudley Digges married Mary, daughter of Sir Thomas Kempe, the heiress of Chilham, near Canterbury; where he built a stately mansion. His wife was a kinswoman of Sir Thomas Smith, both being descendants of Philippa Chicheley, and therefore founder's kin of All Souls. Sir Dudley and Lady Digges had ten children, of whom the eldest, Thomas Digges, succeeded to Chilham, married Mary, daughter of Sir Maurice Abbot, and died in 1687. His son Leonard Digges died in 1718, leaving a son, Thomas, whose eldest son died at Cork in 1787. The second son, West Digges, was a well

---

[1] *Rushworth*, vol. i, pp. 55, 302, 356, 360, 361, 450, 451, 521, 527, 546, 606.

[2] Besides the *Defence of Trade*, Sir Dudley Digges was the author of the *Compleat Ambassador*, London, folio, 1665, which contains the correspondence between Sir F. Walsingham, Burleigh, Leicester, and others respecting the two treaties of the intended marriage of Queen Elizabeth. The frontispiece consists of engravings by Faithorne of Elizabeth, Burleigh, and Walsingham. He also wrote, *Digiti Lingua*, the most compendious way of silent converse ever yet discovered, London, 12mo., 1693.

known comedian, and here I have lost touch of the descendants. Chilham had long before passed away to Colebrookes, Herons, Wildmans, and is now the property of Mr. Charles Stewart Hardy.[1] But the old house, built by Sir Dudley Digges, is still standing. It is beautifully situated on a hill, sloping away on every side. The village of Chilham, consisting of old-fashioned thatched houses, is built round a green, at one end the church, at the other a short avenue, leading to the old manor house. The mansion was finished in 1616, and the names of Sir Dudley Digges, and of his wife Mary Kempe, are carved over the hall door. It is a brick structure, with stone doorway and dressings, square turrets at each angle of the front, and a beautiful oriel window over the carved doorway. The two wings are at an obtuse angle to the front, a peculiar arrangement giving increased space, and the means of arranging most picturesque vistas and angles in the interior. Behind is the ancient keep of the feudal castle of the Badlesmeres, with enormously thick walls. A series of terraces with wall fruit, slope down to a well timbered park, and there are lovely views from the windows. Truly, this patriotic Merchant Adventurer, and bold asserter of his country's liberties, had a most lovely English home. Here, surrounded by wife and children, he retired from the cares of State, and here he died at the age of fifty-six.

Sir Dudley Digges was buried in Chilham church,

[1] In 1724, Thomas Digges sold Chilham to a mercer of London named Colebrooke, whose son sold it to Heron in 1775.

a cruciform edifice with double aisles. Over his grave was erected a magnificent tomb. On a square pedestal of white marble are seated four life-size female figures, and in their midst rises a pillar of black marble surmounted by an urn, with four shields of arms hanging round it.[1] On each side of the pedestal there are black marble tablets with inscriptions. That on the western side preserves the memory of Sir Dudley Digges himself, "whose death the wisest men doe reckon amongst the publique calamities of these times". On the south side there is a genealogical account of his family in Latin. The eastern tablet bears an inscription to the memory of Lady Digges, the heiress of Chilham, while the northern tablet records her virtues. Sir Dudley left £20 yearly to keep this monument in repair, the surplus to be given to the poor. The name of this noble promoter of voyages of discovery is also immortalised by the Cape, on the coast of Baffin's Bay, which is so often mentioned in modern Arctic voyages.

Baffin's most immediate patron, to whom he addressed his letters, was Sir John Wolstenholme. His father, John Wolstenholme, was a native of Derbyshire. He came up to London, and after making a fortune, established himself at Stanmore Magna, near Harrow. His son, Sir John, born in 1562, was a Farmer of the Customs, and a most active promoter of voyages for the discovery of the

[1] The arms of Digges, of Kemp, of Kemp and Digges impaled, and a fourth which I could not make out.

North-West Passage. He was knighted by James I at Whitehall, on March 12th, 1617. He built the church at Stanmore, which was consecrated by Archbishop Laud in 1632, at his sole expense. He died, aged seventy-seven, on November 25th, 1639, and was buried in Stanmore church, where there is a handsome monument to his memory. His second son, Henry, was slain in the Palatinate, while serving under Lord Vere. The eldest, Sir John, was knighted by Charles I, on May 18th, 1633. He succeeded to Nostell Priory, in Yorkshire, which had been purchased by his father. He was a great sufferer during the civil war, having joined the Royalist side, but was created a Baronet at the Restoration, and, dying in 1670, he was buried at Stanmore. His eldest son, John, who died before him, married Dorothy, the daughter of Lord Vere, and sister of Lady Fairfax, but had no children. Both were buried under a stately monument at Stanmore.[1] His second son, Henry, was slain at Marston Moor. The baronetcy became extinct with Sir Francis Wolstenholme, who died in 1780.

Sir William Cockayne, Sir James Lancaster, and Mr. Richard Ball,[2] were also among those liberal patrons of Arctic discovery whose ventures enabled the ships to be fitted out, and whose patriotic zeal

---

[1] For an account of monuments in Stanmore Church, and extracts from the registers, see Lysons' *Environs of London*, first edition, 1795, vol. iii, pp. 395-400.

[2] See notices in foot notes at page 3.

infused a similar spirit into the hearts of the gallant seamen whom they employed.

In Baffin's first recorded voyage, the wealthy adventurers wisely associated with themselves the commander of the expedition; and it is, therefore, necessary to give some account of the brave seaman in whose company our discoverer first appears. James Hall was a Yorkshireman, and almost certainly a native of Hull.[1] We first hear of him as chief pilot of an expedition sent by Christian IV, King of Denmark, to discover the lost colonies of Greenland. It consisted of three ships : the *Trost*[2] (Comfort), with the admiral on board, a Scottish officer named John Cunningham, and James Hall as chief Pilot, was the leading vessel. The second, named *Löven*, was commanded by a Dane—Godske Lindenov; and the third was a pinnace, called *Kathen*, under an Englishman named John Knight. The expedition sailed from Copenhagen, on May 2nd, 1605, and sighted Greenland on the 30th. Soon afterwards, the *Löven* parted company and went home, after hot words. The *Trost* pressed onwards, and came to land under a hill named Mount Cunningham, between the headlands which were called Capes Anne and Sophia, after the Queen and Queen Dowager of Denmark. They were in the neighbourhood of the modern Greenland settlement of Holsteinborg. The Danes had much communication with the Eskimo, and Hall gives an interesting account of them. The *Trost* and *Kathen* safely re-

---

[1] Luke Fox. [2] Purchas calls her the *Frost*.

turned to Elsinore on August 10th.[1] John Knight then went back to England, but Hall continued in the Danish service. Knight commanded an expedition in the year 1606, in which he perished. I printed the narrative of Knight's voyage, from the original manuscript at the India Office, in 1877.[2]

The King of Denmark fitted out a second expedition in 1606, consisting of five vessels. There were the *Trost* of sixty tons, with Godske Lindenov as admiral, and Hall as chief pilot; the *Löven*, of seventy tons, under John Cunningham; the *Ornen* (100 tons), commanded by a Norwegian named Hans Brun, a Scotch vessel of forty tons, called the *Gilliflower*, under Corsten Richardson, and the pinnace *Kathen*, of twenty tons, under Anders Nolk[3] of Bergen. Sailing from Copenhagen on May 27th, 1606, they were beset by mighty banks of ice, and

---

[1] Hall's account of the voyage is given in *Purchas*, iii, lib. iv, cap. xiv, p. 814. There is another brief account in a Danish work, "*Reiser til Grönland om de vigtigste reiser som i nyere tider ere foretagne fra Danmark og Norge for igjen at opsöge det tabte Grönland og at undersöge set gjenfunde*, af C. Pingel," Kjobenhavn, 1845. Pingel quotes a manuscript written on board the *Kathen*. The original is now in a quarto volume, containing various papers about Greenland, in the Royal Library at Stockholm (K. 29). The manuscript was captured by Charles X in the library of Soro in Zealand, and taken by him to Sweden. It consists of six quarto leaves, with the title, "*Sanndferdigh Berettningh om thenn Groenlanndez reise som Konng May 3 Skiff giorde*, anno 1605." It is in the form of a ship's journal, and is signed "Alexander Leyell".

[2] At the end of the Hakluyt Society's volume, *The Voyages of Sir James Lancaster, Knight, to the East Indies*, p. 281.

[3] Purchas calls him Noll.

did not reach Greenland until July, anchoring off Cunningham Fiord, to the north of Cape Sophia. The glittering mica, occurring in the gneiss, was mistaken for silver ore, and the idea of unbounded mineral wealth was indulged in by the explorers. As on the former voyage, several Eskimo were seized with their kayaks, to be taken to Denmark, and some were killed. These outrages led to fatal retaliation when Hall appeared among the Eskimo in a subsequent voyage; while the wretched captives pined away and died. The Greenland expedition returned in October 1606;[1] but King Christian still persevered. In the following year a third expedition, under Carsten Richardson, was despatched with Hall on board the *Gilliflower* as pilot, and "styrmand". But the crews mutinied, and the vessels never got beyond Iceland. Purchas had the journal of this third voyage in his possession, with curious drawings by Josias Hubert[2] of Hull, but he says that he omitted to print it because of the mutiny.[3] Christian IV then gave up his attempts to re-discover old Greenland.

James Hall consequently returned to England, eager to embark once more on discoveries in the

[1] Pingel gives a narrative written by Hans Brun, captain of the *Ornen*, of the second expedition, the manuscript of which is also in the Royal Library at Stockholm.

[2] Afterwards pilot in the *Resolution* in Sir Thomas Button's expedition.

[3] There is a brief account of this third voyage in the work of Claus Christophersen Lyschander, Royal Historiographer of Denmark, entitled, *Den Grönlandsche Chronica* (Kbhvn., 1808).

direction of Greenland, and full of ideas respecting silver ores and other mineral wealth. His faithful follower, a Scarborough lad named William Huntriss, who had accompanied him in all his voyages, and had become so proficient as a navigator that King Christian had granted him a special allowance, came back with Hall. There is, in the British Museum, a manuscript report on Hall's voyages to Greenland, with several coloured maps and sketches of coast lines, which is addressed to the King of Denmark. When Christian IV abandoned the work, Hall probably withheld this report, brought it with him to England, and presented it to King James.[1]

James Hall induced four great Merchant Princes to be venturers with him in a voyage of discovery to Greenland in 1612. His partners were Sir Thomas Smith himself, Sir James Lancaster, Sir William Cockayne, and Mr. Ball. Two vessels, called the *Patience* and the *Heart's Ease*, were fitted out at Hull, and William Baffin first appears in history as pilot on board Hall's ship, the *Patience*.

We are thus first introduced to WILLIAM BAFFIN as an experienced seaman, in the prime of life, and I have been baffled in all my attempts to discover even a single fact respecting his former history. The name is very uncommon, and I am indebted to the

[1] *MS. Bibl. Reg.*, 17 A, xlviii, p. 261. The manuscript contains a narrative, a coloured map of King Christian's Fiord in Greenland, another of Cunningham's Fiord, a third of Brade Ranson's Fiord, a fourth of the "coast of Greenland, with latitudes of havens and harbours as I found them".

obliging kindness of Colonel Chester, to whose research I also owe many facts and dates relating to the Merchant Adventurers, for the very few entries where it occurs. There is no trace of the name at Hull, the place where Baffin first appears to us. From the Parish Registers of St. Margaret, Westminster, Colonel Chester has supplied me with the following entries:—

Baptized 1603. Sept. 30.   Richard, son of John Baffin.
Buried 1609. June 8.   Joseph Baffin.   *Plague.*
 „   „   22.   Elizabeth Baffin.   „
 „   July 11.   William Baffin.   „
 1612 June 8.   Margaret Baffin.   *Child.*

In the Register of the church of St. Thomas Apostle, in the city of London, there is one entry of the name.

Baptized 1609. Oct. 15.   Susan Baffen, daughter of William Baffen.

Colonel Chester has kindly looked at the indexes to his collections from parish registers and monuments, extending all over the kingdom, in more than one hundred folio volumes, comprising upwards of a million and a half of names, and the only instances of the name of Baffin are the above. We are, therefore, justified in the conclusion that it is extremely uncommon. Between 1603 and 1612, we find five individuals named Baffin, three men, a woman, and a child, dying in St. Margaret's parish, Westminster, the three adults of the plague. One is named William Baffin. A child named Richard Baffin is born in St. Margaret's parish in 1603.

Lastly, the child of a William Baffin is baptized in 1609, in the church of St. Thomas the Apostle,[1] in Vintry Ward, within the city of London. This ward includes Queenhithe, a landing-place frequented by sailors, and not an unlikely locality for a seaman to take up his abode in, while on shore.

These meagre facts lead to the conjecture that William Baffin was a native of London or Westminster, that he had relations living in the parish of St. Margaret, and that he himself had established a home for his wife, and for himself when on shore, in the city, in the parish of St. Thomas, and probably in a street near Queenhithe, where his daughter, named Susan, was born in 1609. But Baffin himself must have been constantly at sea, and probably raised himself, by his good conduct and talent, from a very humble position. I gather that Purchas intended to convey such an idea, when he speaks of Baffin as "that learned-unlearned mariner and mathematician, who, wanting art of words, so really employed himself to those industries, whereof here you see so evident fruits".[2] If he was not a Hull man, he probably was not known to Captain Hall, and it may, therefore, be conjectured that, when Hall induced the great London merchants to join in his venture, one of them recommended Baffin to him, as an accomplished seaman. Accordingly, William Baffin was chief pilot of Captain Hall's ship, the *Patience*, when, in company with the *Heart's*

---

[1] The church of St. Thomas Apostle was burnt at the great fire and was not rebuilt.   [2] See page 154.

Ease, she was hauled into Hull Road on April 10th, 1612. Andrew Barker, the master of the *Heart's Ease*, the mate, William Huntriss, and the quartermaster, John Gatonby, were all Yorkshiremen. The expedition finally left the Humber, and made sail for Greenland on the 22nd of April.

The narrative of this voyage was written by Baffin himself, though Purchas has only preserved a fragment, commencing on July 8th in Cockin Sound, on the coast of Greenland. But, in Churchill's *Collection of Voyages and Travels*, there is a journal of the voyage kept by one of the quartermasters named John Gatonby, a native of Hull, and dedicated to Sir Christopher Hildyard of Winestead. I have, therefore, printed the portion of Gatonby's journal from the commencement of the voyage to July 8th, the time when Baffin's fragment, in Purchas, commences. Thus the whole story of the voyage is presented, though only the last half is in Baffin's own words. Captain Hall himself was murdered by the Eskimo, in revenge for the kidnapping perpetrated by the Danes, with whom he served in the two previous voyages, and the expedition returned in charge of Andrew Barker. Baffin relates the events of the voyage while the ships were on the Greenland coast, including the death and burial of Hall, and concludes with some account of the Greenland Eskimo and their country. He examined the west coast, from Godthaab northward to Cunningham Fiord, and, as was his wont, made numerous astronomical observations.

As soon as he returned from Greenland, William Baffin entered the service of the Muscovy Company. This enterprising body of merchants, under the lead of Sir Thomas Smith, began to send ships to fish for whales near Spitzbergen, in 1597. In 1607 and 1608, the Company despatched Henry Hudson on his two important voyages to Spitzbergen and Novaya Zemlya. In the years 1609 and 1610, they sent Captain Jonas Pool, who carefully explored the whole of the west coast of Spitzbergen, naming Bell Sound, Ice Sound, and several other positions. He wrote interesting journals, which are given in Purchas, and had a prosperous career before him. But it was his ill-fate to be "miserably and basely murdered betwixt Ratcliffe and London", after his return in 1611. In the following year the Muscovy Company obtained a charter, excluding all others from the Spitzbergen fishery, native and foreign. The concession of this charter was followed by very high-handed proceedings on the part of the English, and in 1612 a fleet was sent out by the Muscovy Company, which drove away from the Spitzbergen coast fifteen sail of Dutch, French, and Biscayans.

It is remarkable that, although the Biscayans, when in their own ships, were hunted away, the English were obliged to learn the craft and mystery of whale fishing from Biscayans whom they entered on board their own ships. In the middle ages there was a great whale frequenting the Bay of Biscay, and the Atlantic, which is now extinct, known to naturalists as the *Balæna Biscayensis*.[1] The fishermen of Biscay and Guipuzcoa had been engaged in pursuing this whale from time immemorial, and the dangerous occupation had trained up a most expert and daring race of sailors along those coasts. A whale figures in the arms of the Guipuzcoan towns of Fuentarrabia, Guetaria, and Motrico; and the whale fishery was long the chief source of wealth to all the ports from St. Jean de Luz to Santander. The King of Spain, in conceding privileges to San Sebastian, and other whaling ports, retained his own right to a strip of blubber from the head to the foot of the whale, as the royal share.[2] But gradually the Biscayan whale became more and more scarce, and the Basque fishermen began to frequent the Newfoundland banks, where 41 vessels, and 298 boats, employing 1,470 sailors, were annually sent from Guipuzcoa and Biscay, in the early part of the seventeenth century.[3] The Biscayans were still the most expert whale fishers when the Moscovy Company began to send whaling ships to Spitzbergen, and it was the practice to enter a Basque boat's crew, from St. Jean de Luz or San Sebastian, on board one or more of the vessels of each fleet. Orders were given that they were "to be used very

[1] A complete skeleton was found in the peat of Jutland, and is now in the Museum at Copenhagen.

[2] "Et si mactaveritis aliquam ballenam detis mihi unam tiram a capite usque ad caudam sicut forum est."—*Grant of San Fernando*, 1217-1232.

[3] The privileges of the Biscayan fishermen on the Newfoundland banks were recognised by Article 15 of the Treaty of Utrecht.

kindly and friendly, being strangers, and leaving their own country to do us service". At the same time, the Biscayan vessels were forcibly driven from Spitzbergen waters.[1]

A fleet of seven ships was fitted out by the Muscovy Company in 1613, the command of which was given to Captain Benjamin Joseph. He was on board the *Tiger* of 260 tons, with William Baffin as chief pilot; and twenty-four Biscayans were engaged for the voyage. One ship of St. Jean de Luz had permission from the Company to fish, perhaps in return for the two dozen expert whalers. The English found as many as seventeen foreign ships on the Spitzbergen coast—four Dutch, two Dunkirkers, four hailing from St. Jean de Luz, and seven from San Sebastian. All submitted to the English, most were ordered away, a few being allowed to fish on condition of surrendering half their catch to the English ships. The Company's fleet returned safely in September, with full cargoes. The narrative of this voyage was written by Baffin himself, and is given in Purchas. There is a second narrative, probably by Robert Fotherby, which remained in manuscript until it was printed by the

[1] "Todavia la celebre compania de ballenas sostenia en el mayor esplendor el comercio de San Sebastian y aun de toda la provincia, empero los Ingleses, rivales de los Vascongados para alzarse en el beneficio de la pesca de las ballenas, y con tal objeto, enviaron en 1613 dos galeones armados a las costas de la Groenlandia, en cuyo punto se hacia a la sazon, abundante pesca de ballenas, y apresaron doce barcos de Guipuzcoanos."—*Madoz*, ix, p. 163.

American Antiquarian Society.[1] I have reprinted both these accounts of the voyage of 1613, one following the other. Fotherby concludes his journal by giving an interesting description of Spitzbergen, and of the whale fishery.

Baffin served again in the Spitzbergen voyage of 1614, which was also commanded by Benjamin Joseph. This time the fleet consisted of no less than eleven ships and two pinnaces. Fotherby and Baffin were together in a ship called the *Thomasine*, and the former wrote the narrative, which is given by Purchas. During the summer, very persevering attempts were made by Fotherby and Baffin to extend discovery to the eastward, along the north coast of Spitzbergen. Leaving their ship in a harbour, they provisioned two shallops, and, on several occasions advanced eastward, until they were stopped by the ice. At length, in August, they reached Wiches Sound (*Wiide Bay* of modern maps), and walked thence until they came to the entrance of Sir Thomas Smith's Inlet (Hinlopen Strait), encountering much danger on their return. Finally, the ship sailed, towards the end of the season, twenty leagues E.N.E. from Cape Barren (*Vogelsang* of the Dutch), being nine or ten leagues off shore, which brought her off Sir Thomas Smith's Inlet. Such a course and distance from Vogelsang would bring a vessel off Hinlopen Strait; and this identifies the Sir Thomas Smith's Inlet of our old navigators with the Hinlopen Strait of the Dutch. It was the

[1] For an account of this manuscript see p. 54 (*note*).

furthest point reached by Baffin. The year 1614 was very unfavourable for navigation, the ice having been close down on the north coast during the greater part of the season. Baffin returned to London on the 4th of October with the whole crew in perfect health.

After his second voyage to Spitzbergen, Baffin took service with the Company for the discovery of the North-West Passage, which was directed by Sir Thomas Smith, Sir Dudley Digges, and John Wolstenholme. These princely adventurers had, in 1610, furnished out the gallant explorer Henry Hudson, to try if, through any of those inlets which were seen by John Davis, a passage could be found. His ship was named the *Discovery*, and, after discovering the great inland sea which bears his name, and wintering on its shores, he was abandoned to his fate in an open boat, by the villainous crew. The well known story was told by a servant of Sir Dudley Digges, who remained on board, named Abacuk Prickett. The Company next sent out Sir Thomas Button, with Robert Bylot and Abacuk Prickett under him, who had both been with Hudson in his last voyage. Henry, Prince of Wales, took special interest in this expedition. Sir Thomas Button, a talented officer, was selected by the Prince, who drew up the instructions.[1] Button commanded the *Discovery*, and the second ship, under Captain Ingram, was named the *Resolution*. They sailed in

[1] The poor young Prince died on November 6th, 1612, aged eighteen years and a half, before Button returned.

May 1612, and wintered at Port Nelson, on the eastern side of Hudson's Bay. Sir Thomas Button thus made an important discovery, and he returned, in the autumn of 1613, strongly impressed with the idea that a North-West Passage existed. The *Discovery* was sent out, for a third time, under the command of Captain Gibbons, who had been with Button in the previous year. He sailed in the spring of 1614, but only reached the coast of Labrador, where he took shelter in a bay, and remained there so long that his crew named it *Gibbons his hole*. He returned home in the autumn.

This was the record of the Company's proceedings when Baffin took service under it. Three expeditions had been sent out under Hudson, Button, and Gibbons. The two first had made great discoveries, and the Company was not discouraged. The adventurers resolved to fit out the *Discovery* for a fourth voyage. Robert Bylot, who had been in the three previous voyages, was appointed master, and William Baffin was pilot of the expedition. An excellent system of keeping log books, inaugurated by Sebastian Cabot, was enforced by the Muscovy Company, and the officers of its ships were expected to take frequent astronomical observations. Baffin, who had a natural love for such work, was given an excellent training while serving under the Company in his two Spitzbergen voyages, and he continued the same admirable system in his western enterprises under the North-West Passage Company. The whole history of the expedition of 1614 was written by Baffin himself. It is printed by Purchas, but the manuscript, preserved in the British Museum, is fuller. This manuscript was first edited by Mr. Rundall, who very carefully collated it with the narrative in Purchas. Mr. Rundall's edition has now been reprinted, the matter omitted by Purchas being printed in italics, and alterations and additions, in the Purchas version, being noticed in the foot-notes.

Baffin begins with a letter addressed to his patrons, Sir Thomas Smith, Sir Dudley Digges, and Sir John Wolstenholme. He describes his method in preparing the tabulated log book, and in delineating the coast on his map, which is also preserved with the manuscript. As it is the only map, by this accomplished seaman, that has come down to us, it has been thought desirable to reproduce it, as a *facsimile*. It shows Baffin's style of drawing, and is very interesting as a real specimen of his handiwork. The letter to his employers is introductory to a tabulated log book, called *The Breefe Journall*. Then follows "A true relation of such things as happened in fourth voyage for the discovery of a passage to the North-West, performed in the yeare 1615."

In this voyage Baffin carefully examined Hudson Strait and the western end of Southampton Island. Sir Edward Parry passed over the same ground in 1821, and noticed the places named by Baffin with interest. Parry's observations on the tides confirm those of Baffin, and the latitudes of the older navigator were found to be nearly correct. On August 6th, 1821, Parry was nearly on the spot where Baffin left off his search for a passage. Baffin's reasons for relinquishing the attempt in that direction were the increased quantity of ice, the water becoming less deep, and his seeing land bearing N.E. b. E., which led him to conclude that he was at the mouth of a large bay. Parry gave this land the name of Baffin Island, "out of respect to the memory of that able and enterprising navigator". Here Parry's own discoveries commenced.[1]

Returning in the autumn of 1615, Baffin prepared for his fifth and most important Arctic voyage, during which he discovered the great bay which bears his name. The enterprise was again undertaken by Sir Thomas Smith, Sir Francis Jones, Sir Dudley Digges, and Sir John Wolstenholme, and the same good ship *Discovery*, of 55 tons, with 16 men, was fitted out, with Robert Bylot (or Bileth) as master, and William Baffin as pilot. They set sail from Gravesend on the 26th of March 1616, and on the 1st of June, having passed Hope Sanderson of Davis, they entered upon new discoveries. It is an irreparable misfortune that Baffin's papers and maps should have fallen into the hands of old Purchas. It was upwards of two centuries before the mischief done by his suppression of the journal and maps was repaired. We must, however, be thankful for what

[1] *Journal of the Second Voyage for the Discovery of a North-West Passage*, by Captain W. Edward Parry, R.N., F.R.S. Murray, 1824, p. 33.

the Rev. Samuel has spared. He printed Baffin's *Briefe and True Relation*,[1] and his interesting letter to Sir John Wolstenholme,[2] and certainly these two precious documents furnish us with the main incidents of Baffin's great discovery, and with his opinions and conclusions. But when Baffin tells us that "all these sounds and islands the map doth truly describe", we are treated to the following exasperating marginal note by Purchas :—" This map of the author, with the tables of his journall and sayling, were somewhat troublesome and too costly to insert". I shall have to refer to this conduct of Baffin's injudicious editor further on, when we come to consider its consequences.

Baffin had now made five voyages to the Arctic Regions. The fiords and islets of West Greenland, the glaciers and ice floes of Spitzbergen, the tidal phenomena of Hudson's Straits, and the unveiled geographical secrets of the far northern bay, were all familiar to him. He had practically sought out, and deeply pondered over the absorbing questions of polar discovery. As an astronomical observer and navigator, his unwearied diligence was as remarkable as his talent, and in this branch of study he was certainly in advance of his contemporaries. If he was a self-taught man, who had risen from a humble origin, he had so far educated himself as to be able to write letters which are not only well expressed, but graced with classical allusions. He was probably past middle age when, in August 1616,

[1] See pages 138 to 149.   [2] See pages 149 to 155.

he returned from his great discovery, and sought for some new employment.

It was not to be expected that the Arctic problems, so fascinating to all who study them, could be effaced from Baffin's mind. It would appear that the bold navigator, like John Davis before him, conceived the idea of attempting the passage from Japan, and the coast of Asia;[1] and this ambitious hope led him to seek service under the East India Company. The seventh joint-stock voyage was to be undertaken in 1617; and the fleet, which was to be commanded by Captain Martin Pring, was being fitted out during the winter. Baffin obtained an appointment in it, as master's mate on board the *Anne Royal*.

In 1616, the trade of the East India Company was well established; the profits had been very large, and the enterprise was already a great success. Fleets had been annually sent out since 1601; and ships, of a size hitherto unknown, had been built to bring home the rich cargoes from the East. The fleet which was prepared in the winter of 1616, to make the seventh joint-stock voyage, was under the chief command of Captain Martin Pring. The Admiral was a ship called the *Royal James*, of 1,320 tons, with Captain Pring on board, and Rowland Coytmore as master. The *Anne Royal*, of 1,057 tons, was commanded by Andrew Shilling, of whom there was a good report, and who "was not inferior

---

[1] See page 156.

to any man for government". William Baffin served under him as master's mate. The other ships of the fleet were the *New Yeere's Gift*, of 867 tons, "new built of Irish timber",[1] of which Nathaniel Salmon was master; the *Bull*, of 400 tons, Robert Adams, master; and the *Bee*, of 15 tons, John Hatch, master.

In those days the chief commander of a fleet was called the General, and his ship was the Admiral, and the second in command was the Lieutenant-General, sailing in the Vice-Admiral. The captain conducted warlike operations, and the master was responsible for the navigation and safety of the ship, and for the merchandize; but frequently the two offices were united. The purser was also held accountable for the cargo, under sureties, and for the provisions. The *Romager* regulated the stowage. The ordinary food for the sailors consisted of bread, meal, dry salted beef, pickled beef and pork, peas, beans, cod, and stock fish, beer, and cyder. Other articles, coming under the head of "victualling extraordinarie", were cheese, butter, sweet oil, vinegar, aquavitæ, honey, mustard, rice, lamp oil, candles. Great attention was paid to the quality of the meat, the Company slaughtering their own beasts at Blackwall. Special instructions were given for diet and discipline, and strong injunctions were issued on the necessity for cleanliness, and other precautions for preserving health. The most terrible scourge, in the early voyages to India, was the scurvy. In

[1] Sir Dudley Digges' *Defence of Trade*.

a curious little book, called the *Surgeon's Mate*,[1] the prevention and cure of this disease are very fully discussed. The causes of scurvy are said to be infinite and unsearchable; but the chief exciting causes were believed to be long continuance of salt diet, want of sufficient food, and of wine and beer to comfort and warm the stomach, want of changes of clothes, not keeping the clothes clean and dry, and not keeping the cabins sweet and clean. The men were attacked on the voyage from England to the Cape, and on landing they grew strong again, cured by fresh air and fresh food. When deprived of fresh food, the surgeon is recommended to use wine, sugar, and spices, to see that the men's sleeping places are clean and sweet, and to provide themselves with juice of oranges, limes, and lemons, wherever they touch. A quantity of lime juice was always sent on board, by the good care of the merchants; and the instructions were that it should be

---

[1] "*The Surgeon's Mate*, or a treatise discovering faithfully and plainely the due contents of the surgeon's chest, the uses of the instruments, the virtues and operations of the medicines, the cures of the most frequent diseases at sea, namely wounds, apostumes, ulcers, fractures, dislocations, with the true manner of amputation, the cure of the scurvie, the fluxes of the belly, of the collica and *illica passio*, the callenture, with a briefe explanation of sal, sulphur, and mercury, with certaine characters and tearmes of arte. Published chiefly for the benefit of young sea surgeons imployed in the East India Companies affaires, by John Woodall, Master in Chirurgery." London, printed at the Tyger's Head in Paul's Churchyard, 1617, pp. 348, small 4to.

"To the farre renowned, vertuous, and worthy knight, Sir Thomas Smith, Governor of the East India Company, my singular good patrone."

given daily to the men in health, as a preservative. "To that terrible disease of the scurvy, how excellent hath it been approved".[1]

When an East Indian fleet was fully equipped, it was usually inspected by Sir Thomas Smith, or his deputy, before sailing. The fleet, commanded by Martin Pring, left Gravesend on February 4th, 1617, and Maurice Abbot, the Deputy-Governor of the East India Company, with divers Commissioners, came on board on the 6th, mustered the men, and paid the wages. On the 5th of March, the ships weighed anchor in the Downs, and after a prosperous voyage, they arrived at Saldanha Bay on the 21st of June. Captain Pring was obliged to use force, to get a supply of cattle and sheep; but a number were obtained, which overjoyed the hearts of the sick men. In September 1617, the fleet arrived at Surat.[2]

[1] *Surgeon's Mate*, p. 194.
[2] There are three accounts of the proceedings of this fleet in *Purchas*.

I. "Relations and Remembrances taken out of a large Journall of a voyage set forth by the East India Societie, wherein were employed the *James*, the *Anne*, the *New Yeere's Gift*, the *Bull*, and the *Bee*, written by John Hatch, master of the *Bee*, and after of the *New Yeere's Gift*, and lately came home in the *James*." Vol. i, p. 168, lib. v, cap. iiii.

II. "Voyage of the *Anne Royall* from Surat to Mocha in the Red Sea for settling an English trade in those parts, 1618, extracted out of Master Edward Heynes, his Journal." Vol. i, lib. v, cap. v, p. 622.

III. Second voyage of Captain Pring. Vol. i, lib. v, cap. vii, p. 601.

In the India Office there is a manuscript journal written by Robert Adams the master of the *Bull* (No. 20). A very meagre log.

It was then determined to send Captain Shilling to the Red Sea, "for settling an English trade in those parts". Instructions were drawn up by Sir Thomas Roe, the Ambassador at the Court of the Mogul, and three merchants, named Joseph Salbanke, Edward Heynes, and Richard Barber, were selected to conduct the business. The *Anne Royal* sailed from Swally Roads on March 17th, and anchored off Mocha on the 13th of April 1618. The merchants then went on shore with presents to the Governor, and eventually Captain Shilling succeeded in obtaining a Firman from the Pasha, for English merchants to trade at Mocha and Aden. In May, the *Anne Royal* crossed the Red Sea to the bay of Assab, on the African side, for the benefit of the sick men, to procure ballast, and also with a view to exploring the coast; and Baffin was very diligently employed in surveying and preparing charts. On July 21st, the ship returned to Mocha, and on the 20th of August Captain Shilling sailed for India. Later in the year the *Anne Royal* was in the Persian Gulf, and Baffin again made good use of his time, observing and surveying the coasts. Returning to Surat, the *Anne Royal* commenced her homeward voyage in February, and arrived in the Thames in September 1619. She was ordered to unlade at Woolwich.

Baffin had been absent on this voyage to the East Indies for more than two years, from 1617 to 1619, and had won both the confidence of his immediate superior, and the approbation of the Company. In the Court's Minutes of October 1st, 1619, there is the following entry: "William Baffyn, a master's mate in the *Anne*, to have a gratuity for his pains and good art in drawing out certain plots of the coast of Persia and the Red Sea, which are judged to have been very well and artificially performed; some to be drawn out by Adam Bowen, for the benefit of such as shall be employed in those parts."[1]

Captain Andrew Shilling commanded the *Anne Royal* so ably, and conducted important negotiations with such discretion and zeal, that he was selected to have charge of the fleet in the following year. It consisted of four new ships, the building of which was only completed in the end of 1619. The great ship, built at Deptford, was named the *London*, and Captain Shilling was allowed to choose her as his Admiral. The *Harte*, commanded by Captain Blithe, was the Vice-Admiral. The other two ships were the *Roebuck*, under Captain Richard Swan, and the *Eagle*, whose master was Christopher Browne.

William Baffin, at the special recommendation of Captain Shilling, was appointed master of the *London*,[2] and he thus received the command of a ship for the first time. He had worked his way zealously and resolutely, and had become one of the

[1] *Calendar of State Papers (Colonial), East India,* 1617 21, p. 257, para. 748.

Adam Bowen was a clerk in the Company's counting house, and was also employed to draw up sailing directions from the journals, and to prepare fair copies of charts.

[2] *Calendar of State Papers (Colonial), East Indies,* 1617-21, para. 758.

best astronomical observers of his day, a daring and skilful navigator, and even a great discoverer, before his distinguished services were recognised, and he at length became the master of a large ship.[1]

On the 4th of February 1620, the *London* set sail from Gravesend, and on the 25th of March she departed from the Downs, with the rest of the fleet in company.[2] On June 25th they reached Saldanha Bay, and on July 20th Baffin was present at a consultation on board the *London*, as to whether it would be better to go within or without the island of St. Lawrence or Madagascar. After a long voyage they anchored in Swally Road, on the 9th November. Here news was received that a combined force of Portuguese and Dutch ships was waiting off Jáshak, near the entrance of the Persian Gulf, to intercept and attack the English ships. The fleet, therefore, left Swally on November 19th, and went in search of the enemy. On the 16th of December, Captain

---

[1] Officers of the *London*—William Baffin, master; Bartholomew Symonds, surgeon; Nicholas Crispe, purser; John Woolhouse, chaplain; Robert Jefferies, John Barker, Edward Monox, merchants; Archibald Jennison, master's mate; Edwyn Guy, purser's mate.

[2] There are two journals kept on board ships belonging to this fleet, among the manuscript logs at the India Office.

No. 24. "The journal of Archibald Jennison on board the *London*, commanded by Captain Andrew Shillinge, from 1620 to 1622." Thirty-seven and a quarter MS. pages.

No. 25. "The journal of Captain Richard Swan of the *Roebuck* (300 tons) from 1620 to 1622." Sixty-eight pages. This journal of Richard Swan is also given by *Purchas*, vol. i, lib. v, cap. 16, p. 723.

Shilling, with his four ships, came in sight of two large Portuguese ships, and two smaller Flemish vessels, forming a fleet under the command of Ruy Frere de Andrado, with Joam Boralio as Vice-Admiral. The fight commenced at once, and continued, without intermission, for nine hours. The Portuguese then anchored to repair damages, and the English ships, after raking them, put into Jáshak Roads, on the Mekran coast. The two fleets watched each other for ten days, and a second and more decisive encounter took place on the 28th of December.

Captain Swan, in the manuscript journal at the India Office, gives a lively account of the second fight. He says:—"Our broadsides were brought up, and the good ordinance from our whole fleet played so fast upon them that, doubtless, if the knowledge in our people had been answerable to their willing minds and ready resolutions, not one of the galleons, unless their sides were impenetrable, had escaped us. About three in the afternoon, unwilling, after so hotte a dinner, to receive a like supper, they cutte their cables, and drove with the tide until they were without range of our guns, and then their frigate came to them, and towed them away, wonderfully mangled and torn. Their Admiral, in the greatest fury of the fight, was enforced to heale his ship to stop his leakes, his main topmast overboard, and the head of his mainmast. In the *London*, our Admiral and Peter Robinson were wounded; Henry Grand and John Coard slain; in the *Hart*, Edmund Okely wounded, and Walter

David killed. The shot spent in both fights was 1,382 by the *London*; 1024 by the *Hart*; 815 by the *Roebuck*, and 800 by the *Eagle*; total, 4,021."
The calm prevented the two latter vessels from joining in the first part of the battle.

"Our worthy Admiral, in the beginning of the fight, received a great and grievous wound through the left shoulder, by a great shot, which hurt he with such courage and patience underwent, that it gave great hope to us all of his most wished recovery. But having, besides the wound, two of the uppermost ribs on the left side broken, this day, about noon, he departed this life, showing himself, as ever before, a resolute commander; so now, in his passage through the gates of death, a most willing, humble, constant, and assured Christian. His body was interred at Jasques[1] on the 9th, with all the solemnity, decency, and respect the time and place afforded."

Captain Shilling died at noon, on the 6th of January 1621. In the afternoon, "white box No. 1" was opened, and Captain Blithe, according to order, assumed the chief command. It was then arranged, by a consultation, that William Baffin should continue master of the *London*, that Swan should be removed from the *Roebuck* to the *Hart*, that Christopher Browne should go to the *Roebuck*, and that Thomas Taylor should be master of the *Eagle*.

The merchants on board the *London* had a quarrel while the ship was in Jáshak Roads; Mr. Monox

---

[1] Jáshak.

trying to disgrace and excite dis-esteem against his colleague, Mr. Jeffries, which led to a certificate on the subject being signed by William Baffin the master, and countersigned by the Chaplain and the Surgeon.[1] In February the ships returned to Surat.

The fleet, under Captain Blithe, was then to have proceeded to the Red Sea; but it was found to be too late in the season, and the ships shaped a course to the coast of Arabia. The *Hart* and *Roebuck* went to the barren island of Masirah, while the *London* stood onwards, in the direction of Ras al Had, which the English then called Cape Rosselgate. Baffin put into the little port of Súr, on the 'Omân coast, and found water and palm trees. The other ships were ordered to join company, and Súr received the name of "London's Hope". The latitude was found to be 22° 32′ N.[2] Here they appear to have remained at anchor until the 15th of August, when they all set sail for India.

The English now agreed with Shah Abbas the Great, of Persia, to drive the Portuguese out of Ormuz, by a joint attack. The great Viceroy, Albuquerque, had occupied this island in 1515, built a

---

[1] *Calendar of State Papers, Colonial (East Indies)*, 1617-21 p. 414, para. 972.

[2] Lieutenant Wellsted gives the latitude of Súr at 22° 37′ N.; longitude, 59° 36′ E. He was there in November 1835. Súr is the port of the district of Jailan, a large collection of huts neatly constructed with the leaves of date palms, and erected on either side of a deep lagoon, which also serves for its harbour. During the S. W. monsoon the coast of Arabia is a dead lee shore.— *R. G. S. Journal*, vii, p. 104.

strong fort, and exacted an exorbitant tribute from the people, but retained the succession of native kings. The commerce and importance of Ormuz began to decline from the date of the Portuguese occupation, partly owing to their rapacity, and partly on account of the new channel for trade by the Cape of Good Hope. Still, the place was wealthy at the time of the Anglo-Persian attack. The Shah agreed to give the English, for their help, a share of the plunder, and half the customs duties at Gombroon (Bandar 'Abbasi). The English fleet assembled at Surat, and consisted of the *London*, with Captain Blithe and William Baffin on board, the *Jonas*, *Whale*, *Dolphin*, and *Lion*. On the 23rd of December 1621, they arrived at an open roadstead on the Persian coast, near Minab, Ormuz being in sight about ten leagues W.N.W. Here the news was received that the Portuguese had erected a fort on the island of Kishm, to protect some wells, to which the Persians had ineffectually laid siege for some time. On the 19th of January 1622, the English fleet anchored off the town of Ormuz, expecting that the enemy's ships, under Ruy Frere de Andrada, would come out to fight. But it was found that Ruy Frere was in the fort at Kishm, an important post, because it defended the wells for supplying Ormuz. This fort had been built out of the stones of a fine town, containing tombs and mosques, which had been pulled down for the purpose. The wall was of great height, with half moons, and flankers, and a deep dry moat. The Portuguese were already beleaguered by a Persian army, and the English fleet arrived on the 20th of January 1622.

The first operation was to land a certain number of guns from each ship, and to throw up batteries. The siege then commenced, and after two days, William Baffin went on shore with his mathematical instruments, to take the height and distance of the castle wall, so as to find the range "for the better levelling of his piece. But as he was about the same, he received a shot from the castle into his belly, wherewith he gave three leaps, and died immediately". Purchas says:—"In the Indies he dyed, in the late Ormus businesse, slaine in fight with a shot, as hee was trying his mathematicall proiects and conclusions."[1] The death of the great navigator took place on January 23rd, 1622. On February 1st the fort of Kishm surrendered, and the fall of Ormuz followed a few days after.[2]

---

[1] See page 156.

[2] The "Ormuz businesse", as it was called, is related by Master W. Pinder, in *Purchas*, ii, lib. x, cap. ix, p. 1787. Also in a letter to Sir John Wolstenholme from T. Wilson, chirurgeon; and in the journal of the merchant, Edward Monox, both given in *Purchas*.

In the fort of Kishm seventeen guns were captured, and Ruy Frere de Andrada was sent as a prisoner to Surat on board the *Lion*. On the 9th of February, the rest of the English fleet, with about 200 Persian boats laden with soldiers, sailed from Gombroon to Ormuz. About 3,000 Persians landed, occupied the town, and drove the Portuguese into the castle. The English planted batteries, and directed the siege operations, a practicable breach was formed, but the Persian assaults were repulsed. On the 23rd, the Portuguese offered to surrender to the English; and, on the 27th, the garrison embarked for Goa in two of the

Baffin does not appear to have made a will, and he probably left no surviving children, or we should have heard of them, either as claimants of his property, or as recipients of the charity of the Company.[1] But his old widow lived to make claims which were considered troublesome. She is described as a "troublesome impatient woman" who had received £100, and Sir John Wolstenholme, her husband's patron, was moved to cause her to have patience awhile. This was in August 1623. On November 7th of the same year the Court's Minutes record a letter on behalf of Mrs. Baffin for the money due to her deceased husband. The Court "are ready to pay what is due for wages, but to pay £800 which cannot but be gotten by private trade, the Company will not do it. Nevertheless, Mrs. Baffin shall expect their further answer". On the 21st she came in person, accompanied by a Mr. Robert Bourne, and "made demand of her husband's estate, who deceased in the Indies in the Company's service". The Court told them that "if Baffin's estate were questioned it might prove dangerous to the widow, especially if it be true, which she pretends, that he carried £600 out in money, a thing utterly unlawful". The Court proposed arbitration, and Mr. Bourne desired time to consider it.

---

prizes. It was not until September that the English ships left Ormuz in possession of the Persians and returned to Surat. Ormuz was utterly ruined, and has ever since remained desolate.

[1] As in the case of Henry Hudson's son, and scores of other children of men who had served the Company well.

On the 28th, two arbitrators were chosen on either side. The matter lingered on for three years, and, in January 1628, it was ordered that Mrs. Baffin should have £500 in full of all demands, provided that she herself, her friend Mr. Bourne, and her second husband, should join in a discharge to the Company. It was said that Mrs. Baffin was then advanced in years and deaf, and "had made an unequal choice of a man not of the best governed". The Court, therefore, promised so to work with the husband that some honest means might be allotted her out of this grant. This is all that is preserved to us concerning the gallant old sailor's family.[1]

We only know the history of Baffin in the last ten years of his life, from 1612 to 1622. During that period he was engaged in seven important voyages. In the first (1612) he explored the west coast of Greenland. In the second and third (1613 and 1614) he navigated along the coasts of Spitzbergen. In the fourth (1615) he examined Hudson's Strait. In the fifth (1616) he discovered the great bay which bears his name. In the sixth (1617-19) he made valuable surveys in the Red Sea and Persian Gulf. In the seventh (1620-22) he took part in a well sustained sea fight, and fell gloriously in the service of his country. We have seen the place he holds as a brave and able seaman; we will now con-

[1] *Calendar of State Papers, Colonial (East India)*, 1622-24, pp. 140, 175, 181, 184, 189, 219, 231; *Court Minute Book*, vi, pp. 248-267.

sider the position he takes as a scientific observer and as a great discoverer.

We first became acquainted with Baffin in July 1612, at Cockin Sound, on the coast of Greenland, and he is then actively employed on an experimental observation for obtaining the longitude by moon's culmination.[1] The fact of his attempting to take an observation of this kind, the care with which he made all his arrangements, and the interesting remarks with which he accompanied their record, prove him to have been a man who had already devoted much time to self culture, and who was alike thoughtful and ingenious. In the fragment of his journal of this voyage that has been preserved, Baffin records sixteen observations for latitude, and eight for variation of the compass, besides this observation for longitude. In his first voyage to Spitzbergen, Baffin observed for dip as well as for variation; and he tells us that he used a quadrant of four feet semidiameter in taking his altitudes.[2] But his most interesting observation during this voyage of 1613 was for sun's refraction, although there appear to be several mistakes in the record of it. Baffin's method of finding the refraction is most ingenious. He first obtains the latitude, and then takes the difference between the co-latitude and the declination, corrected for the instant when he observed the sun on meridian below the pole to have one fifth of its diameter above the horizon. Then dividing the whole diameter of the sun into fifths,

[1] See page 20, and *note* at page 122.   [2] Page 44.

he calculates that the sun's centre was three-tenths[1] of its whole diameter below the horizon. Subtracting three-tenths of the difference between the co-latitude and the declination from that difference, he gets the approximate refraction.[2]

The second Spitzbergen voyage is recorded by Fotherby, so that the personal work and remarks of Baffin are lost to us; but, during the voyage up Hudson's Strait in 1615, we find him again as active and intelligent as ever. He records twenty-seven observations for variation of the compass, and daily observations for latitude. He also describes a complete lunar observation, the elements being observed altitudes of sun and moon, and angular distance probably measured by difference of azimuth. These elements, cleared from the effects of parallax and refraction, would give the true distance, and the longitude could be found by using the right ascensions of the sun and moon, without the aid of the tables of lunar distances now given in the *Nautical Almanack*.[3] Of course, the distance must have been very roughly observed, and the whole attempt was merely experimental and tentative. But it shows that Baffin was acquainted with the method of finding longitude by observing the altitude of the moon and some other heavenly body, and measuring the angular distance between them; a method first suggested in 1514 by Werner, and again in 1545 by Gemma Frisius. It enables us to claim for Baffin

---

[1] At page 51 (line four from bottom) "foure five" is obviously a misprint for three-tenths.   [2] See p. 51.   [3] See p. 122.

the honour of being the first who ever attempted to take a lunar at sea. Baffin also records, during the voyage up Hudson's Strait, another attempt to find the longitude by lunar culmination.[1] He took tidal observations, and the correctness of his deductions from them was long afterwards confirmed by Sir Edward Parry.[2]

In his fifth voyage, when he discovered Baffin's Bay, the great explorer was especially diligent in observing for variation of the compass, but unfortunately his tabulated journal was injudiciously thrown aside by Purchas, into whose hands it fell. In his narrative he only gives the variation of Smith Sound. Enough has been preserved, however, to show that Baffin takes rank among the foremost scientific seamen of his day, and that he combined perseverance and diligence with painfully acquired knowledge, and remarkable ingenuity and originality of conception. His magnetic observations are of permanent value, for they enabled Professor Hansteen to construct the first of his series of variation maps. His style of drawing is shown in the *facsimile* map which illustrates the present volume; and the great value of his surveying work in the East Indies earned for him special recognition from the East India Company.

As a geographical discoverer, Baffin explored a portion of the west coast of Greenland in 1612, and the west coast of Spitzbergen in 1613. In 1614, Fotherby and Baffin made several attempts to ex-

[1] Page 124.   [2] See *note* at page 132.

tend discovery eastward, along the north coast of Spitzbergen. The season was very unfavourable, the ice being close down on the north shore. But they persevered, and useful work was done, by means of expeditions from their ship in open boats, and by climbing up high hills to obtain more extensive views. In this way they examined the coast from Hakluyt Headland to Wijde Bay of modern maps, and saw a more distant point of Spitzbergen, about sixty miles E.N.E. of the furthest point they reached. Finally, at the end of the season, the ice allowed them to take the ship a distance of about sixty miles E.N.E. from Vogelsang of modern maps, which they called Cape Barren. They were then off the entrance of Hinlopen Strait, and nine or ten leagues from the land.[1]

[1] But there is not the slightest foundation for Dr. Petermann's theory, that Baffin saw the western shore of Franz Josef Land. There is not a word or a syllable in the narrative to justify the notion.

In the *R. G. S. Proceedings*, vol. xix (1874-75), p. 177, Dr. Petermann says:—" I consider it also highly probable that that great Arctic pioneer and navigator, William Baffin, may have seen the western shores of Franz Josef Land as long ago as 1614, for in that year he proceeded to 81° N. latitude, and thought he saw land as far as 82° to the north-east of Spitzbergen, which is accordingly marked in one of Purchas's maps." See also *Mittheilungen*, 18 Band (1872), p. 112, and the map facing page 392 in 20 Band, 1874. From the *Mittheilungen*, it would seem that this notion was conceived by Dr. Petermann, not by referring to the narrative in Purchas, where nothing of the sort is to be found, but by misinterpreting a loose, second-hand statement made by Daines Barrington.

Fotherby and Baffin climbed a high hill at the entrance of Wijde Bay, and saw the coast line of Spitzbergen to the E.N.E.

Baffin's work in Hudson's Strait does not amount to discovery, but it was a painstaking and valuable survey, and was recognised by Sir Edward Parry as praiseworthy and highly creditable.

The fame of Baffin mainly rests upon the discovery of the great bay extending north from Davis Strait. Passing Hope Sanderson, the furthest point reached by Davis, Baffin came to the Women Islands, and the Baffin Islands off Cape Shackleton, at the southern end of Melville Bay. He then crossed Melville Bay, between the 1st and 3rd of July, a most extraordinary piece of good fortune; and, arriving off Cape Dudley Digges, he entered the *North Water*, which "anew revived our hope of a passage".[1] On the 3rd, the explorers anchored off Wolstenholme Sound, but a gale of wind forced them to make sail, and stand out to sea.[2] Their

---

for about twenty leagues distance (see p. 93). This is the single fact on which Petermann's erroneous theory is based. Baffin or Fotherby never proceeded to 81° N., nor thought they saw land in 82° N., nor is such land marked in any of Purchas's maps.

They were never more than thirty miles from the north coast of Spitzbergen, and their highest latitude was 80° 20′ N. The most distant point they could have seen was the North Cape of North-East Land, or possibly one of the Seven Islands. These furthest points are marked correctly on the map in Purchas as a part of Spitzbergen, called Point Purchas, and the island "Purchas *Plus Ultra*".

[1] Page 144.

[2] Sir John Ross says:—"We found the entrances to this inlet, and the general form and appearance of the land to agree extremely well with the description of it given by Baffin, as well as did bearings and distances from Cape Dudley Digges."—*Voyage of the Isabella and Alexander*, Captain John Ross (1818), p. 156.

foresail was blown away, and the wind blew with such fury that they were unable to show any canvas to it. When it cleared they found themselves embayed in an inlet, which Baffin named Whale Sound. The weather then moderated, and the little *Discovery* sailed past Hakluyt Island, to the entrance of Smith Sound. Next, the explorers sighted the Cary Islands; and in the morning of July 10th, they were off Jones Sound, where a boat was sent on shore. This was the first time they had landed since leaving the Baffin Islands. In 74° 20' N., they discovered the entrance of Lancaster Sound, but Baffin failed to realize the fact that it was the opening to a strait of which he was in search. Here his hope of a passage began to be less every day, and he ran south along the edge of the ice, trying to reach the west shore. Giving up this attempt when in 65° 40' N., Baffin stretched across to Greenland, to obtain refreshment for his men, and anchored in Cockin Sound on the 28th of July. This discovery of Baffin Bay was not only very important in itself, but it was achieved by a most remarkable voyage. No other vessel has since been at the entrance of Smith Sound, and recrossed the Arctic Circle within the month of July. The names given by Baffin, during the voyage, were as follows:—

> Women Islands.
> Horne Sound.
> Sir Dudley Digges Cape.
> Wolstenholme Sound.
> Whale Sound.
> Hakluyt Island.

Sir Thomas Smith Sound.
Cary Islands.
Alderman Jones Sound.
Sir James Lancaster Sound.

He thus immortalized the names of his generous patrons.

The omission of Purchas to publish Baffin's tabulated journal and map, led to geographical blunders during the next two centuries, and to such confusion that at length the very existence of Baffin's Bay was doubted. It is interesting to trace the history of these errors respecting Baffin's Bay, and I have, therefore, caused a series of five maps to be prepared, which illustrate the subject.

I. The first is from a very rare circumpolar map, which was drawn to illustrate the narrative of Luke Fox, but is only to be found in one or two copies of his book. The copy in the British Museum has not got it, and a *facsimile* has been inserted. Here Baffin's Bay is shown correctly, and it seems probable that this part of Fox's map may have been copied from the lost map of Baffin. The date is 1635, less than twenty years after Baffin's discovery.[1]

---

[1] *North-West Fox, or Fox from the North-West Passage* (London, 1635).

Luke Fox was a Yorkshire man, an able and intrepid navigator, as well as a quaint and very entertaining writer. In his book he gives a history of discovery in the Arctic Regions down to the time of his own voyage. He then says that he had been itching to start himself ever since 1606, when he was to have gone out as mate to John Knight. Mr. Briggs, the mathematician, encouraged him in

II. But the theoretical map makers, having no sure guide such as Baffin's own map would have supplied them with, soon began to delineate the bay in ways of their own. Hondius first published a map entirely different from that in Luke Fox's book. There is a great prolongation westward, and then a strait leading south into Hudson's Bay. My second map is reproduced from Hexham's edition of Hondius, published in 1636. In the *Atlas* of Vischer (Amsterdam, 1651), and in that of De Wit (1680), the treatment of Hondius is followed. Beyond the Women Islands there is a long strait; then Baffin Bay as a mere indentation, turning north at Cape Dudley Digges, with an opening due south into Hudson's Bay. All Baffin's names are given, except the Cary Islands.

III. My third map is from Moll's *Atlas* (London, 1720), about a century after the discovery. Moll had before him both the delineation of Luke Fox's map, and the later developments of Hondius and his imitators. He, therefore, gives Baffin's Bay, and Davis Strait, according to Luke Fox; but also shows the coast line of Hondius by a shaded line, adding a legend—"Some will have Baffin's Bay to

the idea, and Sir John Wolstenholme, the younger, became treasurer for the voyage. He sailed in May 1631, went up Hudson Strait, and discovered the western shore of the channel leading to Fury and Hecla Strait, which has never been visited since. He conducted the voyage with judgment and energy, and achieved an excellent piece of geographical work.

run west, as far as this faint shadow." Van Keulen (Amsterdam, 1726) was led into still greater confusion. He gives the outline from Hondius and De Wit, but repeats all the names of Baffin twice; first, where the long strait turns to the west, and again in the westward continuation. D'Anville (1761) follows De Wit; but opposite Disco is "James Island", with "Davis Strait" on one side, and "Baffin Strait" on the other. The *Atlas* of Bowles (1765) is copied from D'Anville. In the *Atlas* of Maltebrun (1812) there is a great improvement. A large bay is given northward, in a line with Davis Strait; the Cary Islands are placed close to the north coast, and there is no Hondius opening to Hudson's Bay. The *Atlas* of J. Thompson (Edinburgh, 1817) follows Maltebrun.

IV. But all these discrepancies in the Atlases led to such confusion of ideas that at last the very existence of Baffin's Bay began to be doubted. In the book entitled *The Possibility of approaching the North Pole, asserted by the Hon. Daines Barrington*, which was published in 1818, there is a circumpolar map "according to the latest discoveries". Here the distance between Greenland and Cumberland Land, on the Arctic Circle, is given as about 400 miles. "James Island" is in the centre, with Davis Strait on the east, and Baffin Strait on the west side of it. This seems to have been copied from D'Anville. To the north is a great bay with an enormous westward extension, and a third strait leading into Hudson's Bay. Across the great bay is written, "Baffin's Bay, according to the relation of W. Baffin in 1616, but not now believed".

In the same year Sir John Barrow published a circumpolar map to illustrate his "*Chronological History of the Voyages into the Arctic Regions* (1818) in which Baffin's Bay is entirely expunged. Davis' Strait is made to open northwards on to a blank space. Thus, after many varied methods of treatment, the great discovery of Baffin was at length entirely ignored and discredited.

v. But in the very year of the publication of these incredulous maps, Captain Ross made his voyage in company with Lieutenant Parry, re-discovered Baffin's Bay, and finally cleared away all this mystification. At length the great navigator received full credit for his discovery, and for the admirable way in which he had conducted it. Ross and Parry were as much struck with Baffin's accuracy as an observer, as with his gallantry and skill as a navigator in pushing the little *Discovery* of 55 tons through the middle pack into the "North Water", and bringing her safely back again. My fifth map shows the outline of Baffin's Bay, according to recent charts.

Sir John Ross says, in the narrative of his voyage of 1818, "In re-discovering Baffin's Bay I have derived great additional pleasure from the reflection that I have placed in a fair light before the public the merits of a worthy man and able navigator, whose fate, like that of many others, it has not only been to have lost, by a combination of circumstances, the opportunity of acquiring during his lifetime the fame he deserved, but, could he have lived to this period, to have seen his discoveries expunged from the records of geography, and the bay with which his name is so fairly associated, treated as a phantom of the imagination." Ross identified all the places mentioned and named by Baffin, and bears frequent testimony to his accuracy, especially as regards the latitude of Lancaster Sound.

The main object of Arctic exploration is the extension of scientific knowledge. A secondary, but in many instances an equally fruitful, aim has been the increase of national wealth; in both these respects the work of Baffin gives him pre-eminence. His geographical discoveries were extensive, and his scientific observations were important and of permanent value. At the same time his voyages, and the information he brought home, pointed the way to a new source of commercial profit, and eventually opened up a lucrative whaling trade. Among the naval worthies of the seventeenth century, side by side with Frobisher, and Davis, and Hudson, the devoted zeal and untiring industry, the gallantry and intrepidity of Willam Baffin, and his great services, have secured for him a permanent and an honourable place.

I have added to Baffin's Voyages a discourse inserted by Purchas on the probability of a North-West Passage, because it contains some remarks on

Baffin and a notice of his death by Purchas, and because the remarks of Briggs, the mathematician, show the state of opinion on the subject immediately after Baffin's last Arctic voyage. Purchas adds to his discourse a story heard at Lisbon by a shipmaster named Cowles; a report by Michael Lok on the discoveries of Juan de Fuca; and a Treatise by Henry Briggs on the North-West Passage.

THE FIRST RECORDED VOYAGE

OF

WILLIAM BAFFIN.

PART I.

Written by JOHN GATONBE[1] (ending 8 July 1612).

To the Right Worshipfull Sir Christopher Hilyeards,[1] Knt.

John Gatonbe wishethe in this life the contynvance of health and prosperitie, with great increase of worship, and everlasting felicitie in Christ our Saviour.

PURPOSING with myselfe to present this journall, or travis book, to you, which is ussally kept of seafayringe men and mariners, in ther navigation of long voyagies and unknowne countryes; and having been lett thes two yeares, being travelling upon the sea to mayntayn my poore estat of wife and children; and this winter being at home, and remem-

---

[1] From Churchill's *Collection of Voyages and Travels*, vol. vi [1732], pp. 241-251.

[2] Sir Christopher Hildyard, of an ancient East Riding family, succeeded to his uncle (also Sir Christopher) at Winestead, in Holderness, in 1602. He was High Sheriff of York in 1613, M.P. for Hedon in 1589, 1593, 1597, and 1601, for Beverley in 1620, for Aldborough in 1621, and again for Hedon from 1624 to 1627. He was also a member of the High Commission of York. In 1598 Sir Christopher married Elizabeth, daughter and heir of Henry Welby, of Goxhill, co. Lincoln, by Alice White, whose mother was Anne Cecil, sister of the great Lord Burleigh. Sir Christopher was buried at Winestead, on November 23rd, 1634. The Winestead Hildyards also owned the old palace at Hull, built by the Poles, Dukes of Suffolk. Sir Christopher's son, Henry Hildyard, let it to the king for a magazine of warlike stores. His second son, Robert, was a prominent royalist commander at Marston Moor and elsewhere, and was created a baronet at the restoration. The baronetcy became extinct on the death of Sir Robert Hildyard, of Winestead, in 1814.

bring the manyfold cortesies shewed by you to my anciente father, Nicholas Gatonbe,[1] I thought good this simple labour, such as it is, to offer vnto you, right worshipful, desiring you to accept it, as a gift that proceedeth from such a one who hartily wisheth you well, and would, if ability served, present you with a better, seeing and knowing your worship and your ancesters have been alwayes well-wishers to this towne and the inhabitants of the same; wherefor I intreat your worship to pervse it over.

And, First, you shall see the setting out of our voyage, what adventures we had with our generall.

Secondly. The tym of our saylling.

Thirdly. Our travis upon the sea, with the windes and weyther we had.

Fourthly. The height of the poll observed.

Fifthly. The ice we saylled by, with the coldness of the aire.

Sixthly. The barrenness of the country, with huge mountayns lying full of snow.

Seventhly. The nature and conditions of the inhabitants and salvages of the same.

Eighthly. The thinges we bought of them for old iron, with that which happened vnto vs in the countrye.

Lastly. Of our returne homeward and our safe arrivall.

Thvs craving both pardon for my boldnes, and also requesting your favorable accepting of my simple travell, I cease from further troubling your worship with my rudnes, praying Gode to inriche you with the plentyfull increase of the gifts of his spirite.

From the poore house of John Gatonbe, this 25th day of Februarie, 1615.

[1] Nicholas Gatonby was five times Warden of the Trinity House at Hull, namely in 1587, 1591, 1596, 1602, and 1609; having been elected Steward in 1577. A John Gatonby was Steward in 1570 and Warden in 1578 and 1586. Another Nicholas Gatonby made voyages to Greenland in the *Patience* in 1616 to 1618, and brought home cargoes of oil.

A Voyage into the North-West Passage, undertaken in the Year 1612.

By the Merchants Adventurers of London, Sir George Lancaster,[1] Sir Thomas Smith,[2] Mr. Ball,[3] Mr. Cocken,[4] and Mr. James Hall, being Venturer with them, and General of both the ships.

The 10th of April, being Good Friday, we haled both our ships into Hull road, the one being of the burden of 140 tons called the *Patience*, we being 40 men and boys in her; the other of 60 tons, called the *Heart's-Ease*, containing 20 men and boys. This day we cross'd both our yards, and entred into pay, making fit to take the first wind to sail withal.

[1] There was no Sir George Lancaster. It is a misprint for Sir James, the commander of the first East Indian voyage. James Lancaster was a native of Bishopstoke, in Hampshire. For his voyages and some account of him see *The Voyages of Sir James Lancaster to the East Indies* (Hakluyt Society's vol., 1877). After his return from his last voyage, which was the first voyage of the East India Company, in 1603, Lancaster was knighted, and he afterwards served as a Director of the East India Company. He was possessed of some wealth, lived in something more than comfort in his house in St. Mary Axe, and actively promoted all voyages of discovery. He died in June 1618, leaving his money in numerous legacies, and a larger sum to found a school at Bishopstoke. He appears to have been unmarried.

[2] For a notice of Sir Thomas Smith see the Introduction.

[3] This was probably Mr. Richard Ball, an eminent London merchant, who embarked in various enterprises having discovery as their object. His name appears in the list of adventurers to whom the charter of incorporation of the East India Company was granted, on December 31st, 1600. He was also a member of the Company for the Discovery of the North-west Passage. In 1618 he is mentioned as having fitted out two ships for the discovery of an island in the West Indies. His brother George was a factor for the East India Company at Bantam, and was prosecuted by the Company, on various counts, before the Star Chamber in 1622. Richard Ball was then dead.

[4] This Mr. Cocken, called by Baffin Alderman Cocken, is a name

Monday, April 20, we set sail in Hull road, the wind at E.S.E. and bore down to Cleeness and anchor'd; and towards night the wind came to the N.E., and so we return'd into Paul road again this night, being much wind.

21. This day the wind came to S.S.W., and so at night we went over and rode at the Ness, our pinnace being about business at the town.

Set sail. 22. This day, being Wednesday, we weigh'd and set sail, the wind at S.S.W., and came out of Humber at 12 o'clock at noon, going our course N. and by W.

23. This day the wind southerly, we going the same course, being seven leagues off Whitby at noon, and at six o'clock at night we were 9 leagues off Hunclife,[1] it bearing from us S.S.W., we sailing N.N.W.

April 1612. 24. This day the wind at E.S.E. and very fair weather, we being some 12 leagues off Stabs-head, it bearing W.S.W. from us. At noon we observ'd the sun, and found the altitude of the pole to be 56° 12'.

25. This day the wind at S.E., we sailing N.N.W., and at 9 o'clock in the morning we spake with north sea fisher-

mis-spelt. There was no Alderman *Cocken*, but at this time there was a notable Alderman William *Cockayne*, who is no doubt the personage here mentioned. He was son of William Cockayne, and grandson of Roger Cockayne, of Ashborne in Derbyshire. He was Governor of the Eastland Company, and also of the London planters in Ulster; and it was under his direction that the city of Londonderry was founded. On June 22nd, 1616, King James I dined with him and knighted him, and in 1619-20 he was Lord Mayor of London. He was also an active member of the East India Company, and one of the Farmers of the Customs. His daughter, Martha, with a dowry of £10,000, married that John Ramsay who had the credit of having saved James VI when he was attacked by the Gowries. Ramsay was created Earl of Holderness and Baron Kingston-upon-Thames in 1621, but died childless in 1625. His widow married secondly Montagu Bertie, second Earl of Lindsey, and was mother of the third Earl and other children. She died in 1641. Another daughter, Mary Cockayne, married the second Earl of Nottingham; and the eldest son Charles was created Viscount Cullen. Sir William Cockayne died in 1626. He was buried in Old St. Paul's.   [1] Huntcliff, near Redcar.

men, and had fresh fish of them, they belonging to Yarmouth, being from Bohomness W.S.W. 9 leagues off, the pole being rais'd 58° 30'.

26. This day, being Sunday, the wind southerly, we sail'd betwixt Orkney and Fair Isle and Foullay, leaving the islands and Shetland off our starboard side at 3 o'clock in the morning; and at 6 o'clock we sail'd W. and by N. to the sea, Foullay bearing from us N.E. 5 leagues off; and at noon the wind came southerly, we sailing then W. This day at night the wind came contrary, to the S.W., we sailing to the northward N.W.[1] After we parted from these two islands, we had sight of no other land till we came to sight of Greenland.

27. This day we had much wind at N.W., being forc'd to take in our topsails for our vice-admiral, she being a-stern of us, we sailing W.N.W., and at four o'clock at night we tack'd about to the southward, we sailing S.W. and by S., the wind coming to the W. and by S.

28. This day the wind came to the N.W. with cloudy weather. This day at 6 o'clock in the morning we tack'd about to the southward, sailing W.S.W., and at noon we did observe the sun, and found the altitude of the pole to be 59° 47'.

29. This day, the wind at N.W., we standing to the southward W.S.W., being thick hazy weather.

30. This day calm and misty from 12 o'clock to 6 o'clock in the morning; then the wind came to the S.W., we sailing all the day after W. and by N.

May 1, being Friday, the wind at W.S.W., we sailing to the northward N.W. and by N., being misty and much wind; and at noon it cleared up, and we did observe the sun, and found the pole rais'd 61° 31', we tacking about to the southward, wending S. and by W., having fair weather;

---

[1] Two woodcuts: "Fair-Isle showeth thus 2 leagues off"; "Foullay showeth thus 3 leagues off."

and at 8 o'clock at night we tack'd about and stood to the northward, wending N.N.W.

2. This day stormy weather, with the wind at S.W. and by W., being misty and rain, we standing to the northward N.W. and by W., and at 10 o'clock it fell little wind and calm; and the wind ran to the N.E., we sailing our course W., having a fresh gale of wind at noon.

3. This day we had fair weather, the wind at E.S.E., we sailing W. This day we did observe the sun, and found the pole to be rais'd 61° 46'; and at 4 o'clock at night the wind came contrary, being westerly, we standing to the northward N.N.W.; and at 6 o'clock we stood to the southward again.

4. This day the wind at N.W., we sailing W.S.W., and at 5 o'clock our vice-admiral sprung her fore-mast, whereby she was forc'd to take in her top-sails and fore-sails; and so did we in the admiral, till such time as they had fish'd it and made it strong. This day at noon we did observe the sun, and found the pole rais'd 61° 8', the wind being come to N.N.E., we sailing our course W.

5. This day the wind came to W. and by S., and began to blow, we standing to the northward N.W. and by N.

6. This day the wind at W., and at 6 o'clock in the morning the wind came to N. and by W., and so we steer hence W., the altitude of the pole being 61° 36'.

7. This day the wind at N.W. and by N., we sailing W. and by S., and at 2 o'clock in the afternoon it came up to the N.E., being cloudy and thick, which turn'd to much rain, we sailing our course west.

8. This day much wind and rain at E.N.E., we sailing W., and at noon we had fair weather, the wind being come to the N. This day we hoped to see Friesland,[1] yet did not.

[1] The old navigators were always hoping to see this imaginary Friesland, and were always disappointed. It got into the sea-charts from

9. This day the wind at N.N.E. stormy weather, we sailing our course W., and at noon it grew fair, and we observ'd the sun, and found the altitude of the pole to be 59° 51'. This day our master found by his instrument the compass varied 15°. to the westward of the north, the occasion we had no sight of Friesland sailing to the southward some 12 leagues; so that for our west course we kept, we had made but a W. and by S. way; yet I suppose it to be the current which doth set to the southwestward, and so doth set from the westermost part of Friesland into the N.W. Passage.

10. This day the wind northerly, we sailing W. and by N., and at noon we observ'd the sun, and found the altitude of the pole to be 60° 4', being very fair weather.

11. The wind N., and at noon we sounded, and had no ground of 150 fathom, it being little wind and calm, sometimes southerly, and sometimes at S.W., sometimes easterly; thus it did continue variable all the day, being fair weather and smooth sea, we sailing for the most part W. and by S.

12. This day calm, and at 4 o'clock in the morning the wind came to E.N.E., we sailing W. and by N. This day the water changed of a blackish colour; also, we saw many whales and grampus's.

the old "*Carta da navegar de Nicolo et Antonio Zeno*" (A.D. 1380), first published in 1558, and was placed near the east coast of Greenland. Here it remained in every successive sea-chart for many long years. Frobisher assumed that Greenland was Friesland when he first made the coast. But Davis, when he sighted Greenland, at once saw that this was not the Friesland of the Zeno map; hence Friesland retained a separate place on the charts. Mr. Major holds that the Friesland of the Zeni was the Feroë Islands (see *The Voyages of the Venetian Brothers Nicolo and Antonio Zeno, translated, with Notes and an Introduction, by R. H. Major, F.S.A.*, Hakluyt Society's volume, 1873; and a paper in the *R.G.S. Journal*, xlix, p. 412, entitled, "Zeno's Frisland is not Iceland, but the Færoës"), while Admiral Irminger, of Copenhagen, is of opinion that Friesland was Iceland (see *R.G.S. Journal*, xlix, p. 398, "Zeno's Frislanda is Iceland and not the Feroës").

13. The wind at E. we sailing W. and by N. This day being hazy, we met with ice, the wind being come to N.N.E. Much wind and snow at 9 o'clock at night, so that we were forc'd to take in our sails and stand with our foresail to the eastward, wending E. Also, some of our men spied land, yet we could not well discern it, it snowing so fast.

14. We stood in with the land again at 2 o'clock in the morning, wending N.N.W., and had sight of land betwixt 5 and 6 o'clock in the morning; and our master made it *Cape Farewel*, so called by Captain Davis at the first finding of the country in anno 1585 because he could not come near the land by 6 or 7 leagues for ice.[1] It bearing from us N.N.W., and we sailing along by the ice W.N.W. all the day.[2]

15. The wind at N.N.W. sailing W., and at 4 o'clock in the morning we tack'd about again to the ice, again sailing N.N.E., and at 10 o'clock in the morning we tack'd about again, being hard aboard the ice, having sight of the land, it stretching more to the northward. The ice lieth

---

[1] Cape Farewell, the southern extreme of Greenland, is in 59° 48′ N. This is an interesting statement that it was named by Captain Davis, in 1585; but in his first voyage in 1585, Davis did not sight Cape Farewell. The first land he made, which he called "Desolation", was on the east coast; and he did not sight land again until he was in 64° 15′ N. In his second voyage, in 1586, he did sight Cape Farewell. He says—"And the 15th of June I discovered land in the latitude of 60 degrees mightily pestered with ice and snow, so that there was no hope of landing." But in the narrative written by himself he does not give it any name. On the Molyneux Globe, where the discoveries of Davis are shown, it is called "Reg: Elizabeth Foreland". Still, the tradition mentioned in the text, that Davis originally gave the name of Farewell to the Cape because he could not come near the land, is no doubt true, and is very interesting.

[2] Here there is a woodcut: "The land did rise thus full of snow. The Cape 7 leagues off, N.N.W." "This land is the southermost point in Greenland, the heighth of the Pole there being 59° 15′."

all along it, being as it were a great bay betwixt two head lands.

16. This day a cold hazy wind, it being at N.N.W., we sailing W., and at 7 o'clock in the morning we tack'd about, lying N.E. and by N., and at 2 o'clock we met with ice again; we lying to and fro, hoisted our shallop out; and espying seals lying upon the ice, our shallop rowed to them, and killed one of them; the rest tumbled into the water, being 20 in a company. This day we observ'd the sun, and found the altitude of the pole to be 59° 30′, we being some 70 leagues within the streights, it being 115 leagues between the coast of America and Greenland in the entrance of this passage.

17. The wind at S. in the morning, we sailing N.W. This day we run among the ice, and were inclosed with the ice, so that we could get no passage to the northward; and so we were forc'd to stand out again, and were glad that God had deliver'd us from amongst it; it being 4 o'clock in the afternoon before we were clear of the ice, sailing S.W. to the sea. This day, being Sunday, we had sight of the land called Desolation,[1] it being from us 15 leagues N. and by E.

<small>May 1612. Land of Desolation.</small>

18. This day, at one o'clock in the morning, we had much wind and snow, the wind being westerly; and at six o'clock in the morning it prov'd fair weather. We tacking about into the shore, did wend N. and by W., which did near the land of Desolation: and at noon we tack'd about and stood back again, being ten leagues from the land, it bearing N.N.E. of us: the ice hindering of us this day, we did observe the sun, and found the pole 59° 53′.

19. The wind southerly, we sailing for the most part N.W. by N. and N.N.W. Then the land of Desolation did bear off us N.E. and by E. This day we did meet with great islands of ice. This day we did observe the sun, and found

[1] So named by Davis.

10 THE FIRST RECORDED VOYAGE OF

the altitude of the pole to be 60° 35': also we had a forceable current, which we went along the coast with till we came to bring Desolation point E. of us. This current set from Desolation into America side, and into Hudson's streights, being so called by his men, they leaving him behind them in that country, which was his death in the year 1611.[1]

May 1612.   20. This day, the wind at N. and by E., we sailing E. and by N. to the land, which we had no sight of as this day. This day we did observe the sun, and found the altitude of the pole to be 61° 33', being to the northward of Desolation some 30 leagues. This day we stood to the westward; and at 10 o'clock at night we stood to the eastward, again meeting ice.

21. The wind at N.E. and by E. This day we had sight of land at 2 o'clock in the morning; and our master's mate, John Hemstay and I called it the land of Comfort.[2] And we call'd up our men, and tack'd about our ships, the ice hindering us from coming near the land, we sailing along the land N., and N. and by W., being distant from it 7 leagues. And at noon, we being near the ice, our men went with the shallop to it, and killed four seals, and

The land of Comfort.

[1] Woodcuts with the following notes: "Cape Desolation rises thus 15 leagues off, N.E. by N." (cut). "The land of Desolation rises thus 12 leagues off, N.E. by E." (cut). "This land so called by Captain Davis, it being so desolate and comfortless, with huge mountains of snow lying upon it, such as he had never seen nor any of his men before him."

[2] The two cones of Umanak, off Arsuk Fiord, are the Cape Comfort of the Admiralty chart. The name appears on the map in the English translation of the description of Greenland, by Hans Egede, published in 1745, and also on the map in Crantz's History of Greenland (1757). On the Admiralty chart it is placed in 61° 49' N., but Gatonbe, in the text, gives 62° 33' as the latitude. This is the position of some islets, called Fulluarlalik Islands, between the Danish settlements of Fredrikshaab (62° N.) and Fiskernaes (63° 4' N.). Of course, the Admiralty chart, and the Danish chart from which it is copied, must be wrong, for Gatonbe's evidence as to the point of land named by himself must surely be conclusive.

brought other two aboard quick, we having good sport betwixt them and our mastiff dogs.[1]

22. The wind at N. and by E. This day we turn'd amongst the ice, meeting with many islands of ice, which were very high, like great mountains: some of them we judg'd to be 30 yards from the water, fleeting upon the seas, being 15 leagues off the land. This day we had sight of the land, yet could not come near it for ice. This day we did observe the sun, and found the pole rais'd 62° 55.'

23. The wind at N.N.W. This being calm at noon, we sounded with our lead, and had no ground of 180 fathom, being some 110 leagues within the passage. This day we found the altitude of the pole to be 63°, sailing N.E. and by E. in with the land.

[May 1612.]

24. This day the wind at N. and by E., we sailing N.W. and by W., being thick cloudy weather; and at 8 o'clock in the morning we tack'd about to the eastward, it being little wind, and sometimes calm.

25. This day calm, with little wind and variable; sometimes at N., sometimes at N.W., we sailing for the most part N.E. and by E. This day we sounded by an island of ice with our shallop, and found no ground of 150 fathom, being off the land 21 leagues: and at 10 o'clock at night it was thick and misty weather, so that one ship could not see the other.

26. This day the wind at N., we sailing E.N.E., sailing in with land, being very thick and misty weather; and at 2 o'clock in the afternoon it clear'd up, and we saw the land, being some three leagues from it, it seeming as tho' we were hard by it, being a very high land, having

---

[1] Here another woodcut, with the following note: "Cape Comfort rises thus, the heighth of the Pole being 62° 33', the smoothest land, and best to look to of all the country of Greenland; yet we could not come near it for ice."

much snow lying upon it. Also two of the savages came rowing to our ships in their boats, we sailing in still with the land, sounding, and having with our lead and line 25 fathom, sometimes 20, 18, 15, 12 fathom, it being rocky ground, coming amongst many dry rocks and islands. This day we look'd for a harbour with our shallops, for the ships to ride in safety, and found one, which our general call'd the harbour of Hope; for here we came to land with our ships; the which we could not come near, the time we sail'd along the land, from the sight of Cape Farewel until we came to this place.[1]

Harbour of Hope.

27. The 27th day we harboured in the harbour of Hope (the islands we call'd Wilkinson islands; the mountain we call'd Mount Hatclife[2]) at 2 o'clock in the morning; praising our God for our safe arrival in this unknown country, having been from home 5 weeks and 2 days.[3]

28. The 28th day our general found a convenient place

Inhabitants of Greenland.

[1] The southern part of the western side of Greenland is blocked by the stream of ice drifting down the eastern side from the north, and then turning northwards round Cape Farewell. The current sets into Davis Strait, keeping close to the coast, but gradually decreasing in strength as it advances northward and disappears in about 64° N. The pack ice follows the track of this current, pressing upon the coast with southerly winds, and dispersing with those from the north. This belt of ice is often found to be quite impenetrable, though of no great width, and it sometimes locks up the southern coast for the greater part of the summer.

[2] A misprint, I think, for Huntcliff, a point on the coast of Yorkshire, near Redcar; so named, no doubt, from a fancied resemblance.

[3] This anchorage was the Gilbert Sound discovered by Davis in 1585, and visited in his two subsequent voyages. (See *Voyages of John Davis*, pp. 6, 15, 16, 17, 22, 35, 38, Hakluyt Society's vol., 1880). Davis gives the latitude 64° 15' N. Here, in this Gilbert Sound, the "Harbour of Hope" is now the modern Danish settlement of Godthaab, in 64° 8' N., the principal station in South Greenland. The Godthaab-fjord runs in a north-eastern direction for 70 miles, and sends off a branch to the south-east 25 miles long. The greater part of the coast is sheltered by clusters of low islands. Godthaab was founded by Hans Egede in 1728.

to land the quarters of our pinnace for our carpenters to set together, it being an island hard by our ships. This day also our general caused our ship's boat to be mann'd, and our shallop, and went himself to discover the country, and what rivers he could find in the main; the savages rowing to and fro to our ships, holding up their hands to the sun, and clapping them on their breasts, and crying, *Elyot*,[1] which is as much to say, in English, Are we friends? thus saluting us in this manner every time they came to us, and we offering the same courtesy to them, making them the more bold to come to our ships, they bringing with them sealskins, and pieces of unicorn horn, with other trifles, which they did barter with us for old iron.

29, 30, 31. These days our carpenters made haste with our great pinnace to get her down, the weather being fair, and the wind for the most part easterly; for our general was minded to make what speed he could for to sail along the coast further to the northward, being as yet not come to the place where he was at afore by 70 leagues.

June 1. Our general return'd aboard again, having found two rivers in the main, the one he call'd Lancaster river; the other, Ball river;[2] for Greenland is like Norway, having many islands and rocks along the main.

2. Our master and Mr. Barker,[3] master of the *Vice Admiral*, went in the shallop and rode amongst the islands, and to one of the rivers where they were afore, having their fowling-pieces with them to shoot fowl with, which that country affordeth small store.

[1] See the list of Eskimo words given by Davis. (*Voyages*, p. 21). He has *Yliaoute*—" I mean no harm".

[2] These were the two deep branches of Godthaab-fjord, called after two of the merchant adventurers who set forth the voyage—Sir James Lancaster and Mr. Richard Ball. (See notes at p. 3.) The latter name got corrupted into Baal's River, but it is correctly spelt on the Danish chart of 1832.

[3] Andrew Barker, master of the second ship, was a seaman of repute at Hull. (See note further on.)

3. This day we employ'd ourselves in searching the country, which affordeth nothing as yet for the profit of our voyage.

4. At night one of the savages stole a musket from our men which kept the island, where our great pinnace was set up, they keeping a bad watch, and leaving their musket where they kept centry, being at the fire in the coy, the weather being cold, it was taken away by one of the wild men, they could not tell when. The cause of our watching was, for that the salvages will steal all things they can come by, but chiefly iron.[1]

5. This day we launch'd our great pinnace, which our general call'd the Better Hope. This day also James Pullay catching hold of one of the salvages, another did cast a dart at him, and struck him into the body with it, on the left side, which gave him his death's wound. Also the salvage he took we haul'd into the ship, and by him we had our musket again; for two of the salvages being aged men, and rulers of the rest, came with great reverence to know the occasion we had taken one of their men; we with signs and other tokens did shew them the occasion, being the best language we all had amongst us, delivering their man, his boat, oar, and darts. Our general gave unto him a coat, a knife, and a seeing-glass also, to requite the injury we had done; yet he, with a frowning look, desiring to be gone from us, we let him go out of the ship, and helping him into the chains, he leapt over-board, and the other two did help him ashore; and when he was ashore, the salvages cut off the coat our master gave him, from his back, so little did they regard it. It was made of yellow cotton, with red gards of other cotton about it.

[1] Here there is a woodcut of a kayak: "The fashion of the salvages rowing in their boats, the boat being made of seal skins, and clos'd all but the place where he rows in her, and that is clos'd about him when he sits in her, from his waste downward. His oar hath two webs, and he useth both hands to row with. (Wilkinson's Islands, The Harbour of Hope, and Mount Hatcliffe)."

6. James Pulley departed this life to the mercy of God, at three o'clock in the morning, and we bury'd him at noon upon one of the islands we rode by. This day also we carry'd the quarters of Mr. Barker's small shallop to be set together by the carpenters ashore, that we might have our shallops ready to go with us along to the northwards.

7, 8, 9. Rainy weather, otherwise our shallop had been done, and we gone from hence to the northwards.

10. The shallop was done and launched this day. Mr. Hall, being general of both the ships, did hold a parley with all the company of both ships, strictly commanding that none of us should barter for anything, but Mr. Wilkinson, who was merchant for the venturers, and them that were appointed by the merchant, in pain of forfeiting their wages; which articles were wisely answer'd by the officers of the ships.

11. We cross'd our yards, and got an anchor home, but the wind came contrary, spending our time in rowing from island to island, and the salvages came to and fro to our ships, bringing us fresh fish, which we bought for iron nails.

13. One of the salvages brought two young seals, which he had kill'd at sea, and our master bought them, and we haul'd them into the ship, we wondering he could kill them at sea, it blowing so much wind at S.W.

14. This day, being Sunday, we came out with the wind N.N.E., and the salvages rowed to us, being 6 leagues off the land into the sea; and for that our captain gave one of them a knife. This day we observed the sun, and found the pole's altitude to be 64°, being the height of the place we came out of, being the harbour Hope; Wilkinson's islands and mount Hatcliffe we rowed under, they bearing off us E.

15. The wind at E.S.E., we sailing along the land to the northward N. by E., being fair weather.

16. The wind at N. by W., we sailing into the shore N.E. by E. This day Mr. Hall and Mr. Barker took their shallops, being well mann'd, and rowed into the land to discover the country, and to see what traffick they could have with salvages. This day, lying off and on with our ships, they being ashore with the shallops, the wind came out of the sea, and we stood of, sailing N.N.W. The wind being come to west, and the vice-admiral following of us, struck on a blind rock, and took no harm, praised be God! our shallops not coming to us till we were 5 or 6 leagues off the land.

17. The wind at S.E., we sailing along the land to the northward N. by E. This day, being Wednesday, we row'd with both our shallops into the land, and sounded the harbour we anchor'd in, being the second harbour we came in.[1]

18. At 8 o'clock at night we had a sore storm off the land at S.E., with such mighty whirl-winds, which came from the mountains, that all our cables we had, being new ones, we bent to our great anchor, and let it fall to keep us from the rocks.

19. In the morning we broke one of our cables, and we rode by our great anchor, having much wind and rain.

20. The weather faired, and our general caused our great pinnace to be made ready, and to row along the coast, he going with us himself, we being in her 22 men and boys. This day we rowed some 4 leagues, and came to a great island, and anchor'd there 3 hours; and from thence we went into a river lying E. by N. up the river.

---

[1] This second anchorage was named Cockin (Cockayne) Sound, after one of the four merchant adventurers who set forth the voyage—Alderman Sir William Cockayne. (See note at p. 4). Baffin gives the latitude 65° 20′ N. This is nearly the latitude of the Danish settlement of Sukkertoppen, which was founded in 1755. Sukkertoppen (Sugar-loaf) is in 65° 25′ N., and is situated on an island, the conical elevations of which present the appearance expressed in its Eskimo name *Manitsok* (uneven). It is the most populous place in Greenland, and has a fine stone-built church.

21. We rowed up the river still, and we found nothing in it for any profit, rowing some 3 leagues into it, the ice stopping that we could get no further.

22. We being left by ice, return'd and rowed out again, and the salvages follow'd and row'd after us, and so along with us, intending to do us some harm; for when we came near any island they did throw stones at us with their slings.

23. The wind at N.N.W., and we row'd amongst the islands to the northward, and so came to a great river, which troubled us to row over, there went such a forceable tide of flood, it being within a league of Queen Anne Cape,[1] and came to an island, and rested us there till the flood was done; and then we rowed about the cape, and came to an island, whereon was a warlock, and rowed into it, and found it a good harbour for ships. This day we rowed into a river, as we supposed, but found it to be a bay, we being 3 leagues to the northward of the cape. This day our men went ashore and kill'd 6 partridges, and spy'd in a valley 7 wild deer, yet as soon as they did see us, they did run away as fast as their feet could carry them.

24. We row'd out again, and so along the land. This day we came to a mountain, where we rowed to it amongst the islands, taking it for a river our master had been at afore, yet it was not: the mount we call'd Gabriel mount. *Gabriel mount.*

25. We row'd from thence to an island which lieth two leagues off the land, with many broken rocks about it, that stretch from the main, and so to the sea-board; and there we rested all that day, the wind blowing very much at N., it being against us. This island our master call'd by the

---

[1] Cape Anne, so named by Hall during his former voyage with the Danes, after the queen of Christian IV. Hall, on his map accompanying his report to the Danish King, gives the latitude of Cape Anne 66° N. On the modern charts it is in 66° 24′ N., just to the south of Cockin (Cockayne) Sound.

name of Throughgood island. Here we got great store of mussels, being of a great bigness. Here one of our men killed a fox with a fowling-piece, being many in this island that run from the main, and feed upon fish they got off the island.

26. It being very fair weather we row'd from thence, amongst many broken rocks, and so along the land; and at noon we came to the river our master had been at afore, he naming it the King's-ford;[1] there is a mount he named Cunningham mount;[2] we had traffick with the salvages; and at night we anchor'd in a haven, on the south-side of the river, call'd Denmark haven, there being in the entrance 40 fathom deep, and had traffick with the salvages for seal skins, and some salmon trout.[3]

27. We rowed over to the north-side of the river, and sought for a roadstead for our ships, and found one, having 12 fathom deep, meaning to bring our ships thither, with God's help.

28. We rowed to our ships again, having but two days victuals; none could we get, being from our ships, the salvages eating raw meat do kill with their darts, both fowl, fish, and flesh, so that there was little to get but that they brought us.

29. We came to our ships again, being from them nine days, having had much tedious weather, with thicks and snow, as we rowed along the coast, it being some 25 leagues betwixt the ships and the King's-ford. The vice-

---

[1] King Christian's Fiord was discovered and named by Hall during his first voyage with the Danes. He gives the latitude 66° 25′ N., close to Cape Anne.

[2] So named in Hall's first Danish voyage, after the commander of the expedition. This majestic peak is called *Kœrlinghœtten* by the modern Danes, and *Nusasak* by the Eskimo.

[3] "Cunningham Mount; the height of the Pole 66¼°; King's-ford" (this river was the first harbour he anchored in when he was pilot of the King of Denmark's ships); "and Throughgood Islands."

admiral welcomed us to our ships with a volley of small shot, being all in health, God be thanked.

30. We made ready to sail to the river we had been at with our pinnace; fetching home an anchor, and getting our yards across.

1. This day, being the 1st of July, the wind northerly, July. yet at night it came southerly, and we set sail, hoping to have got to the sea, but the wind came westerly, with rain, and so we came in again.

2. The wind northerly, and rain, we riding in this harbour still.

3, 4, 5, 6, 7, 8. The wind northerly, we rode still, being wind-bound, and much rainy weather; we buying of the salvages such things as they brought us, being fresh fish, namely, salmon-trout, muskfish, codfish, and butfish, a little quantity serving for our victuals.

THE FIRST RECORDED VOYAGE

OF

WILLIAM BAFFIN.

PART II.

Fragment written by BAFFIN himself, beginning 8th July 1612.

The fourth Voyage of James Hall to Groenland, wherein he was set forth by English Aduenturers, Anno 1612, and slaine by a Greenlander.[1]

WEDNESDAY, the eighth of July 1612, in the morning I perceiued the sonne and the moone, both very faire aboue the horizon, as I had done diuers times before. At which time I purposed to finde out the longitude of that place, by the moones coming to the meridian. Most part of this day I spent about finding of the meridian line; which I did vpon an Iland neere the sea, hanging at the extreames of my meridian line two threeds with plummets at them, instead of an index and sights.

Thursday, the ninth day, very early in the morning, I went on shoare the iland, being a faire morning, and obserued till the moone came iust vpon the meridian. At which very instant I obserued the sunne's height, and found it 8° 51′ north; in the eleuation of the pole 65° 20′. By the which, working by the doctrine of sphericall triangles, having the three sides giuen, to wit, the complement of the poles eleuation; the complement of the almecanter;[2] and the complement of

[1] From *Purchas*, Part 3, lib. IV, cap. xvii, pp. 831-836.
[2] An almicanter is a circle parallel to the horizon—a circle of altitude.

the sunne's declination, to find out the quantitie of the angle at the pole. I say, by this working, I found it to be foure of the clocke, 17 minutes and 24 seconds. Which, when I had done, I found by mine ephemerides, that the moone came to the meridian at *London* that morning at foure of the clocke, 25 minutes, 34 seconds: which 17 minutes, 24 seconds, substracted from 25.34, leaveth 8.10 of time, for the difference of longitude betwixt the meridian of *London* (for which the ephemerides was made) and the meridian passing by this place in *Groenland*. Now the moone's motion that day was 12° 7′, which, conuerted into minutes of time, were 48 minutes, 29 seconds; which, working by the rule of proportion, the worke is thus: if 48 minutes, 29 seconds; the time that the moone commeth to the meridian sooner that day then she did the day before, giue 360, the whole circumference of the earth; what shall 8 minutes 10 seconds giue, to wit, 60 degrees, 30 minutes, or neere there about which is the difference of longitude betweene the meridian of *London* and this place in *Groenland*, called *Cockin's Sound*, lying to the westward of *London*.[1] 60° 30′ difference of longitude betweene the meridian of London and Cockins Sound in Groenland.

This finding of the longitude, I confesse, is somewhat difficult and troublesome, and there may be some small errour. But if it be carefully looked vnto, and exactly wrought, there will be no great errour, if your ephemerides be true. But some will say, that this kinde of working is not for marriners, because they are not acquainted to work propositions by the table of signes,[2] and an instrument is not precise enough to find out the houre, minute, and second. For the losse of one minute of time is the losse of 7 degrees of longitude. I answere, that although the most part are not vsed to this worke, yet I Objection. Answere.

---

[1] Baffin's result is a longitude too far to the westward. It is, in fact, nearly the longitude of Cape Walsingham, on the other side of Davis Strait. Cockin Sound is in 52° 50′ W. [2] Sines.

know some of the better sort, which are able to worke this and the like propositions exactly. And those which yet cannot, and are desirous to learne, may in short space attaine to such knowledge as shall be sufficient for such things. And how necessary it is that the longitude of places should be knowne, I leaue to the iudgement of all skilfull marriners, and others that are learned in the mathematicks.

This afternoone it was agreed by the chiefe of our company, that our master, *James Hall*, should goe in the smaller ship farther to the northward.

The foresaid Thursday, in the evening, he departed out of the *Patience* into the *Harts-ease*,[1] to get forth of the harbor, which our master called *Cockins-ford*, in remembrance of Alderman *Cockin*, one of the aduenturers; which place is in the latitude of 65° 20'.[2] And the variation of the compasse is 23° 28' to the westward. That evening was very calme, and we towed our shippe forth with the shallops and ship's boat. But within an houre or two after we were got into the offin, the winde being at north, it blew a great storme, which continued all that night.

Cockins Ford, in 65° 20'. Variation, 23° 58'.

The fourteenth, our master turned the ship vp to the river againe, toward the riuer where the supposed mine[3] should

---

[1] Gatonbe, the quartermaster, who wrote the preceding account of the voyage, printed in Churchill's collection, says the arrangement was that Hall, with twelve men of the *Patience*, should go on board the *Heart's Ease* to explore to the northward. Baffin and young William Huntriss were of the number. Two masters' mates and two quartermasters were left on board the *Patience*, and she was to follow from Cockayne Sound to King's (or Christian's) Fiord. The boats and shallops towed the vice-admiral (*Heart's Ease*) out to sea.

[2] The Admiralty Chart places Cockin Fiord in 65° 10' N. The Danish settlement of Sukkertoppen is really Cockin Fiord, in 65° 25' N.

[3] The main object of the expedition appears to have been to visit and collect ores from a supposed silver mine which Hall had discovered during his voyage with the Danes. Like Frobisher, he had mistaken the glittering pieces of mica occurring with the granite for silver ore.

be. But the tyde was so farre spent that we could not get to sea, but were constrained to anker in a roade at the south side of the riuer, some three leagues from the *Patience*, in which place are many good rode-steeds to be found.[1] Many good Rodes.

Thirsday, the sixteenth day, the winde was at north-west, and blew so stiffe a gale that we could not get to sea that day. That night, eighteene of vs went into the ilands to looke for some deere, but found none. But we perceiued the foote-steps of some great beast, which wee supposed to be of some great elke; the foote was as bigge as any oxe foote. Great footing.

Tuesday, the twentie-one, the weather still continued in such sort that wee could not by any means get to the riuer, where the supposed myne should bee. Wherefore our master bare roome for Ramels-ford,[2] being a river southward of another, called *Cunninghams-ford*,[3] some twelve leagues. And we came to an anchor at the entrance on the south side of the ford, about seuen of the clocke. Ramels River.

Wednesday, the two and twentieth day, about nine or

---

[1] According to Gatonbe, there was a quarrel between Hall and William Gordon, the master's mate of the *Patience*, while the two ships were at anchor in King's Fiord. "Our general, being angry, would not come aboard of us, but was in the vice-admiral."

[2] Henrik Rommel's Fiord was discovered by the Danes when Hall was with them in 1605, and so named. Hall, in his report to King Christian IV, places Rommels Fiord in 66° 35' N. latitude. Further on, in a marginal note, Baffin gives 67° as the latitude. Rommels Fiord is the harbour of Holsteinborg. The settlement on the south side is in 66° 54' N. The original settlement of Holsteinborg was founded, on the north side of the harbour, in 1759, in a spot now overgrown with willows and overshadowed by the lofty range of the Prœste-fjeld. This is exactly in Baffin's latitude. It was removed to its present site, on the south side, in 1771, and the church was founded by Paul Egede on January 6th, 1775.

[3] North of Rommels Fiord is the promontory named Cape Sophia by Hall, in 1605, after King Christian's mother; and beyond it is Cunningham's Fiord, which Hall places in 67° 25' N. The Danish chart of 1832 places its entrance in 67°15' N.

ten of the clocke, the sauages came to barter with vs, being about fortie of them, and continued about an houre and an halfe: at which time our master, *James Hall*, being in the boate,[1] a sauage with his dart strooke him a deadly wound vpon the right side, which our surgeon did thinke did pierce his liuer. We all mused that he should strike him, and offer no harme to any of the rest; vnlesse it were that they knew him since he was there with the *Danes;* for out of that riuer they carried away fiue of the people, whereof neuer any returned againe;[2] and in the next riuer they killed a great number. And it should seeme that he which killed him was either brother, or some neere kinsman to some of them that were carried away; for he did it very resolutely, and came within foure yards of him. And for ought we could see, the people are very kinde one to another, and ready to reuenge any wrong offred to them. All that day he lay very sore pained, looking for death euery houre, and resigned all his charge to Master *Andrew Barker*, master of the *Harts-ease*, willing him to place another in his room master of the small ship.[3]

James Hall deadly wounded by a Sauage.

[1] Gatonbe says that William Huntriss and two others were in the boat with Hall, when he was murdered.

[2] There is a sad account of the kidnapping of natives during the Danish voyages of 1605 and 1606, in which Hall was engaged. In the first voyage Hall's people seized four Eskimo, but killed one to strike terror into the rest, who were untractable. Two were seized by the crew of the other ship. These poor people were brought to Denmark, but constantly cast an eye northward with sorrowful countenances and pitiable sighs. At last they took to flight in their kayaks, but were caught and brought back to Copenhagen, where two of them died of grief. One of the Eskimo used to weep bitterly whenever he saw a little child hanging on its mother's neck, from which it was concluded that he must have had a wife and children. But no one could speak with them. Two died on the voyage back to Greenland. The last once more fled in his kayak, and was not overtaken until he was sixty or seventy leagues from land. On being brought back he also died of grief. See *Crantz's History of Greenland*, i, p. 277; and *Peyrere*, p. 150.

[3] Doubtless Hall named his constant and faithful attendant William Huntriss to be Master of the *Heart's Ease*.

Thursday, the three and twentieth, about eight of the clocke in the morning he dyed, being very penitent for all his former offences. And after wee had shrowded him wee carried him in the shallop, to burie him in some out iland,[1] according to his owne request while he was liuing. After we had buried him, we went in the shallop to seeke for the mine, which we had expected so long. All that day we rowed along toward the north, passing by a cape called *Queen Sophias cape*. That night we staied at an iland, some three leagues short of the river. The death of James Hall.
Queene Sophias Cape.

Friday, the four and twentieth, in the morning, wee rowed along and came to the place which is on the south side of the entrance of *Cunningham's* river. And we found diuers places where the Danes had digged; it was a kinde of shining stone, which, when our goldsmith, *James Carlisle*, had tried, it was found of no value, and had no mettall at all in it, but was like vnto *Moscouie fludde*,[2] and of a glittering colour. That day, after we had dyned, wee rowed vp that riuer some foure leagues, where diuers of our company went vp into the mountaines, and found a valley more pleasant than they had seene in the countrey. That euening we returned, and came to the place where the *Danes* had digged their supposed mine, and tooke some of it in our boate to carry with vs, and returned toward our ship. That night we rowed and sailed, and the next morning, about nine of the clocke, we came to our ship.

Saturday, the fiue and twentieth, being Saint *James* his day, in the forenoone, we came to our shippe, lying on the south side of the riuer called *Ramels* river. And as soone as our master found that the people came no more to trade with vs, he determined to depart with the shippe into the Kings Ford to the *Patience*; and rowing about the harbour, where we lay to finde some neerer way out to the sea, we

---

[1] One of the Knight Islands, outside Holsteinborg.
[2] Mica.

Many of their winter houses in Ramels River. The fashion of their greater Boates.

found among the Ilands where many of their winter houses had bin, and some of their tents were but lately carried away. In which place wee also found one of their long boates, made of wood, and bound together for the most part with shiuers of whales fins, and covered with scales skinnes, being some two and thirtie foote in length, and some fiue foote broad, having tenne thoughts or seates in it.

Ramels ford in the latitude of 67°. The variation is 24° 16'.

That day, about twelue of the clocke, we weighed anchor, and departed out of Ramels Ford, which lieth in the latitude of 67°, and the variation of the compasse is 24° 16', being a very faire riuer, and one of the most principall which we saw in that countrey, stretching in east and east and by south. This night, about one of the clocke, we came to the *Patience*, lying in the Kings Ford.[1]

Sunday, the sixe and twentieth, Master Andrew Barker, and our merchant, Master Wilkinson, with other of the company, were in conference about returning home, because that since our master was slaine, none of the sauages would trade with us as they were wont.

Wednesday, the nine and twentieth, we were likewise occupied about taking in of ballast, for our shippe was very light; and that evening it was agreed that *Andrew Barker*,[2] master of the *Harts-ease*, should goe master of the *Patience*, which was sore against the minde of *William*

---

[1] Gatonbe says: "This day at night came our vice-admiral, with our great pinnace at her stern, her flag hanging down, and her ancient hanging down over the poop, which was a sign of death."

[2] The appointment of Andrew Barker, to succeed Hall, appears to have been unpopular with the two master's mates, William Gordon and John Hemsley, and with some of the men. There was a display of mutinous feeling. Several called out for Hemsley to be general; but the quartermasters, boatswains, gunner, and other officers declared for Barker. Gatonbe says that Barker was an old and experienced seaman, having before been ruler and overseer of many good men in ships in Hull, besides other places, and having been one of the chief masters and wardens of the Trinity House. The officers

Gourdon;[3] and *William Huntrice*[4] was appointed master of the *Harts-ease;* and *John Gatenby*,[5] one of the quarter-masters of the *Patience,* was masters-mate of the *Harts-ease.*

eventually succeeded in persuading the two crews to accept Barker as general of the expedition and the arrangements made by him.

Through the kindness of Mr. Wilson, of the Trinity House, at Hull, I am able to give the following additional particulars respecting Andrew Barker. He was admitted a younger brother of the Trinity House of Hull in the year 1594, and was three times Warden, namely, in 1606, 1613, and 1618. In 1611 Barker made a voyage to the northern seas, and brought back a cargo from Wardhous (Vardö in Norway).

Among the Lansdowne Manuscripts in the British Museum (923), there is a collection of pencil-notes on Hull and the neighbourhood by Warburton, made in the summer of 1724. From one of these notes it appears that Andrew Barker presented one of the compartments of painted glass in the east window of the old chapel of the Hull Trinity House. The figure was that of St. James-the-less. This has disappeared; but there still hangs in the Hall of the Trinity House the

---

[3] William Gordon was afterwards employed in Spitzbergen voyages. He cannot have been the same William Gordon whom the Muscovy Company sent to reside at Pustozera on the Pechora river in 1611 as one of their traders. This William Gordon wrote an interesting report, in 1615, on the Samoyeds, their dress, sledges, tents, customs, etc., which is published in *Purchas,* iii, p. 553.

[4] William Huntriss, or Huntrice, was a Yorkshire lad. Purchas says he came from "Stoneborough". But there is no such place in Yorkshire. It is probably a misprint for Scarborough. Huntriss is a Scarborough name, and there is Huntriss Row in the old town. Young William Huntriss went the first voyage to Greenland with James Hall. This expedition, under Captain Cunningham, was sent by the King of Denmark, and sailed from Copenhagen on May 2nd, 1605. Hall was master of the *Troost,* Cunningham's ship, and Huntriss was Hall's boy. The ship anchored off the Greenland coast, and Hall went to explore in the pinnace, attended by his boy. On this occasion young Huntriss, when in the boat, was shot through both buttocks by an Eskimo arrow.

He went with Hall in his second and third voyages, and was allowed £30 a year by the King of Denmark for his skill in navigation.

When Hall left the Danish service his faithful boy accompanied him, and went out in this Greenland voyage from Hull, of which Baffin is the historian. Now we find him promoted to be Master of the second

28   THE FIRST RECORDED VOYAGE OF

<small>They come out of harbour.</small>

Tuesday, the fourth of August, in the morning, the winde being northerly, a very small gale, we got to sea, where the winde came to the southward, and we tacked sometime on the one boord, and sometime on the other, making small way on our course.

<small>Thick and foggie weather, the winde being south.</small>

Munday (sic), the tenth, was raine and foule weather, as it had continued euery day since wee came from harbour, sauing the seuenth day, which was somewhat faire; for commonly, while the winde is south, it is very thick and foule weather. We tacked sometimes on one boord, and sometimes on the other, making a south-by-west way, at noone six leagues.

<small>Burnils Cape.</small>

Wednesday, the twelfth, it waxed calme, we being somewhat southward of a cape, called *Burnils Cape*;[1] and about

model of a *kayak*, with an Eskimo in it, which was presented by Andrew Barker. It has the following inscription:—

"*Andrew Barker, one of the Masters of this House, on his voyage from Greenland, anno domini 1613, took up this boat and a man in it, of which this is the effigy.*"

In the accounts for the second quarter of Andrew Barker's third Wardenship, A.D. 1619, are the following entries:—

" Item to Edward Ffewlis for c rving the Greynlander   v⁸

" Item to the paynter for the Greynlander   . iiij."

And in the succeeding Warden's accounts (A.D. 1620) is the following entry:—" Item to Andrewe Barker, wᶜʰ he paid about the Grenlandman more than he accompted for at the auditt .   viijˢ."

Kayaks from Greenland were also brought home by Frobisher and Davis, and there was one hanging in the hall of Sir Thomas Smith's house. In the curious old *Schiffer-gesellschaft*, at Lubeck, there is an old *kayak* hanging from the beams, which appears, from the inscription, to have been brought to Europe by the Danish Expedition of 1607.

[1] Burnil's Cape is the Cape Burnitt of the Admiralty Chart, which is copied from the Danish Chart of 1832. The name was given by Hall

ship, the *Heart's Ease*. Further on we shall find that Baffin's ship, the *Patience*, lost sight of the *Heart's Ease* in a gale on September 2nd. She arrived safely in the Thames on September 19th, and I have not been able to find any further trace of young Huntriss.

[5] Or Gatonbe, writer of the other account of the voyage in Churchill. See note at page 2.

three or foure of the clocke in the afternoone, the winde came to the north and by west, an easie gale, with faire weather.

The eighteenth, at noon, we were in 58° 50′. The seventeenth day I tooke the variation of the compasse, finding it to be 13° 22′, contrary to the obseruations of others in this place. And if any doe doubt of the truth thereof, they may with a little paines prove it. The eighteenth of August, the declination of the sunne was 9° 58′, for the meridian of London. But we being almost foure houres of time to the westward thereof, there are three minutes to be abated from the rest: and so the declination was 9° 55′; and his height aboue the horizon was 24° 40′ in the latitude of 59° 0′; and his distance from the south to the westward, by the compasse, was 81°. And for truth of the first obseruation, I tooke another shortly after, finding them not to differ above 4′. *Variation 13° 22′.*

Wednesday, the nineteenth, the winde still continued with thick and hasie weather, we being at noone in the latitude of 58° 30′, or thereabout, making a south southeast way, about ten leagues.

Thursday, the twentieth, was faire weather, the wind at east north-east, wee steered away south-east and south-east and by east, making at noone a south-east and by south way, about thirtie leagues, being at noone in the latitude of 57° 20′. This day, in the afternoone, I tooke the variation of the compasse, and found it about 11° 10′. *Variation 11° 10′.*

Friday, the one and twentieth, faire weather, with the winde at north and north by east, and we made an east

in the voyage of 1605, and I think it probable that it should be Cape Brunel, after Oliver Brunel, the Dutch explorer, who was for some time in the Danish service. For a full account of Brunel, and of the difficult questions connected with his history, see Lieut. Kooleman Beynen's Introduction to the *Barents' Voyages* (Hakluyt Society's vol. 1876). See also the note at the end of the Voyage of Knight (Hakluyt Society's vol. *Voyages of Lancaster*).

south-east way, half southerly, some twentie-foure leagues, being at noone, by obseruation, in the latitude of 56° 50′.

Saturday, the two and twentieth, faire weather, the wind at north and north by east, wee made an east way half southerly, some twentie-two leagues, being at noone in the latitude of 56° 47′.

Sunday, the three and twentieth, faire weather, the wind at west north-west, we making an east and east by north way, about twenty-four leagues. This day I tooke the variation of the compasse, and found it to be 7° 23′, being at noone in the latitude of 57° 26′.

<small>Variation 7° 23′.</small>

Munday, the foure and twentieth, being *S. Bartholomewes* day, faire weather with a north north-west, wee making an east north-east way, halfe northerly, about twenty-seven leagues, and were at noon, by observation, in the latitude of 58° 4′. This day I obserued and found the compasse to be varied 7° 20′.

<small>Variation 7° 20′.</small>

Tuesday, the fiue and twentieth, faire weather and calme; the winde at north, wee made a north-east and by east way, seuenteene leagues, being at noone in the latitude of 58° 30′. This day I found the common compasse to be varied one point, and the true variation to be 6° 4′.

<small>The true variation 6° 4′.</small>

Wednesday, the sixe and twentieth, faire weather also, with the wind north north-west, wee made a north-east and by east way halfe, about twentie two leagues, being in the height of 59° 10′.

Thursday, the seven and twentieth, indifferent faire weather, with a stiffe gale of wind at the north north-west, we making a north-east way about thirty-one leagues, being at noone in the latitude of 60° 10′.

Friday, the eight and twentieth, the wind at south-east, with a stiffe gale, wee made good about noone a north-east and by east way, about twenty-nine leagues. This day, in the afternoon it blew so greate a storme that we were in great distresse, the winde at east south-east. But about eleuen of the clocke it came to the north-west, and north-west by north. And we ranne some twentie leagues.

Saturday, the nine and twentieth, it blew so stiffe that wee could beare none but our foresaile, making an east and by south way, halfe southerly, about thirtie leagues.

Sunday, the thirtieth, all the forenoone it blew a very stiffe gale, and about noone the winde came southerly; and it blew a very great storme, which continued all that day and that night, in such sort that we could not saile at all, but all that night lay at hull.

Monday, the one and thirtieth, in the morning about foure of the clocke, the winde came to the south-west a very stiffe gale, at which time we set our fore-saile. The wind continued all this day and night; we steered away east and by south, making at noon an east north-east way, about thirtie foure leagues.

Tuesday, the first of September, the wind still continued at south-west, blowing a very stiffe gale; we steered away east and by south, making an east way about fiftie leagues. This day, at noon, we were in the latitude of 60° 45′.

Wednesday, the second, faire weather, with the wind at south-west; wee made an east and by south way, half a point southerly, about fortie-two leagues, being at noone in the latitude of 60° 10′. This day I obserued, and found the compasse to be varied three degrees to the westward.

Thursday, the third day, faire weather, the wind at south-west; wee made an east by north way at noone, about twentie leagues. This day, in the after-noone, the winde being at north north-west, it blew a very stiffe gale for two watches; and toward seuen or eight of the clocke the storme so increased that our shippe was not able to beare any saile. And all that night wee lay at hull.[1]

Friday, the fourth, the storme still continued, and we

[1] Lying-to.

could beare no saile all that day till about foure of the clocke in the afternoone, at which time we set our fore course and our maine course. The night before, in the storme we lost the *Harts-ease*.[1] This day wee made some twelue leagues east and by north, and we fell to lee-ward, lying at hull some fiue leagues south by west.

The lose company of their consort, the Hartsease.

Saturday, the fift, calme weather, but very thicke and close all the fore-noone : the wind continued still at north north-west; we making, from the time wee set our courses the day before, about twentie leagues east half southerly, beeing at noone in the latitude of 59° 53'.

Sunday, the sixt, faire weather, the wind at north north-west, we steering away east north-east, and east and by north, made an east by north way, half northerly some 29 leagues, being at noone in 60° 10'. This day the compasse was varied to the east sixe degrees. This afternoone it was almost calme, and wee sounded, and found ground at sixtie eight fathomes. This evening, about ten of the clock, the wind came to the south-east.

Variation 6 degrees to the East. Ground found.

Munday, the seventh, very faire weather, the wind south-east and south-east by east; wee tacked in the morning to the northward, and ranne east north-east and east by north vntill seuen or eight in the afternoone, at which time we tacked vp to the southward, and went away south-west till toward twelue a clocke that night, twentie leagues.

Tuesday, the eight, in our morning watch I found our selues to be in 59° 20', and about fiue of the clock I espied land, which wee supposed to bee the Isles of *Orkney*, as

---

[1] The *Heart's Ease*, under command of young William Huntriss, with John Gatonbe on board, diligently writing his journal, lost sight of the *Patience* on the 4th of September, as here recorded by Baffin. On the 8th she sighted Fair Isle, and on the 15th arrived in Yarmouth Roads, proceeding to London instead of going to Hull, as the *Patience* did. The *Heart's Ease* entered the Thames on the 19th of September, and Huntriss caused the flags to be hoisted half mast, in token of the death of his beloved commander, James Hall. He brought the ship up to St. Katherine's Pool.

afterward we found them to be the same; and toward three of the clocke we came to an anchor in a channell running betweene the Ilands, where the people came to vs, and brought vs hennes, geese, and sheepe, and sold them to vs for old clothes and shoes, desiring rather them then money. There are about eighteene of these Ilands, which are called by the name of the Orkneis. *The Iles of Orkney.*

Wednesday, the ninth, it was thicke weather, and the wind so easterly that wee could not weigh anchor.

Thursday, the tenth, faire weather, and the wind came to the north-west, and about noone we weighed anchor; and towarde fiue of the clocke we were cleere off the Iles. The channel, for the most part, lyeth north-west and south-east. All that night we stood away south-east. *The lying of the Channel in Orkney.*

Friday, the eleuenth, faire weather, with the wind at north north-west; and about nine of the clocke in the morning we steered away south south-east, at which time wee had sight of Buguham-nesse,[1] and about two of the clocke we were thwart of it. The seuenteenth, we came to an anchor in Hull Road, for which the Lord bee praysed. *Buguham-ness. They arrive at Hull.*

Here I thinke it not amisse briefly to relate the state and manner of the people of Groenland, forasmuch as I could learne; as also what likelihood there is of a passe into the sea, which lyeth vpon Tartarie and China.

The north-west part of Gronland is an exceeding high land to the sea-ward, and almost nothing but mountaynes, which are wonderfull high all within the land, as farre as wee could perceiue; and they are all of stone, some of one colour, and some of another, and all glistering, as though they were of rich value, but indeed they are not worth anything; for our gold-smith, James Carlisle, tryed very much of the Vre, and found it to bee nothing worth.[2] If there bee any mettall, it lyeth so low in the mountaynes *No profitable Vre.*

[1] Buchan Ness, the east point of Aberdeenshire.

[2] The mica, often found in masses in clefts of the gneiss, was mistaken for silver ore.

34   THE FIRST RECORDED VOYAGE OF

<small>Continuall snow.</small>

<small>Grasse.</small>

<small>No trees.</small>

<small>Balls River.</small>

<small>A grove of small wood.</small>

that it cannot bee well come by. There are some rocks in these mountaynes, which are exceeding pure stone, finer, and whiter then alabaster.[1] The sides of these mountaynes continually are covered with snow for the most part, and especially the north sides, and the No[r]th sides of the valleyes hauing a kind of mosse, and in some places grasse, with a little branch running all along the ground, bearing a little black berrie; it runneth along the ground like three-leaued grasse heere in England. There are few or no trees growing, as farre as wee could perceiue; but in one place, some fortie miles within the land, in a river, which wee called *Balls* River. There I saw, on the south side of an high mountayne, which we went vp, and found (as it were) a yong groue of small wood, some of it sixe or seuen foot high, like a coppice in England that had beene some two or three yeers cut; and this was the most wood that wee saw growing in this country, being some of it a kind of willow, juniper, and such like.[2]

We found in many places much angelica. We suppose the people eate the roots thereof, for some causes, for we haue seene them have many of them in their boats.[3]

[1] Quartz.

[2] The largest tree ever seen by Dr. Rink, in Greenland, was a birch fourteen feet high, in the Tasermiut fjord, in 60° N. lat. This *Betula alpestris* is only found south of 62° N. South of 65° N. the alder (*Alnus repens*) grows scantily.

[3] The *Quan* (*Archangelica officinalis*) is found in the fjords of South Greenland, and more rarely in Disco. The word *Quan*, now used by the Eskimo, is Norse, and hence it is supposed that angelica was introduced by the Normans. The young stalks are eaten raw, being brittle and sweet. In sheltered spots the plant will grow to a height of six feet. Angelica was well known in the kitchen gardens of England in the days of Baffin. Gervase Markham, in his "*Country Farm*" (published in 1616), includes it among the physic herbs, which should, he recommends, be grown in certain borders below the kitchen garden, near the wall of the orchard. The root was believed to be sovereign against the plague and all sorts of poisons, and Englishmen then used the leaves and stalks in sauce with their meats, because it was supposed to help digestion

There are a great store of foxes in the Ilands, and in the Mayne, of sundry colours; and there are a kind of hares, as white as snow, with their furre or haire very long. *Foxes. White hares*

Also there be deere, but they are most commonly vp within the Mayne very farre; because the people doe so much hunt them that come neere the sea. I saw at one time seuen of them together, which were all that wee did see in the country. But our men have bought diuers coates of the people, made of deeres skinnes, and have bought of their hornes also. Besides, we have diuers times seene the footsteps of some beast, whose foote was bigger than the foot of a great oxe. Furthermore, the inhabitants haue a kinde of dogges, which they keepe at their houses and tents, which dogges are almost like vnto wolues, liuing by fish, as the foxes doe. But one thing is very strange, as I thought; for the pizzles of both dogges and foxes are bone. *Deere. These seeme to be elkes, or Loshes. Dogges like Wolves. The pizzles of Dogges and foxes are bone; so also is the Morses pizzle, of which I have by me one of stone.*

The people, all the summer time, vse nothing but fishing, drying their fish and seales flesh vpon the rockes, for their winter prouision. Euery one, both man and woman, haue each of them a boate, made with long small pieces of firre-wood, couered with seales skinnes very well drest, and sewed so well with sinewes or guts that no water can pierce them through, being some of them aboue twentie foot long, and not past two foot, or two foot and an halfe broad, in forme of a weauers shittle (*sic*), and so light, that a man may carrie many of them at once for the weight. In these boates they will row so swiftly, that it is almost incredible; for no ship in the world is able to keepe way with them, although shee haue neuer so good a gale of wind; and yet they vse but one oare, who, sitting in the middle (*sic*) of their boate, and holding their oare in the *The great swiftnesse of their Boats. Their Oares broad at both ends.*

very much. The leaves were held to be good against sorcery and enchantment. For notices of angelica in Greenland, see *Crantz*, i, p. 61; and *Egede*, p. 45.

middle, being broad at each end like our oares, will at an instant goe backward and forward as they please.¹

In these boates they catch the most part of their food, being seales and salmons, morses, and other kinds of fishes. Some they kill with their darts, and other some with angles, hauing a line made of small shiuers of whales finnes, and an hooke of some fishes bones, with which·lines and hookes we also have caught very much fish.

<small>Salmons and Morses, etc. Angles and Lines.</small>

Also they haue another kinde of boate, which is very long; for wee haue seene one of them thirty-two foot in length, open in the toppe like our boates, hauing tenne seats in it; in which, when they remooue their dwellings, they carrie their goods or house-hold stuffe; for they remooue their dwellings very often, as their fishing doth serve, liuing in the summer-time in tents made of seales skinnes, and in winter in houses somewhat in the ground.

<small>Their great Boats 32 foot long.</small>

Wee could not particularly learn their rites or ceremonies; but generally they worship the sunne, as chiefe authour of their felicitie. At their first approach vnto vs, they vsed with their hands to point vp to the sunne, and to strike their hands upon ther brests *Ilyout*²; as who would say, I meane no harme; which they will doe very often, and will not come neer you vntil you do the like, and then they will come without any feare at all.

<small>They worship the Sunne.</small>

<small>Their salutation.</small>

They burie their dead in the out-Ilands neere the seaside. Their manner of buriall is this:—vpon the tops of the hils they gather a company of stones together, and make thereof an hollow caue or graue, of the length and breadth of the bodie which they intend to burie, laying the stones somewhat close like a wall, that neyther foxes nor other such beasts may deuoure the bodies, couering them

<small>Their burials.</small>

---

¹ Both Frobisher and Davis brought home kayaks, and one was hanging in the hall of Sir Thomas Smith's house.

² Davis, in his list, gives the same word with the same meaning—"*Yliaoute*", "I mean no harm" (Hakluyt Society's ed., p. 21).

with broad stones, shewing afar off like a pile of stones.
And neere vnto this graue where the bodie lyeth is another, wherein they burie his bow and arrowes, with his darts and all his other prouision which hee vsed while hee was liuing. Hee is buried in all his apparell; and the coldnesse of the climate doth keepe the bodie from smelling and stinking, although it lye aboue ground. *[They burie the weapons and all other furniture of the dead.]*

They eat all their food raw, and vse no fire to dress their victuals, as farre as wee could perceiue. Also wee haue seene them drinke the salt-water at our shippes side; but whether it be vsuall or no, I cannot tell. Although they dresse not their meate with fire, yet they vse fire for other things, as to warme them, etc. *[They vse fire.]*

Diuers of our men were of opinion that they were maneaters, and would haue deuoured vs, if they could haue caught vs. But I do not thinke they would; for if they had bin so minded, they might at one time haue caught our cooke, and two other with him, as they were filling of water at an Iland a great way from ovr ship. These three, I say, were in the ships boate, without eyther musket or any other weapon; when, as a great company of the sauages came rowing vnto them with their darts and other furniture, which they neuer goe without, and stood looking into the boate for nayles, or any old iron, which they so greatly desire, while our men were in such a feare that they knew not what to doe. At length our cooke remembered that hee had some old iron in his pocket, and gaue each of them some, as farre as it would goe, with his key of his chest. And presently they all departed, without offering any harme at all: but this I speake not that I would haue men to trust them, or to goe among them vnprouided of weapons. *[They are not Man-eaters.] [Nailes and old Iron greatly desired of the Sauages.]*

SECOND RECORDED VOYAGE

OF

WILLIAM BAFFIN.

I.

A Journall of the Voyage made to Greenland[1] with sixe English ships and a Pinasse, in the yeere 1613.

Written by MASTER WILLIAM BAFFIN.[2]

Ascension day.
BY the prouidence of Almightie God wee departed from *Queenborough* the thirteenth day of May with sixe good ships, viz., the *Tigre*, admirall; the *Matthew*, vice-admirall: the *Sea-horse*, called the *Gamaliel*, the reare-admirall; the *Desire*, the *Annula*, and the *Richard and Barnard*, with the *John and Francis* shortly to follow.[3]

---

[1] Spitzbergen.

[2] From *Purchas*, Part III, lib. IV, cap. V, pp. 716 to 720. There is another account of this voyage, believed to have been written by Fotherby, which follows this journal.

[3] The Fotherby Narrative tells us that Mr. Benjamin Joseph, of London, was chief captain—"a man very sufficient and worthy of his place". There were twenty-four Biscayners, the most expert whale fishers of those days, in the fleet. The *Tiger*, of 260 tons, was admiral; the *Matthew*, of 250 tons, vice-admiral; and the *Gamaliel*, 200 tons, rear-admiral. The other vessels were the *John and Francis*, 180 tons; *Desire*, 180 tons; and *Annula*, 140 tons. The *Richard and Barnard* was a pinnace of 60 tons, intended for further discovery. The fleet dropped down to Gravesend on April 30th, and on the 4th of May "wee entered into the Swaile at Quinborowe". On the 7th, the Royal Fleet, returning from landing the Count Palatine and the Princess Elizabeth, passed them, and there was an exchange of salutes. On the

The one and twentieth day, faire weather, the winde southwarde, wee still making to the northwards. This morning wee had sight of land on the coast of Norway, it lying east and by north off about twelue or fourteene leagues. This day, at noone, we were in the latitude of 61° 30′, the variation of the compasse at Scoutes-nes is eight degrees east, it being about ten or twelve leagues off; wee hauing made a north way halfe east, about thirtie leagues.

The three and twentieth, at noone, in the latitude of 65° 45′, in which plaçe the needle of declination doth dippe vnder the horizon 63° 30′ by that instrument, which declineth 54 at London.

The thirtieth day, about three of the clock,[1] wee espied the land of Greenland,[2] being about eight or nine leagues off. The southwardest part of it bare south-east and by east off it, which shortly wee perceiued to bee the land lying in 76° 55′, which is called Horne-sound.[3] This land

<small>Greenland attayned in eighteen dayes.</small>

13th of May the exploring fleet sailed from the Swale. Benjamin Joseph, the general of the voyage, was a man in high repute for skill and conduct. After his return from Spitzbergen he commanded a small ship of Bristol, and brought timely relief to Waterford, when Captain Downton arrived there from the East Indies in October 1613, in sore need of provisions. At that very time the Court of Directors was recognising his claim to command one of their fleets. He appears to have made demands at first which were considered unreasonable; but an agreement was arrived at, and in December 1613, Benjamin Joseph was appointed to command the East India Company's fleet. He himself was in the *Charles*, on board of which a journal was kept by Henry Crosby, master's mate *(preserved at the India Office—No. 23)*, and his vice-admiral was the *Unicorn*. In 1617 Captain Joseph was slain in a fight with a Portuguese karrack. His widow Isabell petitioned the Company for a gratuity, and a sum of £40 was granted, and thankfully accepted by her son-in-law, Mr. Maddocks.

[1] The Fotherby Narrative says four o'clock in the morning, all the ships being in company.

[2] Spitzbergen.

[3] Discovered and so named by Jonas Poole in his voyage in the *Amity* for the Muscovy Company, in 1610.

lyeth, by our common compasse, north north-west. Within two houres after we had sight of land, it began to snowe, and was very cold. This euening the compasse was varied thirteene degrees west.

The one and thirtieth day, variable weather with snowe, and very cold, and the winde also variable; and in the afternoone the winde was at the north-east. In the morning wee espied a ship, and about noone wee spoke with her, and their master and pilot came aboord of vs; and wee knew them to bee that ship of Saint John de Luys, which had leaue of the Companie to fish; and they told vs that there were eight Spaniards on the coast. Also wee espied another ship, which we supposed to be a Frenchman, and had one Allan Sallas to their pilot.

<small>A ship of Saint John de Luz.</small>

<small>Eight Spaniards on the Coast.</small>

The second of June, in the morning, about fiue of the clocke, our generall sent our shallop to a small pinke, that all this night we saw along the shoare, to bid their master and pilot come aboord vs, which presently they did. The masters name was Clais Martin of Horne, and his ship was for Dunkerke, and he told vs that he was consorted with another ship that was his admirall; the captaines name was Fopp of Dunkerke, and that he was on the coast. Wee kept the master and pilot aboord of vs, and sent some of our men aboord of her, and brought her vnder our lee; and then wee sent their master aboord againe, charging them to follow vs. This afternoone we took their shallop, with fiue or sixe men, whereof two were English men, and one Scot, at the Faire foreland.[1]

<small>The Generall was Captain Beniamin Joseph, after slaine in a fight with a Carrike.</small>

The fourth day, also faire weather. This morning was the first whale killed.[2] We had no night since the three

<small>Dutch ship.</small>

<small>No night the 23 May.</small>

---

[1] The northern point of Prince Charles Island, so named by Jonas Poole in 1610.

[2] Fotherby, who was in the *Matthew*, says that they ran before a fresh gale to the north end of Prince Charles Island, and then beat up into Sir Thomas Smith's Bay, where the fleet anchored. Then the Bis-

and twentieth of May. The fift day, faire weather, but very cold, the winde north.[1] We sayled along the Iland, being about eighteene or twentie leagues in length, lying for the most part, by the common compasse, north and by west half westward. About nine of the clocke in the afternoone we saw our other three ships, viz., the *Gamaliel*, the *Desire*, and the *Richard and Barnard*, which lay there to and fro, because they could not goe into their harbour by reason of the ice; and also because there were foure other ships in a bay or coue, called Pooppy Bay, or Nickes Coue; and also other ships on the other side in Greene Harbour. We sailed along the drift ice vntill about one or two of the clocke in the morning, at which time we came to an anchor in the entrance of the sound, because the ice came driuing out so fast.

The sixt day, faire weather, the wind variable till the afternoone, at which time it came to the northwards. About three in the afternoone we weighed anchor, and about ten of the clocke we came to the foure ships lying in Pooppy Bay, two of them being Hollanders, and one a Rocheller, and the other a ship of Burdeaux. The masters of the Hollanders came aboord of our ship to speake with the generall, both of them being of Amsterdam, and

Divers strangers.

cayners, "our whale stickers", went away in their boats to look out for whales off the Foreland. The rest of the men took the coppers for melting blubber, and the casks on shore, and got everything ready for boiling down. Then came the news that the Biscayners had killed a whale, and from that time the work of boiling down went briskly forward.

[1] On the 5th, word was brought from Green Harbour that five ships, Spanish and French, were come into Ice Sound, intending to fish for the whale. So the *Tiger* weighed anchor and made sail for Ice Sound. "Then did our Admiral continue as a *wafter* alongst the coast, till the 27th of June, and then he came to us againe into Sir Thomas Smyth's Baye." A "*wafter*" was a term applied to ships of war, probably from their carrying flags or *wafts*.

brought a commission granted by the Graue Maurice, for to fish in this country. But, when they saw our Kings Maiestys Commission granted to the worshipful companie, they told our generall that they would depart this coast, hauing our general's ticket to shew to their aduenturers that they were there, and had made their port, and how he would not suffer them to fish. We anchored close by the French ship, wherein was Allane Sallis,[1] being ready to fight if they refused to come aboord vs. So when we sent our shallop, the master came presently, and their surgeon, who could speake English. At the first, they denyed that Sallas was aboord of them; but, being hardly urged, they confessed that hee and one Thomas Fisher, an English man, was aboord, who were both presently sent for. This Sallas was their pilot, and Fisher was their gunner.

The seuenth day, faire weather, we road still at anchor. This day I obserued the latitude of the place, and found it in 78° 24′. The variation of the compasse is, in this place, 15° 21′ west. About a north sunne, a small ship of Biscay came into the harbour where we roade.

<small>Lat. 78° 24′.</small>

<small>Ship of Biscay. Snowe.</small>

The eight day, for the most part snow, the winde southward. This day the master of the French ship, being a ship of nine score, or two hundred, called the *Jaques* of Burdeaux, agreed with our generall that he might fish on the coast: our generall was to have halfe the whales he could kill. Also, this day the master of the ship of Rochel, and the master of the small ship of Biscay, were agreed to depart from the coast.

The ninth day, faire weather. This morning the *Gumaliel*, our rear-admirall, and the *Desire*, weighed anchor to goe for Greene-harbour, where two ships lay, one of Dunkerke, and the other of Saint Sebastian in Biscay. The captaine of the Dunkirke, called Fopp, had beene with our generall, and told him that he would depart from this coast. Our generall gaue him leaue to take the pilot of the small

[1] Allen Sallowes, an English pilot.

pinke, and the other Dutch men he had taken of his, keeping only the English men and the Scots; also the two ships of Holland, with the ship of Biscay, and that of *Rochel* weighed anchor, and departed from this harbour. About sixe of the clocke in the afternoone came the master of the ship of Saint Sebastian aboord of vs, being brought by one of the masters mates of the *Desire* (they hauing taken two of his shallops) to know our generals pleasure, whether he should haue them againe or no. Our generall gaue them him againe, vpon condition that he would depart the coast. About a north north-west sunne, we weighed anchor to goe for Horne-Sound, where we heard that there were diuers ships; the wind northward; a small gale.

The tenth day, faire weather, the winde at north, being very close weather. About a north sunne, we came to an anchor, in the entrance of Low Sound, where we saw two ships ride at anchor. Our generall sent our shallop to see what ships they were, who found them to bee the two ships of Holland. Also our long boate went on shoare, to set vp the Kings Maiesties armes vpon a low point of land, lying a great way off, called Low-nesse. We set vp a crosse of wood, and nayled the armes vpon it. {Low Sound. His Maiesties Armes and a Crosse set up at Lownesse.}

The thirteenth day, in the morning, it snowed very fast, being very thicke weather, the winde variable, we standing off from the land. About seuen of the clock it began to cleere vp, at which time we espied three ships; and making toward them, at length we perceiued them to be the three ships which came from the bay where we road; the winde also was at east and by south, and blew a very stiffe gale. Then we stood in for the shoare, and spent most of this day in turn vp Horne-Sound. And about a north northwest sunne, at ten a clock, wee espied six ships lying at anchor on the south side of the Sound, in a small bay. The one of them was Captaine Fopp, the Dunkerker, who came in before vs, and was appointed by our generall to come into this harbour, and there to stay for vs, and to goe to the Foreland, to haue his other ship which we kept there. Foure of them were Biscaines of Saint Sebastian; and one of them was in the harbour where we road and found the French ship. The sixt was a ship of Amsterdam wherein Thomas Bonner was master and pilot, and aboue twentie English men more. All the Biscaines came aboord of vs, as soone as we were at an anchor; but Thomas Bonner refused to come, being sent for by our generall. Our generall commanded our gunner to shoot at him, he himself discharging the second ordnance. Then presently he began to set saile, and cut his cable, thinking to get from vs; but wee hauing shot him through three or foure times, they began to weaue vs, so we sent our shallop and he came aboord. There were fiue or sixe more of the English men fetched aboord, and some of our men sent to bring her to an anchor, where she might ride safe, for shee was almost run ashoare. This was about a north sunne, or eleuen a clocke. The Biscaines were charged presently to depart, so soone as they had filled fresh water, which they said they wanted; and to bring what whale finnes they had found, or had taken, or other things.

The fourteenth day, faire weather, the winde at east north-east. This morning, one of the Biscaines brought a few whale finnes aboord of vs, and the skin of a beare, which they had killed. Then was our boate-swaine sent aboord of them to search their ships, and to bid them depart. Our generall kept the Holland ship, wherein was Thomas Bonner, to the vse of the Companie. This day I oberued the latitude of this place by a quadrant of foure foote semi-diameter, and found it to stand in 76° 55′: the declination of the needle vnder the horizon is 67° 30′, pointing to the northwards; but pointing to the southwards, it is 80°. The variation of the compasse is 12° 14′ west, from the true meridian; but from our common sayling compass it is

17°, because the compasse is touched five degrees and a halfe to the eastward, and the variation is to the westward. This day, in the afternoone, the foure ships of Biscay departed from this harbour, which is called Horne-sound; and about a north sunne, I, with the master, Thomas Sherin, went ashore with other, to set vp another crosse with the Kings Maiesties arms, cast in lead, nayled vpon it. Then I obserued the sunne vpon his north meridian, by my foresaid quadrant, and found it eleuated aboue the horizon 10° 30'; but because his height at the south meridian, and his height at the north, did not agree in finding of the latitude, I did abate fiue minutes from each, as the meane betwixt both; for his altitude at the south meridian was 36° 40', the declination 23° 29'.

The fifteenth day, faire weather; the winde in the morning south, but almost calme. This day, about noone, we weighed anchor with the ship of Amsterdam, and diuers of her men were fetched aboord vs with their shipper, and some of our men were sent aboord her with one of our masters mates, called Master Spencer. All this day it was so calme, that wee were faine to towe our ship. Our carpenter did trim vp two of the Biscaine shallops, which they did leaue behind them, and they did leaue diuers hoopes and caske [s?] staued ashore.

The eighteenth day, faire weather; the winde variable, we stearing away northward. This afternoone wee met with another ship of Biscay, being a ship of two or three hundred tunnes. Our generall, as he did to the rest, caused her master and pilot to come aboord vs, to whom he shewed his commission, charging them to depart this countrey. They, seeing no remedie, were content, so soone as they had filled fresh water. We met with them off the southward part of the Iland. Our generall being so neere Greene Harbour, where the *Gamaliel* and the *Desire* road, wee went into the Sound to see them, with this great ship of Biscay, and the ship of Amsterdam. We found that the entrance of Greene Harbour was quite stopped with ice, and ran our ship into it, thinking to get through, but wee could not. Then wee got her out againe and came to the bay, where we roade on the other side of the sound in Pooppy Bay, or Nickes Coue.

<small>Abundance of Ice.</small>

The nineteenth day, faire weather, the winde northward. This day, about twelue of the clock, we came to an anchor in the foresaid bay. This afternoone there came another ship of Saint Sebastian into the bay where wee roade; and about seuen of the clock the captain came aboord of vs, who told us that he had lost six of his men and a shallop vpon the coast of Groineland, vpon an Iland in the latitude of 72°, or thereabouts. This was the master which had beene here last yeere, and made a great voyage, Master Woodcocke being their pilot. His making so great a voyage was the cause that so many ships were here this yeere.

<small>An Iland in 72° on the Coast of Groinland.</small>

The twentieth in the morning we had news that the *John and Francis* was come about two days agoe, and that they had killed one and twentie whales at the Foreland, and had also killed two at Greene harbour. This day it was very close weather with some snowe; the winde north-west. This afternoone the captains of the two Biscay ships were commanded to depart this coast.

The one and twentieth wee perceiued another ship standing toward vs. Wee lessened our sailes, and stayed for her to see what she was. At length we perceiued her to bee another Biscaine. About a north sunne we came to an anchor in Greene harbour, by the *Gamaliel* and the *Desire*, and the ship of Burdeaux, and the Biscaine followed vs. So soone as they were come to an anchor, their captaine came aboord of vs, to whom our generall shewed his commission, as he had done to the rest, charging him to depart those coasts, and told him that hee would take away some of their shallops. They earnestly intreated him not to take them away, and they would depart; the captaine offering his bond to our generall, that if he stayed either in Greenland, Groineland, or Cherie Iland, he would willingly forfeit all he was worth. There was another whale killed in Greeneharbour, in the killing whereof there was a man slaine, and a boate ouerwhelmed by too much haste of following him, after the harping iron was in him. ^{A man slaine.}

The three and twentieth day, faire weather, the winde northward. This day and the last night I obserued the latitude of the place where we roade, and found it by both to bee in the latitude of 78° 7'; the skie at both obseruations being very cleere, where I find that there is no sensible error betweene a south obseruation and a north, the skie being cleare. But if the skie be hasie, there will be some difference as of eight or ten miuutes, being obserued on shore by some large quadrant or other instrument for the purpose; also a south south-west moone, by the common compasse, maketh a fulle sea in this place.[1] ^{Lat. 78° 7'. Note.} ^{A South South west Moone maketh a full Sea here.}

The ninth of July, faire weather, the winde at north. This day wee stood to the southward along the Iland; but toward night it fell calme, and then the winde came to the west. The tenth day, faire weather, but thicke and close, the winde south south-west. All this day we stood for Bel-sound.[2] Our generall went on shoare this afternoone, and killed foure deere, and brought a young morse aliue with him aboord.

The eleuenth day, faire weather, but calme. This afternoone wee perceiued fiue shippes in a bay in Bel-sound.

---

[1] On the 27th of June the *Tiger* returned to Sir Thomas Smyth's Bay, rejoining the *Matthew*. During her cruise as a *wafter*, she had met seventeen ships,—four from Holland, two from Dunkirk, four from St. Jean de Luz, and seven from San Sebastian. All their commanders had submitted to the English commander, and had agreed either to leave the coast or to remain upon such conditions as he proposed to them.

[2] So named by Jonas Poole in 1610.

The winde was so calme that wee were faine to towe in our shippes, and about a north north-west sunne we came to an anchor by them, with our three ships, *viz.*, the *Tigre*, admirall; the *Matthew*, vice-admirall; and the *Richard and Barnard*, hauing made all things readie for to fight. These fiue shippes which rid here, the one was a great shippe of Biscay, of seuen hundred tunnes,[1] and two Hollanders, which we found the sixt of June in Pooppy-bay, and one small pinke of Amsterdam, and another smal shippe of Rochelle. This great shippe of Biscay, which we expected would have fought with vs, sent their captaine aboord of vs before we came to an anchor, and submitted themselues vnto the generall. The two ships of Amsterdam, whose masters names were these, viz., Cornelius Calias, William Vermogan, admirall, and John Jacob, vice-admirall; these two would gladly haue stood out with vs, if the Biscaine would haue assisted them.

<small>A Biscayan ship of 700 tuns.</small>

The twelfth day, faire weather. This day the ship of *John Jacobs* was vnderladen of such goods as shee had in her; as oyle, blubber, and morses skinnes. The thirteenth day I was sent in a shallop to Greene Harborough.

The foureteenth day, thicke close weather, the winde northward; but towarde noone it began to cleare vp, and then it blew more winde. About a west sunne, we came to a small Iland, or rather a rock, where morses vse to come; where we found seauen which we killed, and knocked out their teeth, and let them lye. In this place are many of these rockes, where are great multitudes of foule, and they are called Lizets Ilands. The land all along is so full of rockes, that it is vnpossible for any shippe to come neere the maine, but in the sands, which are very deepe and good to come in. All this euening and night wee rowed betweene this Iland and Ice-sound.[2]

<small>Many rockes full of Fowle.
Lisets Islands.</small>

---

[1] She was a ship of St. Jean de Luz, of 800 tons, called the *Michael de Aristega*.   [2] So named by Jonas Poole in 1612.

The fifteenth day, about nine or tenne o'clock, we came to the shippes in Greene Harborough, where we found that they had killed eighteene whales in all. Foure of these ships were French-men, which had killed eight whales for the Companie, according to the agreement which the generall had made with them; which was, that they should kill eight for vs, and after, what they could kill should be for themselues. Our English men had killed three in this place, and the Baskes in the *Desire* also three. The *Desire* had taken in an hundred tunnes of oyle when wee came there, and she was to be laden so soone as she could. *[margin: Eighteen Whales killed. Three Whales killed by the English]*

The seauenteenth day, also faire weather, the winde northward. This day, toward a west sunne, the master of the French shippe came from Sea-horse Bay, who went thither to speak with our generall; because Master Mason and Master Cooper had stayed his shallops from going to sea, in regard they would not obserue the orders which the generall had appointed them; which were, that those whales which our Englishmen did chase, they should not follow; nor our men should not follow the whales they chased. For the order of the Biscaines is, that whoso doth strike the first harping iron into him, it is his whale, if his iron hold. This euening, I say, he returned from Sea-horse Bay, hauing lost his labour; for the generall and Master Edge were in Bell-sound. We vnderstood by him, that they had killed some eight and thirtie whales in all; and that there was one hundred and sixtie tunnes of oyle ready made. The fiue and twentieth day in the morning, the *Desire* weighed anchor to go to the generall, and the master of the French ship also this morning went from thence to speake with the generall, because of a whale which was in strife betweene his Biscaines and ours; when, for pilfering, and for some peremptorie speeches, two of the *Rochellers* were ducked at our yard arme, the one on the one side, and the other on the other. This day I also *[margin: Eight and thirty Whales killed.]*

August 1.   obserued the latitude of this place, and found it to be
Latitude 77° 40'.   77° 40'. Also, the variation of the compasse is 13° 11'
Variation, 13° 11'.   west. This variation was obserued the third of August, in
the morning; the height of the sun above the horizon was
17° 24', and the declination was 14° 41' north in the latitude of 77° 40', and his magnetical azimuth was 63 from
south to east. The ninth day we had sight of Master
Bonners ship, wherein was Master Marmaduke,[1] who had
beene to the northward as farre as Faire-hauen; and now,
as he said, he was bound to the southward, to discouer
beyond Point Looke-out, hauing his direction from Master
Edge, as he said. Our generall told him that hee had
hindered the voyage more by his absence then his discouerie would profit; and that it were best that he went
back with him to the Foreland, and that he would giue no
licence to go now for discouerie, because the yeare was far
spent; but bad him, according to his commission, so to
proceede. The twelfth day I obserued, and found the
latitude of this place, by an exact obseruation, to be in
Latitude 79° 14'.   79° 14'. They in the Pooppy Bay had seen a ship of Eng-

This was Ma. Cudners ship of London.

[1] Fotherby says that Thomas Marmaduke was Captain of the Vice-Admiral. He was a Hull man, and Jonas Poole mentions that in the previous year, 1612, he had gone as far north as 82°, in a ship called the *Hopewell*. In 1611 he was in the Spitzbergen Sea, in command of a Hull vessel, and gave the shipwrecked crew of Poole's ship, the *Elizabeth*, a passage home.

Captain Markham (*Northward Ho!* pp. 42, 43) thinks that there is a mistake with regard to Marmaduke having reached 82°; arising from his commanding the *Hopewell*, the same vessel in which Hudson, in 1606, nearly reached that latitude.

In 1617 Thomas Marmaduke of Hull presented a petition to King James. He represented that he could prove the shortest way to Cathay to be by the north-east, which for six months in the year is navigable, without impediment. He asked to be set out to make the passage at the king's charge, or for leave for himself and friends to undertake it. I cannot find what was the fate of this petition, or the subsequent history of Marmaduke.

land off Black-point, and had spoken with her, who told them that they were come from Kildeene.

The foureteenth day, faire weather, the wind at north north-east. This day, about tenne a clocke in the forenoone, we waied anchor to goe homeward, being sixe ships in company, viz., the *Tigre* admirall, the *Gamaliel* vice-admirall, the *John and Frances*, the *Annula*, the ship of Burdeaux, which the generall agreed to fish in Greene-harborough, and the Biscay ship which fished in Sir Thomas Smith's Bay.[1]

The fifteenth day very faire weather, all the forenoone almost calme; in the afternoone an easie gale at north-east. This day, about twelue a clocke at noone, wee were against Faire-Foreland, which is in the latitude of 79° 8'. Latitude 79° 8'. This night was very cleere and faire weather, and also calme, by which meanes I had very good opportunitie to finde the sunnes refraction. For, beholding it about a north Sunnes refraction. north-east sunne, by the common compasse, at which time the sunne was at the lowest, it was but one fifth part of his body aboue the horizon, hauing about foure fifth parts below, so neere as I could gesse. His declination for that instant was 10° 35' north, being at noone in the 2° 7' of Virgo, his daily motion was 58', whose halfe beeing nineteen[2] to bee added to the former, because it was at twelue houres afore noone. I say his place at that instant was 2° 26' of Virgo, whose declination was as before, 10° 35'; the latitude of the place was 78° 47', whose complement was 11° 13', the declination being subtracted from the complement of the poles eleuation, leaueth 38', foure fiue part of which 12'; which, being subtracted from 38, leaueth Note. 26' for the refraction. But I suppose the refraction is more or lesse according as the ayre is thicke or cleare, which I

---

[1] The *Matthew*, *Desire*, and *Richard and Barnard*, had previously sailed for England on the 31st of July, and arrived safely at Blackwall on the 23rd of August, well laden with oil and skins.

[2] Twenty-nine?

leaue for better schollers to discusse: but this I thought good to note, for the better helpe of such as doe professe this studie.

The sixteenth day also very faire weather, and for the most part calme; the winde that was, was at north-west. This morning we espied a ship out in the offen, ouer against Cold cape, which we stood with, and she also stood with vs; and when we came to her, wee found her to be the *Desire*, a shippe of Alborough. Our generall sent for the master and merchant aboord of vs, who certified him that they came from Killedeene, and that they had made but a bad voyage of fish; and they were come to see if we could fraight them home. The merchant was of London, whose name was Master Cudner; the masters name was Fletcher, who also brought sixe men, which Thomas Bonner had left at Cherie Iland. These sixe men had killed but one morse all this yeere at the Iland; who also told vs that William Gourdon was gone to the northwards. At noone, the three and twentieth day, I obserued the variation of the compasse, and found it to be 1° 5' east.

<small>Mr. Cudner of London.</small>

<small>William Gourdon.</small>

<small>Variation, 1° 5'.</small>

The three and twentieth day faire weather, with a fine gale at north and by east, we stearing away south and by west halfe south, being at noone, by supposition, in the latitude of 69°, no minutes, hauing sailed, since yesterday noone, some thirty leagues south, true.

The foure and twentieth day, very faire weather and cleere, the winde all the fore-noone northwards, but about noone it came to the south-east. This morning I obserued the middle starre in the great beares tayle, and found it to be in the latitude of 68° 24' about two a clocke, at which time that starre was on the meridian vnder the pole. Also I obserued the starre in the beares rump about one a clock, and found the like latitude. Also all this day we had sight of Rost Ilands,[1] being about ten or eleuen leagues off vs.

<small>Rost Ilands or Rosten.</small>

---

[1] Roost, the most southern of the Lofoden Islands.

Also at noone I obserued the latitude by the sunne, and found vs to be in the latitude of 68°, no minutes, which did agree with the former obseruations by the starres. Also the variation of this place is 4° 8' east from the true meridian, wee hauing ranne, since yesterday noone, some two and twentie leagues south and by west. Almost all the afternoon it was almost calme. *68° no min.* *Variation, 5° 3' East.*

The fiue and twentieth day also very faire weather, the winde this morning came to the east south-east a fine easie gale. We steered away south and by west half west ten leagues, being at noone in the latitude of 67° 5'. The variation of this place is 5° 3' east, neere to the set of our compasse. This euening the winde came to the south south-west, which continued about two watches. *Variation, 5° 3' East.*

The nine and twentieth day faire weather, with a good gale of winde at north north-east. From two this last night to sixe we stood away south-west and by south; and at sixe we steered away south south-west, being at noone, by obseruation, in 62°, no minutes. The land about Scoutes- nesse lyeth in this sort: from sixtie three toward sixtie two, it is nineteen leagues south south-west halfe westward; from thence ten leagues south and by west, which is two or three Ilands, which are the westwardest land in Norway, lying in the latitude of 62° 44'. But whether these Islands, or a point of land which lyeth about three or foure leagues more to the north, be called Scoutesnesse, I know not. The sixt of September we entered the Thames. *The lying of the land about Scoutesnesse.*

SECOND RECORDED VOYAGE

OF

WILLIAM BAFFIN.

II.

Another account, probably written by ROBERT FOTHERBY.[1]

A Short Discourse of a Voyage made in the Yeare of Our Lord 1613, to the Late Discouered Countrye of Greenland; and a Briefe Discription of the same Countrie, and the Comodities ther raised to the Adventurers.

IN the month of May 1613, seauen good ships bound for Greenland,[2] were sett forth from the port of London, beeing furnished with victualls and other prouision necessarie for the killing of the whale, and twenty-four Basks, who ar men best experienced in that facultie, at the chardge and aduenture of the right worshipfull Sir Thomas Smith, knight, and of the rest of the companie of merchants tradeing into Moscouia, called the Merchants of Newe Trades and Discoveries.

[1] The manuscript of this journal was formerly in possession of Deacon James Green, a merchant of Boston, who died about the beginning of the present century. His daughter, Mrs. Nabby Richmond, gave it to Benjamin R. Howland in 1808. From him it passed to the Honourable John Howland, the late President of the Rhode Island Historical Society, who transferred it to the American Antiquarian Society in 1814. The manuscript is a folio, with wide margins, neatly written and illustrated with a map of Spitzbergen (mutilated), and sketches in water-colour. The leaves are stitched into a thick parchment cover. It was first printed in the *Transactions and Collections of the American Antiquarian Society* (1860), vol. iv, p. 285, and edited by Mr. Samuel F. Haven, who gives reasons for the belief that Robert Fotherby was the author.

[2] Spitzbergen.

In this fleet, Mr. Beniamin Joseph, of London, was chiefe captaine and commissioner, a man very sufficient and worthy of his place. A shippe called the *Tiger*, of burthen 260 tonnes, was admirall; the *Mathew*, of 250 tonnes, vice admirall; and the *Gamaliel*, of 200 tonnes, rere admirall; the fourth, the *John* and *Francis*, of 180 tonnes; the sixth, the *Anula*, of 140 tonnes; and the seuenth, the *Richard and Barnard*, a piniace of 60 tonnes, intended for further discouerye.

Wee came to Grauesend the 30th of April, where we staied but one tide, and then weyed anchor about 6 a'clock at the euening, and plied to Tilberry Hope, remaining there all night. The next morneing, beeing the first of Maye, wee anchored againe in Lee Roade, where we continued till the 4th of Maye, the wind keeping contrarie to us, blew betwixt north and north-east.

The 4th daie, about 3 a'clock afternoone, wee entered into the swaile at Quinborowe,[1] and rid at anchor there till the 13th of Maye. In which time, namelie, on the 7th of Maye, the kings ships came by us on their retourne out of Holland, from transporting the Count Palatine, and the Ladie Elizabeth, the kings onely daughter. Before they came neere us wee caused our flaggs to be furl'd up, and when they passed by us, our admirall shott off 7 peeces of ordnance, our vice admirall 5, and our rere admirall 3; and the rest of our fleet, ech of them, one. The Great Admirall of England, called the *Prince*, gaue us 3 peeces, and the rest of the kings ships each of them one.[2]

The 13th of Maye, about 9 a clock in the morneing,

---

[1] Queenborough.

[2] The Princess Elizabeth, who was destined to experience so much misfortune, was married to the Count Palatine, Frederic V, on St. Valentine's Day, with an expense and magnificence before unknown in England. They were conveyed to Flanders in great state by the Lord Admiral, the Earl of Nottingham, with eight of the king's ships, besides transports for baggage.

wee came forthe of the Swaile, and passed by the Sandes called the Spitts, holdeing our course north-east and north north-east.

Our departure from England.
The 14th daie, about noone, wee lost sight of the Cromershield, which is a cape on the coast of Norfolke, and was the last land of England that we sawe, being outward bound. Then wee stear'd awaie north, maintaineing that course till the 22nd of Maye.

On the 21st daie wee had lost sight of land againe upon the coast of Norwaye, before wee came to the bay of Rosse, beareing from us east and by north, and distant about nine leagues, in the latitude of 61° 20', found by obseruation. Then, on the 22nd wee directed our course more easterlie, as north-and-by-east, and north north-east.

The 24th, wee were in the latitude of 67° 36', while the sunne was in the horison, at the time of midnight, and after that time wee had continuall dailight dureing our voyage; till, in our retourne homeward, wee had the sunne againe in the circle of the horison, when he came to the north of our meridian, in the latitude of 75°, on the 2nd of August.

Wee ariued on the coast of Greenland.
The 30th of Maye, about 4 a clock in the morneing, wee descried our wisht-for coast of Greenland,[1] being all our ships in company; and wee had bene but 17 daies at sea, viz., from the 13th till the 30th of Maye, haueing sailed, according to the difference of latitude and longitude, by an arch of a great circle 500 leagues, and according to the ship's way, by our account on dead reckoning, 514 leagues.

Then we plied nearer to the shoare, and discerned the mountains to be couered with snowe; notwithstanding, wee had no trouble with ice all this while, as wee expected; for it was almost all voided er wee came ther. Nowe wee coasted along towards Sr. Thomas Smyth's Baye, passing

[1] Spitzbergen.

on the west side of Prince Charles his Iland, by reason of a barre that is betwixt the iland and the maine continent of the land, which hinders us to passe with our ships that waie.

The 1st of June, wee were becalm'd on the south-west side of the iland, about fiue leagues from the shoare, where I obserued the north sunne, at the time of midnight, to be 11° 15′ high; so, concludeing the latitude in that place to be 78° 5′ (the sunne's declination for that daie being 23° 10′).

The 2nd of June, haueing gotten a little more northward, and beeing on the best side of the iland, againe becalm'd, about three leagues distant from the shoare, I and Joh. Wilmote, one of the master's mates, with 6 more of our sailors, went ashore in a Biska shallop, purposeing to kill some deare and some wild fowle; and to that end wee took with us such dogs as wee had in our ship,[1] viz., a grewhownd, a mastiffe, and a water spaniell, and two fowleing-pieces, with shott and powder.

We landed upon a hard shingle, comeing close to the shore with our boat, there being no ice to keep us off; notwithstanding, upon fiue or six rocks, near the shore side, there laie a great quantitie of ice, which couered them in such sorte, that the hollowness or distances betwixt one rock and another, appeared under the ice like vaulted caues. After that wee were landed upon the shingle, the ice or congealed snowe was so high upon the shoare, that it withstood vs like a strong wall, to pass anie further; wherefore wee wer faine one to help up another, it beeing mor than a man's height in thickness, and haueing manie long isicles hanging in diuers places.

When wee were up, and had gone about two roods, wee might perceaue that wee were upon the ground or sand; yett could not see it by reason of the snowe. Then wee

[1] The *Mathew*.

did look about if we could see any deere; and presentlie espied one buck, whereupon we dispersed ourselues seuerall waies, to gett betwixt him and the mountaines, slipping sometimes to the mid leg into the snowe, which, for the most part, did beare vs above. In our waie wee went ouer two or three bare spots that were full of flatt stones, whereon ther grew a certaine white mosse, which, it seems, the deare doe feed upon at the first beginning of their somer; for theise spotts were full of their ordure; and besides, wee then sawe not any other thing for them to liue on.

Before that wee came near the buck which wee first espied, wee sawe four more not farre from him, and two in another place, and therefore we hounded at the fairest heard; but then they came all one waie together, and (avoideing all circumstances) we kill'd three of them, being all bucks, which we found then to be but pore rascals, yet verie good meat, as we presentlie made tryall and tasted. For, finding ther (as ther is in all places of the countreye) great store of drift wood, which the sea bestowes on the barren land, and being also well prouided of hunter's sauce, wee made a fier and broiled some of our venison, and did eat thereof with very good appetites; much like to that in Virgil, of Æneas and his companions:—

> "Ac primum silici scintillam exaudit *Achates*[1]
> Susceptiq. ignem *lignis*[2]
> Pars in frusta secant *verubusque*[3] trementia figunt
> . . . .
> Tum victu reuocamus vires."

Beeing thus well refreshed, wee were willing to have killed more venison, because wee needed not to use much labour in hunteing for our game; for the deare that had latelie escaped us were not gon farre from us. But the

---

[1] Master's mate.
[2] "Folia enim nulla cadunt ubi est neq flos nec arbos."
[3] Wooden spit.

aire began to be so thicke and foggie, that wee aduised better to goe presentlie a-board with that which wee had alreadie gotten, least that the fog, increasing, might haue made vs lose sight of our ship; therefore wee made speedie waie towards her, and came aboord about 11 o'clock, before the time of midnight.

Then wee continued still becalm'd till the next morning, and then were so befriended with a fresh gale of winde that wee sailed to the north end of the iland with a flowen sheat; and makeing manie boards, wee plied into Sir Tho. Smyth's Baye, where we anchored about 8 a clock that euening.

When we came to an anchor, then the Basks, our whale strikers, went presentlie back againe to the Foreland[3] with their shallops, ther to attend the coming-in of the whales; and when our men had taken some rest, they carried ashoare our coppers cask, and other prouisions for makeing of oile, and prepared all things ready for use as speedilie as we could. For newes was brought us in the morneing, that the Basks had kil'd a whale; therefore we hasted to sett up our fournaces and coppers, and presentlie began work, which we continued (God be thanked) without any want of whales, till our voyage was made; not receaueing anie intermission of rest, but onlie on the Saboth daie. For when some slept, others wrought; and haueing a continual daie, wee alowed no time of night for all men to sleepe at once, but maintained work from Sundaie about 5 a clock afternoone, till Saturdaie at 12 o'clock, in time of midnight, dureing which time our men receaued no other recreation from work and sleep, but onlie the time of eateing their meat, whereof they had sufficient, thrice in every twenty-four howers; and besides, some of them had alowed aquauitæ at ech four hower's end.

The next daie after that we came into harbour, word was brought our general from Green Harbour (a place where

Wee harboured in Sr. Tho. Smyths Baye.

[1] The northern extremity of Prince Charles's Island.

three ships of our fleet put in to make this voyage) that fiue ships, French and Spanish, wer come into Ice Sound, and intended there to fish for the whale; upon which occasion the *Tiger*, our admirall, weyed anchor the 5th of June, and being well man'd with sixty sufficient men, went out of harbour from us towards Ice Sound, where, when he came, he found the aforesaid ships, according to the information, and anchored close by them. Then he hailed the captains and masters of theise ships to come presentlie aboord him, which they performeing accordinglie, he shewed them the King's Majesties patent, graunted to the Merchants of Newe Trades and Discoueries, and therwithall his comission, forbidding them, by the authoritie thereof, to make anie longer aboad ther, or in anie parte of the countrey, at their perills. Whereupon they, not knowing how to remedie themselues, did all promise to departe, desireing a note from our general, wherby they might certefie their setters-forth, that they had bene in the countrye, except one ship of Burdeux, called the *Jaques*, wherof was Maister Peirce de Siluator, who was permitted to staie, upon condition that he should first kill 8 whales for us, and then to kill more what he could for himself, and by this conclusion he made a good voyage; for he kil'd 12 whales in all, wherof we had eight, and he had 4.

Then did our admirall continue as a wafter alongst the coast till the 27th of June, and then he came to us againe into Sir Thomas Smyth's Baye. In which time of his absence he had mett with 17 ships, viz., 4 of Holland, 2 of Dunkirk, 4 of St. John de Luz, and 7 of San Sebastian's. The commanders of all those ships had submitted to our general; and were content either to departe out of the country, or els to staie upon such condicons as he propounded unto them.

On the 8th of June, about 11 a clock, before the time of midnight, Mr. Marmaduke, who was captaine of our vice admirall, and I, with 6 or 7 sailors, went in a shallop to the beach at the barre, marked with a^9,[1] to cause our men gather drift wood together, and laie it readie at the waters side, to lade a small Flemish flie boat, that was to come hither to fetch it. Upon this beach, wee saw lieing ther, by our estimacion, neare 300 morses, at the verie point or end of it; but wee could not go too near them, for disturbing them. When the flie boat came to take in the wood, Mr. Marmaduke and I came awaie in the shallop; and haueing present occasion to use a peece of straight timber about our crane, before the flie boat could be loaded, wee caused the men that rowed the shallop to towe a tree after them. Nowe, when wee had put off a little from the shoare, there came fiue or six morses swimming hard by us and about us; some of them coming so near the sterne of the bote that we called for our launces, purposeing to strike them. They would, diuers times, laie their teeth upon the tree which we towed (as it were scratching the wood with their teeth), but wee still rowed awaie, and at length they left us. Then we passed through a great deale of small ice, and sawe, upon some peices, two morses, and upon some, one; and also diuers seales, layeing upon peices of ice.

The 19th of June wee had a verie great storme, the winde beeing at south south-west, which was like to haue driuen our ships upon the shoare; and haueing three dead whales floating at the sternes of our ships, wee were glad to cut the hawsers that they were tyed in, and to lett them driue a shoare; because we feared that otherwise they would haue caused our ships either to break their cables, or to haile home their anchors, and to be driuen upon the shoare. When the storm ceast, haueing continued about 6 howers, the water fell from the shoare, and wee saw two of the whales lie cast upon the shoare, and the water faln from

A storme in harbour.

[1] The bar may be see on the map, but the "a" is wanting.

them againe. The third whale was driuen further off, but wee found him againe cast upon the shoare, hauing lost all his finnes[1] out of his mouth. Ther was also, at the same time, 5 whale's heads driuen ashoare, with toungs and finnes in them, wherby some labour was saued, which should otherwise haue been bestowed about hailing them ashoare, for the cutting out of the fins.

The 21st of June, there came a white beare down from the mountaines, and took into Fresh-water Baye, which is the water you see marked with *e*, within Sr. Thomas Smith's Baye,[2] and Thomas Wilkinson, one of the master's mates in the *Matthew*, vice-admirall, went forth in a shallop, and shott him with a peece as he was swimming, and kil'd him, and brought him to the shoare.

In this harbour ther haue been killed mor whales than in anie other, but verie fewe deare; notwithstanding ther haue been slaine in this country, this voyage, about four hundred deare. Wee kil'd very few morses, by reason the whales came so fast, that wee could not have a fitt opportunitie to goe about that buisines; although ther was said to be at one time about 500 morses upon the beach before mencioned; to which place wee went, prepared for their slaughter, the sixt of Julie, and found ther but about 40, wherof wee killed 32, and wee took their hides, their fat, and their teeth.

We killed also good store of wild fowle, as wild geese, culuerdumes, willocks, and such like, and some white land partridges. Wee caught manie young foxes, which wee made as tame and familiar as spaniell-whelpes. I brought one of them out of the country, till we came to the coast of England, and ther he died.

[1] Whale-bone they called whale's fins.
[2] The position here referred to, belonged to a part of the map that was mutilated; and, although the outline has been restored, the locality above-mentioned cannot be precisely indicated.

On the 24th of June, the *Mathew* began to take in hir ladeing, and was fully freighted the 6th of July with 184 tonnes of oyle, and 5,000 finnes, which wer in 100 bundles, each containeing 50.

On the 8th of July the *Mathew*, and the *Richard and Barnard* (which was laded with oile and finnes), weighed anchor forth of Sir Thomas Smyth's Baye, with purpose to come presentlie for England; and the *Tiger*, our admirall, came also forth with us to waft us alongst the coast of Greenland.[1] But, putting into Bel Sound the 11th of July, expecting to find some strangers there, wee espied accordinglie 5 ships at anchor on the west side of Joseph's Baye. One of them seemed unto us to be a verie great ship, as indeed she was; and other two of them seemed also to be good stowt ships. And therefore wee, supposing them to be such as would withstand vs, resolued to feight with them, and made spedie preparation accordinglie, hanging our waist-cloths and clearing our decks, that the ordnance might have room to plaie; and made readie all our munition, ech one addressing himself with a forward resolucion to perform a man's parte so well as he could.

<small>We wayed anchor out of Sr. Tho. Sm. Baye.</small>

This was about 9 o'clock, before the time of midnight, the sunne shining very bright, and the aire being very cleare, and so calme that wee caused ye saylers with boats and shallops to rowe ahead of our ships, and towe them into the harbour. When wee came neare them, the captain of the great ship, whose name was Michael de Aristega (his ship being of St. John de Luz, of burthen 800 tonnes), came in a shallop abord our admirall, submitting himself and his goods unto our generall, and tould him that ther were two ships of the Hollanders, who had insulted over him, and would not suffer him to fish for the whale but upon such condicons as they propounded unto him, namely, that the Hollanders, hauing but 3 shal-

---

[1] By Greenland, in this narrative, is always meant Spitzbergen.

lops, and he 7 furnished with whale strikers, they
should all joine together; and the Hollanders not onlie
to haue the one-half of all the whales that. should be
kil'd, but also to haue the first whale that was stricken
wholie to themselues, ouer and besides the half of the rest.
And he further tould the general that the Hollanders would
haue persuaded him to combine with them against us, and
to beate us out of the countrye. Then the generall willed
him to goe aboard againe of his own ship, and keepe his
men in quietnes, and he would deale well enough with the
Hollanders. So, passing further on, they were knowen to
be 2 ships of Amsterdam, which our admirall had formelie
mett withall, and dischardged to staie in ye country. Then,
comeing by close to them, our admirall anchored on one side of
them and our vice-admirall on the other; but they, as men
unwilling to be depriued of the ritches they had gotten,
allthough unable by force to hold them, kept out their flags
—the one in the maine-top, and the other in the fore-top,
as admirall and vice-admirall. Then our generall comanded
the maisters to come aboard his ship, which they, doeing,
he chardged them with the breach of their promise formerlie made unto him—viz., that they would departe out
of the country. Then, after some other speeches, he, not
finding them willing to resigne the goods they had gotten—
as whale oil and finnes—tould them that they must not think
to carrie anie of it awaie, seeing that they did so sleightlie
esteeme the King's ma'ties grant formerlie shewed them;
therefore, he bad them go againe to their owne ships, and
they should have half an hower's space to consider and
aduise with themselues what to doe; and if they thought
fitt to give him further answer before the glasse were runne
out, then good it were; otherwise, if they would not then
yield their goods, he would feight with them for them.
So ech of them went aboard his own ship, and, without anie
long deliberation caused their flags to be taken in; and

Wee an-
chored
againe in
Joseph's
Baye.

retourning to our generall, yeilded their goods to our disposing. Nowe, although it was intended that our two laded ships should go presentlie for England notwithstanding, it was thought fitting not to leave our admirall alone amongst his offended neighbours; and, therefore, wee staied till the two Hollanders were gon, who (being dispossessed of some oile and finnes they had alreadie stowed in their ships, and also of some dead whales that were floateing at their ship's side) went forth of harbour, one of them the 15th, and the other the 18th of July.

The great ship of St. John de Luz staied still, the captaine of hir being content that his men should hould on their work, and his whale-strikers to continue fishing, upon condicõn granted that he should onelie haue one-half the oile he should make. There were also in the same harbour 2 small ships, the one of Biska, and the other a Flemish flie boat; besides another little pinace of St. John de Luz which was on the east side of the iland, within L. Elesmere Baye, marked with *b*.

On the 23rd of July, about 9 o'clock in the euening, wee sent forth two shallops with men, to goe kill some venison, who retourned againe with 17 bucks and does slaine; yet had they no dog with them, onelie peeces; and they brought also aboard the skinne of a white bear, which they had kil'd.

The 25th July, the *Desire* came to us in to Joseph's Bay, out of Green Harbour, and tooke in thirty tonnes of blubber, to make up hir full ladeing; for shee was to come with us, one of the first, for England.

The 29th of July wee had some trouble with great ice; the waters being verie rough, and the winde bloweing hard at east south east, which brought some ilands of ice towards our ships, wherof some fell 'thwart our hauses, so that wee were faine, with pikes and oares, to keepe it cleare of our

_{Wee were troubled with ice.}

ships; and also glad to lett fall our sheat-anchor, to keep us from being driuen upon the lee shoare.

In this harbour, ther was killed a great store of venison, 3 or 4 white beares, and some sea morses, which the Hollanders had slaine and flayed before wee came thither; for ther laie their bodies, without either fatt, skinnes, or teeth.

One thing more I obserued in this harbour, which I haue thought good also to sett down. Purposeing, on a time, to walk towards the mountaines, I, and two more of my companie, ascended up a long plaine hill, as wee supposed it to be; but hauing gon a while upon it, wee perceued it to be ice. Notwithstanding, we proceeded higher up, about the length of half a mile, and as we went, sawe manie deepe rifts or gutters on the land of ice, which were crackt downe thorowe to the ground, or, at the least, an exceeding great depth; as we might well percciue by heareing the snowe water run belowe, as it does oftentimes, in a brook whose current is somewhat opposed with little stones. But for better satisfaĉon, I brake down some peeces of ice with a staffe I had in my hand, which, in their falling made a noise on ech side, much like to a peice of glasse throwen downe the well within Douer Castle, wherby wee did aestimate the thicknes or height of this ice to be thirty fathomes. This huge ice, in my opinion, is nothing but snowe, which from time to time has, for the most parte, bene driuen of the mountaines; and so continueing and increasing all the time of winter (which may be counted three quarters of the yeare), cannot possiblie be consumed with the thawe of so short a somer, but is onelie a little dissolued to moisture, wherby it becomes more compact, and with the quick succeeding frost is congealed to a firme ice. And thus it is like still to encrease, as (I think) it hath done since the world's creation.

On Saturday, the 31st of Julye, about 5 o'clock in the

afternoone, wee weyed anchor out of Joseph's Bay to come for England, namelie, the *Matthew*, the *Desire*, and the *Richard and Barnard;* leauing ther our admirall the *Tiger*, and the great ship of St. John de Luz. At 9 o'clock that euening wee weare at sea, about 6 leagues from the land, and then directed our course for Cherrie Iland, south and by east. The next daie, being the 1st of August, about 8 a clock before noone, there came a shallop aboard the *Desire*, with 11 Dutchmen that belonged to one of the Hollander's ships that we had latelie sent forth of Bel Sound. The reason of their so comeing was this: sixe of these men had gon ashoare from their ship to kill some venison, and landeing at the time of a high water, they made fast their shallop, and so left her, safe enough, as they supposed, and went up into the land; but when the water fell againe, the shallop was splitt upon a rock, and by that meanes they were forced to staie ther; nowe, they that were in the ship, considering that their fellowes staied verie long, began to doubt of some unwelcome euent, that hindered their retourne; and therfore they sent 5 men more, in another shallop, to knowe the cause of their so long absence. When these men last sent forth came ashoare, they found the other men, who tould them the occasion of their staie. Then went they all aboard the shallop, and rowed towards their ship; but the aire was growen to be verie mistie, and such a thick fog increased, that they could not by anie meanes find their ship, wherfore they were faine to row to the shoare againe.

Then followed stormie weather, the winde bloweing of the shoare, which caused the ship to haile further of to sea; so that when the aire was cleeare, notwithstanding, they could not see her; wherby they were much discouraged, being in a place that could yeild them but little comforte. And there they contynued 8 daies, in which time they lieued with the flesh of 2 bucks and a beare, which they had

Wee came for England.

killed, being eleuen men; and mor they could not kill, because their powder was spent. Then seeing our ships come by, they rowed fast and came aboard of us; and so wee brought them into England, wher they had some monie alowed them for their work at sea, by the Company of Moscouy Merchants, although (God be praised) wee neuer stood any need of their helpe; and so they were free to departe homeward, when they could gett shipping.

On the 3rd of August wee were about 10 leagues distant from Cherry Iland, but could not see it by reason of ill weather; the winde being contrarie, not suffering us to touch ther, as wee intended; therfore wee steered awaie, south-and-by-west and south-south-west, for England. After this daie the sunne began to sett, and to be depressed under the horizon at midnight; the nights began to lengthen, and starres to beare vewe. On the 16th of August, Mr. Greene, one of the master's mates, died in the Matthewe, about 10 a clock before noone; and, about 4 a clock in the afternoone he was cast ouerboard, and a peice of ordnance shott of.

<small>Wee arrived on the Coast of England.</small> The 18th of August, about 5 aclock in the morneing, wee fell in with the coast of England, and descried land about Huntcliff Foot, which is northward from Scarborough, on the coast of Yeorkshire, and was the first land that wee sawe after wee lost sight of Greenland.

<small>We anchored in Winterton Road.</small> The next daie, about 3 a clock afternoone, wee anchored in Winterton Roade, which is six miles from Yarmouth. Then I caused the shallop to be taken out, and 6 sailors to sett me ashoare, within 2 miles of Yarmouth, wher I lodged that night; and having prouided a horse, I rid out of the towne the next morneing at 9 o'clock, being Friday, and came to London at 3 a clock afternoone, on Saturday, not haueing receaued anie sleepe at all betwixt Yarmouth and London. Our ships came up to Blackwall on the Tuesday next after; and, so soone as they had deliuered

their goods, the other 4 ships of our fleet came also safe home with their ladeings; and thus, by the mercie of God, we ended our voyage with good successe. To God, therfore, be praise and glory for euer. Amen.

A Briefe Description of the Country of Greenland, otherwise called King James his New Land.

Greenland is a countrie beareing from England northward, nearest upon the pointe of the compasse north-and-by-east. The south-most parte of it is distant from the Arcticque Circle 10° northwards namelie, in the latitude of 76° 30'. This country hath bene discouered by the English almost to the parallel of 83°, which is but 7° eleuation distant from the North Pole, and therefore but 140 leagues from that point, upon the superficies of the earth or water (whither it be), where the Pole shal be our zenith, and the æquinoctiall our horizon.

In the latitude of 76° (which wee made the greatest parte of our voyage this yeare), the sunne, when he entereth into the 1° of Cancer, makeing the longest daie and shortest night to all places betweene the Equator and the Polar Circle, is in his meridinal altitude, or greatest distance from the horizon, 34° 30' high; and at the time of his comeing to the north, is still apparent aboue the horizon 12° 30'.

The compasse varieth on this place, from the true meridian, or line of north and south, neare 20°, the north end of the needle inclineing so much towards the west. _{Variation of the Compasse W.}

The nature and condicõn of this country of Greenland is verie much different from the name it hath; for I think ther is no place in the world, yett known and discouered, is lesse green than it. For when wee first arriued ther, which was on the 30th of Maye, the ground was all couered with snowe, both the mountaines and the lowe lands, saue onelie some few spotts that were full of flatt stones, wheron ther grewe a certaine white mosse which, it seems, the deere doe feed upon at the first beginning of their sommer; for theise bare spotts wer verie full of their ordure; and besides, wee could not see anie other thing for them to feed upon.

The thawe began this yeare about the 10th of June, at which time there began to spring up, in some places where the snow was melted, a certaine stragling grasse, with a blewish flower, much like to young heath or ling, which grows upon moreish grounds in the north parts of England. And this is that wher with all the deare, in a short time, become exceeding fatt; but how they liue in the time of extreame winter, when al is couered with snowe, I cannot imagine. Yet the meanes of their preseruacon is not more strange to man's capacitie than is their creation; and therfore we must knowe that He who made the creature, hath also ordained that he shal be fed; although, to our understandings, ther is not any food to sustaine them.

In the moneths of June, Julye, and the beginning of August, ther is often times warme and pleasant weather; but, in the other moneths, certainlie uery uncomfortable. For the temperature of the winter time maie be iudged, by the qualitie of the place, to be extreame could, especiallie dureing that time wherein the sunne shal be altogether depressed under the horizon, which, in the former latitude of 79°, continues from the 11th of October till the 10th of Februarye, and contrarilie it is eleuated altogether aboue the horizon from the 9th of April till the 14th of August; the rest of the time is an intercourse of long daie and short night, and contrarilie of short daies and long nights.

The country afoardeth great plentie of fresh water in all places, which proceeds from the snowe, and therfore there can be no want thereof at anie time, for ther is alwaies snowe, and (I think) euer hath bene since snowe first fell upon the earth. Besides, I found ther, within Sr. Thomas

Smyth's Baye, a very pleasant spring, neare the water side, boiling (as it were) and workeing up sand, euen as our springs doe in England; being as pleasant water as anie I euer tasted in England.

The comodities of the countrie, hitherto knowen, are chieflie whales and sea morses. The whale yeilds oyl and finnes; and the morse yeilds oyl, hydes, and teeth of good valewe, whereof he hath but two, and they growe in his uppermost jawe. Ther be also white whales and seales, which were thought not to be worthy of time and labor to kill them, seeing that wee wer imploied about the aboue mentioned comodities. Wee sawe very fewe fishes ther, or rather none at all; saue onelie one cod, which was caught with a baited hook in Green Harbour. But the Basks, our whale strikers, doe saie that they haue sundrie times seene good store of salmon.

Upon this land ther be manie white beares, graie foxes, and great plentie of deare; and also white partridges, and great store of white fowle, as cueluerduns, wilde geese, sea pigeons, sea parots, willocks, stint, guls, and diuers others, wherof some are unworthy of nameing as tasteing. The land also doth yeild much drift wood, whales finnes, morses teeth, and some times unicorn hornes, which are supposed to be rather of some sea creature, than of anie land beast. And theise things the sea casteth forth vpon the shoare, to supplie the barrenes of the fruitles land, which, by the Diuine Prouidence, hath sufficient to maintaine these unreasonable creatures which ther wee found, but by all likelihood was never yet inhabited by anie natiues that beare the shape of man, the country being altogether destitute of necessaries, wherewithall a man might be preserued in the time of winter.

I haue thought good but to sett downe what was written concerning this country by one of Amsterdam, that was this yeare in Greenland (with whom I thus sometimes conuersed).

as it is sett forth in printe by some of Holland, and (with other things concerning this present voyage) is inserted in a late edition of *Hudson's Discoueries* :—" Hæc pessima et frigidissima est regio mundi, undique rupes, montes, lapides ; tanta ibi aquarum terram inundantium copia, ut vestigia hominum non admittat ; maxima glaciei ibi copia, tantaque montium glacialium multitudo, ut ab ipsa natiuitate Christi, concreuisse videantur ; tanta enim niuium abundantia, ut fidem superet. Ceruis abundat et vrsis, et vulpibus ; cerui planè sunt albi coloris. Admiror tantos ceruorum greges, vnde viuant, cum regio niuibus tegatur, et planè sit sterilis. Auibus luxuriat, maximè annséribus minoribus qui turmatim conueniunt."[1]

The manner of killing the whale, and of the whole proceedings for performing of the voyage.

The whale is a fish, or sea beast, of a huge bignesse, about 60 feet long, and 18 feet thick. His head seems to be one-third parte of his whole quantitie. His finnes (which wee call whale bone in England) doe growe, and are wholie included within his spacious mouth, being fastened, and, as it were, rooted in his uppermost jawe, spreading on both sides of his toung, in number more than 260 on one, side, and as manie on the other side. The

[1] The following note is by Mr. Haven, the American editor:—
"The title of the book here referred to is ' Descriptio ac Delineatio geographica Detectionis Freti, sive Transitus ad Occasum, supra Terras Americanas, in Chinam et Japonem'. Amst., 1613, 4to. In it the above passage occurs as a quotation, in italics, preceded by the following remark : ' Hæc vera esse, fidem faciunt testes oculati reduces, etiam literæ Navarchi Thomae Bonaert et Semmij, cujus hæc verba, sub finem, in literis ad patrem de qualitate hujus regionis.' "

This Thomas Bonaert may be no other than Thomas Bonner, who commanded a Dutch ship at Spitzbergen, which was captured by the English, and sent northward for discovery under Master Marmaduke. (" Baffin's Narrative" in *Purchas*, vol. iii, pp. 717, 719).

longest finnes are placed in the midest of his mouth,[1] and the rest doe orderlie shorten, more and more, both backwards and forwards, from 12 feet to less than 3 ynches in length. His eies are not much bigger then the eyes of an oxe, and his bodie in fashion round, with a very broad spreading taile, which is of a rough and solid substance, and therefore it is used for to make chopping blocks, to chop the whales fatt upon (which we call blubber); and of other like matter, are also his two swimming finnes, which serue, at some times, for the same use.

The whale comes often aboue water, and will comonlie spowte 8 or 9 times before he goe under againe, by which spowteing of water wee maie discerne him when he is 2 or 3 leagues distant from us. When he entres into the sounds, our whal killers doe presentlie sallie forth to meet him, either from our ships, or els from some other place more conuenient for that purpose, where to expect him, makeing very speedie waie towards him with their shallops. But, most comonlie, before they come near him, he will be gon downe under water, and continue, perhaps, a good while er he rise againe; so that some times they rowe past him, and therfore are they alwaies very circumspect,

[1] The description given by Purchas begins as follows: "The whale is a fish or sea-beast of a huge bignesse—about sixty-fiue feet long and thirty-fiue feet thicke. His head is a third part of all his bodie's quantitie; his spacious mouth contayning a very great tongue and all his finnes, which we call whale finnes. These finnes are fastened or rooted in his upper chap, and spread over his tongue on both sides of his mouth; being in number about two hundred and fifty on one side, and as many on the other side. The largest finnes are placed in the midst of his mouth", etc.

Mr. Haven, the American editor, observes:—" The above extract will suffice to show the resemblance between the description of Purchas relating to this subject and those of this narrative. The inference appears to be a reasonable one, that, if Fotherby was the author of the notes used by Purchas in compiling his account, he was also the author of this narrative, as the similarity of it, in the two, is too great to be accidental. Purchas has not improved the accuracy of the statement by altering the figures.

lookeing if they can discerne his waie under the water
(which they call his wake), or els see him further off by his
spowteing, being risen. Then, comeing neare him, they
rowe resolutlie towards him, as though they intended to
force the shallop vpon him. But so soone as they come
within stroak of him, the harponier, (who stands up readie
in the head of the boat,) darts his harping iron at him out
of both his hands, wherwith the whale being stricken, he
presentlie discends to the bottom of the water, and therfor
the men in the shallop doe weire out 40, 50, or 60 fathoms
of rope—yea, sometimes 100, or more, according as the
depth requireth. For vpon the sockett of harping iron
ther is made fast a rope, which lies orderlie coiled up in the
sterne of the boat, which, I saie, they do weire forth untill
they perceaue him to be riseing againe, and then they haile
in some of it, both to giue him the lesse scope, and also
that it maie be the stronger, being shorter. For when he
riseth from the bottom, he comes not directlie up aboue the
water, but swimmes awaie with an uncontrowled force and
swiftnes, hurrying the shallop after him, with hir head so
close drawen downe to the water, that shee seemes ever
readie to be hailed under it. When he hath thus drawn
hir perhaps a mile or more—which is done in a verie short
time, considering her swiftnes—then will he come spowteing
aboue the water; and the men rowe up to him, and strike
him with their long launces, which are made purposelie for
that use. In lancing of the whale, they strike him as near
his swimming finne, and as lowe under water, as they can
conuentlie, to peirce into his intralls. But when he is
wounded, he is like to wrest the launce out of the strikers
hand; so that sometimes two men are faine to pluck it out,
although but one man did easilie thrust it in. And now
will he frisk and strike with his tail very forceablie, sometimes hitting the shallop, and splitting hir asunder, sometimes, also, maihmeing or killing some of the men. And

for that cause, ther is alwaies two or 3 shallops about the killing of one whale, that one of them maie relieue and take in the men out of another, being splitt. When he hath receaued his deadlie wound, then casteth he forth blood where formerlie he spowted water; and before he dies he will sometimes drawe the shallops 3 or 4 miles from the place wher he was first stricken with the harping iron. When he is dyeing, he most comonlie tourneth his bellie uppermost, and then do the men fasten a rope, or small hauser, to the hinder parte of his bodie, and with their shallops (made fast one to another) they towe him to the ships with his taile foremost; and then they fasten him to the sterne of some ship apointed for that purpose, while he is cutt up in manner as followeth. Two or three men come in a boat, or shallop, to the side of the whale, one man holdeing the boat close to the whale with a boat-hook, and another, who stands either in the boat or upon the whale, cutts and scores the fatt, which we call blubber, in square-like peices, 3 or 4 feet long, with a great cutting knife. Then, to raise it from the flesh, ther is a crab, or capstowe, sett purposelie upon the poop of the ship, from which ther discends a rope with an iron hook at the end of it, and this hook is made to take fast hould of a peice of the fatt, or blubber, and as, by tourning the capstowe, it is raised and lifted up, the cutter, with his long knife, loosest it from the flesh, even as if the larde of a swine were, by peece and peece, cut off from the leane. When it is in this manner cleane cutt off, then doe they lower the capstowe, and lett it downe to float vpon the water, makeing a hole in some side or corner of it, wherby they fasten it vpon a rope. And so they proceed to cutt off more peeces, making fast together 10 or twelue of them at once, to be towed ashoare at the sterne of a boat or shallop. Theise peices, being brought to the shoare side, ar, one by one, drawen vpon the shoare by the helpe of a high crane ther placed, and at length are hoised up from the ground over a vessell which is sett to receaue the oile that runnes from it as it is cutt into smaller peices; for whilest it hangeth thus in the crane, two men doe cutt it into little peices, about a foot long and half a foot thick, and putt them into the forsaid vessel from which it is carried to the choppers by two boies, who, with little flesh-hooks, take in ech hand a peice, and so convey it into tubbs, or ould casks, which stand behinde the choppers, out of which tubbs it is taken againe, and is laid for them, as they ar readie to use it, vpon the same board they stand on.

The choppers stand at the side of a shallop, which is raised from the ground and sett vp of an equal height with the coppers, and stands about two yards distant from the fournaces. Then a fir-deale is laid alongst the one side of the shallop within board, and vpon it doe they sett their chopping blocks, which ar made of the whale's taile, or els of his swimming finne. Nowe the blubber is laid readie for them by some apointed for that purpose as before is sett downe, in such small peices as the boies doe bring from the crane; and so they take it vp with little hand-hooks, laieing it vpon their blocks, where, with chopping knives, they chop it into verye small peices, about an ynch and a halfe square. Then, with a short thing of wood, made in fashion like a cole rake, they put the chopt blubber off from the block downe into the shallop, out of which it is taken againe with a copper ladle, and filled into a great tubb which hangs vpon the arme of a gibbet, that is made to tourne to and again between the blubber boat and the coppers. This tubb containeth as much blubber as will serue one of the coppers at one boiling, and therfore, so soon as it is emptied, it is presentlie filled againe, that it maie be readie to be putt into the copper when the frittires ar taken out. Theise frittires, as we call them, are the small peices of chopt blubber, which, when the oile is sufficientlie boiled, will look browne, as if they were fried; and they are taken out of the coppers, together with some of the oile, by copper ladles, and put into a wicker basket that stands over another shallop, which is placed on the other side of the fournaces, and serues as a cooler to receaue the oile being drayned throwe the said baskets. And this shallop, because it receaues the oile hott out of the two coppers, is kept continuallie half full of water, which is not onlie a meanes to coole the oile befor it runnes into cask, but also to cleanse it from soot and drosse, which discends to the bottome of the boat. And out of this shallop the oile runneth into a long trough, or gutter of wood, and therby is conveyed into butts and hogsheads, which, being filled, are bung'd up, marked, and rowl'd by, and others sett in their place. Then is the bung taken out againe, that the oile maie coole; for, not with standing the shallop is halfe fulle of water, yet, the coppers being continuallie plied, the oile keeps very hott in the boat, and runs also hott into the cask, which sometimes is an occasion of great leakage. Now concerning the finnes.

When the whale lies floating at the sterne of the ship, where he is cutt up, they cut off his head, containing his toung and finnes, comonlie called whalbone; and by a boat or shallop they towe it so neare the shoare, as it can come, and ther lett it lie till the water flowe againe; for at high waters it is drawn further and further upon the shoare, by crabs and capstowes ther placed for that purpose, untill, at a lowe water, men maie come to cutt out the finnes, which thing they doe with hatchets, by 5 or 6 finnes at once. And theise are trailed further vp from the shoare side, and then are seuered ech from another with hatchetts, and by one, at once, are laid upon a fir deale, or other board, raised up a convenient height for a man to stand at, who scrapeth off the white pithie substance that is upon the roots or great ends of the finnes, with such scraping irons as coopers use, being instruments very fitting for the purpose. Then are they rubbed in the sand, to cleanse them from grease, which they receauve when the heads are brought to the shoare side; for whilst the whale is in cutting up, his head is under the water, and his finnes remaine cleane; but being brought near the shoare and grounded, then does the grease cleaue vnto them at the ebbing or falling of the water, which is alwaies fattie with blubber that floats upon it continuallie. When the finnes are thus made cleane, they are sorted into 5 seuerall kindes, and are made up into bundells of 50, contayneing of ech sort 10 finnes. These bundles are bound vp with coards, and upon ech of them ther is tied a stick whereon is written some number, and the Companies mark sett, and so they are made readie to be shipped.

Nowe a little concerning the sea morse (of manie called the sea horse), which, indeed, maie seeme to be rather a beast than a fish, and partakes both of the sea and the land. He is in quantitie about the bignesse of a oxe.

Theise morses used to goe ashoare upon some beach or pointe of lowe land, which the snowe doth soonest melt or dissolue; and there will they lie upon the sand close together, grunteing much like hoggs, and sometimes creeping and tumbling one ouer the other. They neuer goe farre up from the water side, and therfore the men that goe to kill theise strike the first that are next the water, that their dead bodies maie be a hinderance to barre the rest from escapeing, for they all make towards the water, with out anie feare, either of man or weapon that opposeth them.

Theise also are killed with launces, which are verie broad headed to the end, so that they maie make the more mortal wound, for the speedie killing of them, because they are so neare the water, and also many in nombers; for in some places there will be 400 or 500 morses all together.

This sea beast being dead, his teeth are taken out of his

upper jawe; and his skin, or hide, is fleyed of him, first on the one side, and his fat or blubber, which lies next to his skinne, aboue his flesh, is also taken off; and then is his other side tourned up, and ye like againe done with it. Then is the blubber put into a cask, and carried to the choppers, and by them it is chopped and put into the coppers, and then it is tryed and reduced to oile.

THE THIRD RECORDED VOYAGE

OF

WILLIAM BAFFIN.

A Voyage of Discouerie to Greenland,[1] etc., Anno 1614.[2]

Written by RO. FOTHERBYE.[3]

THE ship *Thomasine* went downe from Black-wall to Woolwich the sixteenth of April, and from thence to Grauesend, the three and twentieth, where shee remayned vntill the eight and twentieth of the same; and, weighing from thence, she anchored againe in Tilberie Hope, with ten

---

[1] Spitzbergen.

[2] *Purchas*, Part III, lib. ii, cap. iv, pp. 720 to 725.

[3] There was a family of Fotherbys at Grimsby in Lincolnshire. Martin Fotherby of Grimsby had a brother Robert, and two sons—Charles, Dean and Archdeacon of Canterbury, who died in 1619; and Martin, Bishop of Salisbury. Archbishop Whitgift was also a native of Grimsby, which accounts for Dr. Fotherby's Kent preferment. There is a very elaborate altar tomb to Archdeacon Fotherby's memory in Canterbury Cathedral—the marble sides being carved with skulls and bones in high relief. Our Robert Fotherby probably belonged to the Grimsby stock. He was in the Spitzbergen Voyages of 1613, 1614, and 1615, and wrote narratives of them all, the first in manuscript until it was printed in 1860 in the *Archæologia Americana*, the two others in *Purchas*. These narratives afford evidence that their author was a man of classical, as well as of mathematical culture. After his return in 1615, a Court's Minute of the East India Company, dated in the October of that year, records the opinion that Robert Fotherby is "a very fit person to be employed upon a discovery for the south side of the Cape". He probably went on a voyage to the Indies, but in November 1618 he was appointed the East India Company's overseer for making cordage, to reside at Deptford. In 1621 he was confirmed in his place and salary, and in August of that year he was removed to Blackwall, to act as the Company's Agent there. In October 1624 his wages were increased.

ships more of good burthen, and two pinnasses, all of the Greenland fleet, set forth also at the charge of the said Company, vnder the command of Master Beniamin Joseph, chiefe captayne and generall of the said fleet.

We set sayle out of Tilberie Hope the fourth of May, and came to an anchor the same day in Lee Road, where we stayed till the next morning, then wee set sayle againe, and went forth to sea before night. We proceeded in company of the fleet, and met with stragling ice the fiue and twentieth of May, in lat. 75° 10', thro' which wee passed without danger, holding on our course all that day, till time of midnight; then we found the ice so close packt together, that we were forced to tacke about and stand to the westward, till wee found more open passage; wee plyed through it without any great danger, till the eight and twentieth day; but then, being in sight of land, we passed amongst very much ice all the fore-noone, which lay in great abundance on both sides of vs; but a desire (as it seems) to get through it drew vs on to be the more intangled with it, for about noone we could neither find a passage to goe forward, nor way to retyre backe againe, but being nine ships and two pinnasses (for the *Prosperous* and the *Desire* lost company through foule weather, the one and twentieth of May, otherwise we had beene thirteene sayle), we began very suddenly to bee inclosed, and shut vp with ice. Now euery one wrought the best meanes he could for the saftie of his ship; our master, in the *Thomasine*, caused a hauser and a grapnell to be carried forth, and laid vpon a great iland of ice, and so we rid as at an anchor, and by that meanes wee stayed from forceable rushing against other peeces; afterward we laid forth an anchor for surer hold, and made fenders of an old cable, which was hung ouer the ships sides to keepe the ice from piercing of her plankes. Wee rid thus from the eight and twentieth of May till the second of June, still floating as the wind droue vs, with our anchor holding iland,

_{Eleven Sayles fast in the Ice.}

_{M. Th. Sherwin.}

which now we accounted as the shoare, and made vse thereof accordingly, for vpon it our carpenter sealed and trimmed our lesser shallop.

<small>June.</small>

On the second of June we had a great homeming[1] sea, the wind being at north-west, whereby we iudged we were not farre from an open sea to windward of vs; there wee resolued to make tryall what we might doe to free our selues out of the ice. In the afternoone, about three a'clock, we got aboard our anchor, letting fall our fore top-sayle, and putting forth our mizen; and so droue a sterne for a while, till the floating iland gaue way; then wee filled our top-sayle, and attempted diuers places where to passe, but had repulse, and fell asterne againe; notwithstanding, at the length we preuayled, and with much adoe we attayned an open sea at a north and by west sunne, parting very gladly

<small>Wee got cleere off the Ice.</small>

from these ill neighbouring ilands; which, at our parting from them, gaue vs, or rather receiued from vs some knockes; but whilest we remayned amongst them, they seemed much more perillous than they proued hurtfull, so wee prayed God for our safe deliuerance, wishing that the rest of the ships which we left in the ice were as cleere out of it as was the *Thomasine*.

Hauing attayned the open sea to the westwards, we proceeded to the northwards, keeping the ice still on our starboord side, and met with the *Mary An-Sarah*, that got also

<small>Wee meet with the Mary An-Sarah.</small>

free of the ice the same day that we came forth of it; we kept company together till the next day, when being as high as Prince Charles Iland, we both stood in for the shoare, the *Mary An-Sarah* going for Bel-sound, her assigned harbour; but we proceeded to the Fore-land, where,

<small>Wee came to the Fore-land.</small>

when wee came the sixt of June, wee met with two shallops that belonged to the *Desire*, wherein was Cuthbert Appleyard and William Sunmes, harponiers; by whom we vnderstood that the *Prosperous* and the *Desire* had more desiredly prospered then all the rest of the fleet; they es-

[1] A misprint. Perhaps "hummocking".

caped the danger that all the rest fell into, and came to the Foreland the third of June, finding the harbour open.

Here was yet no worke begunne, for they had not seene one whale since their comming into the harbour; so that for vs there was no cause of stay to bee helpfull vnto them; and therefore we proceeded to the northward, hoping to find the shoare still as free from ice as it was at this place; but it fel out contrary to our expectations, for being come as farre as Maudlen Sound, in the latitude of 79° 34′, we met with some stragling ice, and from the mayne top we saw much ice lye betwixt vs and Hackluyts Headland, which seemed to bee close to the shoare, therefore we sent some men in a shallop to Maudlen Sound, to see if it were open, that wee might harbour our ship there, and search for a leake which wee found her subject vnto in foule weather. Wee proceeded to the Northwards.
Maudlen Sound.
Hackluyts Headland.

The Sound was open, and we anchored in a good harbour, but the ice was not gone cleere from the shoare, therefore we could not hale our ship aground, but we carined her, and set vp our *Biscaine* shallop, which we carried with vs out of England in pieces. We anchored in Maudlen Sound.

The next day after our comming hither, I went forth in a little shallop (the other being then vnset together), to see how the ice lay at Hackluyts Headland, and whether we might passe with our ship that way or no. Being come forth of the harbour, we perceiued that it was very foule weather at sea; notwithstanding, I proceeded into Faire Hauen, where the south harbour was then open, but much ice lay then in the Sound, vnbroken from shoare to shoare; otherwise wee might haue passed that way to Hackluyts Head-land, betwixt the iland and the mayne land; we stayed here till the next morning, then the weather beganne to cleere vp, and we put forth to sea againe, intending to goe without the Ilands; but being out of the harbour, wee found the foule weather to be such as our little weake shallop was not able to endure; therefore we returned I went forth in a shallop.

againe to our ship into Maudlen Sound, where we killed two female morses, and took their teeth, hides, and blubber.

We set sayle out of Maudlen Sound, and followed the Ice.

On the tenth of June we set sayle out of Maudlen Sound, and coasted along to the northward till we were past Hackluyts Headland, but then we saw the ice lye before vs, extending close to the shoare, so that for us to passe further that way it was not possible; therefore wee turned to the westward, to see if wee could finde passage further from the shoare. Wee sayled as the ice trended, west and south-west, till the thirteenth day, and, keeping still alongst it, we found it to trend neerest south and south south-west. We proceeded well thus far, till we came vnder the latitude

Prince Charles Iland in 78° 40'.

of Prince Charles his Iland in 78° 40', being eight and twentie leagues from shoare; but then we altered our

Wee stood againe for shoare.

course, and stood in for the foreland, to goe and be helpfull to the other ships there, for the furthering of their voyage, according to our instructions (as some did vnderstand them), but contrary, I am sure, to some of our desires. When we

Eleuen Holland ships.

came neere the Foreland, we saw eleuen ships of Hollanders vnder sayle, plying to the southwards. One of them came roome, and struck her top-sayles twice, whereby we supposed they took vs for some of their fleete which they wanted, but wee held on our course still into Sir Thomas

We anchored in Sir T. Smiths Bay.

Smiths Bay, where we came to an anchor the fifteenth of June by the *John-Anne-Francis* and the *Desire*, the *Mary Margaret* being then vnder sayle to go to the Foreland.

Here was yet no need of any helpe that we could make them, for they had hitherto neyther killed one whale since their first comming in hither; therefore we thought it best not to stay here, but rather goe to Faire Hauen, where wee should bee more readie to proceed on our discouerie when the ice would giue vs leaue, and in the meane-time wee might bee helpfull to the two ships thither assigned for the making of their voyage; and so much the rather wee hasted, because we vnderstood that the Hollanders also set forth a ship on discouerie.

We set sayle the seuenth of June, and met with the *Prosperous*, that came from Cross-road, and was going into Sir Thomas Smith Bay, there to get some bricke and lime to mend their furnace, as Nicholas Woodcocke,[1] the master, told vs. Then we went forth to sea, and, being about foure leagues from the shoare, the winde began to blow so hard from the north-west, that wee were forced back againe to seek harbour, and came to an anchor the nineteenth of June in Crosse-road. Here we stayed two dayes, much wind blowing at the north north-east, till the one and twentieth of June, and then, in the after-noone, the wind came to the east and by south, and the weather was faire; therefore, at a north north-west sunne, we weighed and set sayle againe, and so did the *Thomas Bonauenture*, that came to an anchor by vs this morning, beeing also bound for Faire Hauen.

<small>We went forth of Sir T. Smiths Bay</small>

<small>We were driven back againe into Crosse-road.</small>

<small>We set sayle out of Crosse-road.</small>

This next day, in the afternoone, we were thwart of Maudlen Sound, and, the weather being faire and calme, we sent a shallop to the northward, to see what alteration there was amongst the ice, and to seeke out some good harbour for a ship, and also to set vp the kings armes at Hackluyts Headland, or some other conuenient place.

<small>One shallop to the North ward.</small>

When Master Baffin was gone from the ship in the foresaid shallop, I went presently into the other shallop into Maudlen Sound, there to set vp the kings armes, and also to see if there were any morses come ashoare. When I was within the Sound, I found no beeches bare for morses to come vpon, for ice and snow lay yet vndissolued from the shoare side; but I went to the harbour, and there caused a

<small>The other into Maudlen Sound.</small>

<small>The Kings Armes set vp in Trinitie Harbour</small>

---

[1] There was a seaman of this name, which is not a common one, sent out by the Muscovy Company in 1568, on a voyage to reach the river Ob, but the particulars have not been preserved. Nicholas Woodcock may have been a grandson of this earlier namesake. He was pilot in Jonas Poole's voyage of 1610, but in 1612 he piloted a Spanish ship, and is said to have been the cause of so many Dutch ships having gone to Spitzbergen in 1613. For that offence he was arrested and suffered imprisonment. (*Purchas*, iii, p. 466.)

crosse to be set vp, and the kings armes to be nayled thereon, vnder which also I nayled a piece of sheet lead, whereon I set the Moscouie Companies marke, with the day of the moneth and yeare of our Lord. Then, cutting vp a piece of earth, which afterward I carried aboard our ship, I took it into my hand and said, in the hearing of the men there present, to this effect:

I take this piece of earth, as a signe of lawfull possession of this countrey of King James his New-land, and of this particular place, which I name Trinitie Harbour, taken on the behalfe of the company of merchants called the Merchants of New Trades and Discoueries, for the vse of our Souereigne Lord James, by the grace of God King of Great Brittaine, France, and Ireland, whose royall armes are here set vp, to the end that all people who shall here arriue may take notice of his Maiesties right and title to this countrey, and to euery part thereof. God saue King James.

Trinitie Harbor is vnder the parallel of 79° 34′.

This is a good safe harbour, and is vnder the latitude of 79° 34′, as I haue found by good obseruation, and haue of westerly variation 25°. When I had here set vp the kings armes, I returned toward our ship, which was come to an anchor at the entrance of Faire hauen, staying the floud came, because that at the tide of ebbe there runnes a great current out of the Sound; so, at the next floud, we came into Faire hauen, and anchored by the *Gamaliel* and the *Thomas Bonauenture* the three and twentieth day of June.

We came to an anchor in Faire Hauen.

Then John Mason, master of the *Gamaliel*, came aboord of our ship, and I asked him if he had any worke for our men, for I would cause them to come a shoare. He told me that hitherto he had not seene a whale come in; but his furnaces and coppers were already set vp, and therefore as yet he had no neede of helpe, but when occasion serued he would imploy them. This day, about eleuen a clocke, Master Baffin returned in the shallop from the northwards. He said that he had beene at Cape Barren, which is the point of an iland three or foure leagues from Hackluits

No Whales were yet come in.

The shallop returned from the Northwards.

Cape Barren.

headland; but further than that he could not passe for ice which lay close to the shore, and he had not set vp the kings armes in any place.

On Munday, the seuen and twentieth of June, I went forth againe in the shallop to the northward, partly to see what alteration there might be in the ice with the easterly windes, which had blowne hard since the shallop last returned, but chiefely to set vp the kings armes in some place conuenient, because there was none set vp to the northwards of Maudlen Sound.

We rowed to Cape Barren, where formerly Master Baffin had bin, and, finding the ice there gone from the shore, we proceeded further, to an iland which now we call the Saddle, *Saddle Iland.* in respect of the forme thereof, more than a league distant from Cape Barren. In our way thither it began to snow, and grew to be a great and vehement storme from the *A Storme.* west north-west; therefore we hasted and got to the lee side of the aforesaid iland, and there made fast our shallop with a grapnell laid vpon the icie shore, vsing the best meanes we could with our shallops saile to keepe vs from the extremitie of so cold an harbour. We staid here eight houres, and the storme continued driuing the ice still eastward in great abundance, and with wonderfull swiftnesse. When the weather began to cleere, I caused the men to rowe to leewards to another iland, a league distant, which seemed then to be a cape of the maine land, purposing there to set vp the kings armes; but afterwards wee found it to be an iland, and to the maine wee could not come for broken ice.

This stormie weather continued from Munday night till Friday morning, during which time we had beene but eleauen leagues at the furthest from our ship; yet went we so farre as we could haue gone had the weather beene neuer so faire, for at foure leagues distance from Cape Barren the ice lay firme and vnbroken two or three miles from the shore, and close againe to it lay the shattered ice,

Julii.

thronged together with this present storme. On Friday morning we came backe againe to Hackluit's Headland, and there I set [up?] the kings armes in the like manner as at Trinitie Harbour. From thence we rowed towards our ship; and as we entred into Faire-hauen, there came a whale that accompanied vs into the harbour, leaping and aduancing himselfe almost quite out of the water, falling headlong downe againe with greate noise. We hasted aboord our ship, and I sent forth both our shallops to strike this whale, if they could, and told Master Mason of her comming in, who also went forth in his shallop; but it seemes the whale past vnder the ice which lay yet vnbroken betwixt the north harbour and the south harbour, for they could not see her againe.

The Whales began now to come in.

The next day there came more whales in, and Robert Hambleton, our masters mate, strucke two, which vnluckily escaped, the first for want of helpe, the *Gamaliel's* shallop being in chase of another whale, and our owne little shallop not able to row against a head sea to assist the other; so that at length, the whale hauing towed the shallop forth to sea, the harping iron came out; the second was also strucken within the sound, and ranne vnder the ice, which lay yet vnbroken at the east end of the Sound, and drew the shallop vpon it cleane out of the water, by which meanes the harping iron came forth. Here we remained till the sixt of Julie, our men and boates being helpefull at all times to further the voyage.

Two Whales escaped.

The sixt of Julie we set saile forth of Faire-hauen, intending to make triall if we could to get to westwards of the ice, and so proceede to the northwards, hauing sent away one of our shallops the day before, prouided with twentie dayes bread, to coast along the shoare, search the beach for commodities, and set vp the Kings armes at places conuenient, hoping thereby to preuent the Hollanders, who now rid in the north harbour of Faire-hauen, and were

We came forth of Faire-hauen.

ready for the first opportunitie to discouer and take possession of other harbours, hauing two ships to goe forth onely vpon discouery.

We sailed westwards from Faire-hauen seuen leagues, and then met with a maine banke of ice, which trended north and south, the sea appeared to the northwards to be open, so far as we could see, therefore we plied that way. When we had run seuen or eight leagues more, the ice lay so thick on euery side, that we were bard from proceeding any further; then we stood in toward the shore, and being a little to the northwards of Cape Barren, our shallop had sight of vs, and came rowing to vs through the broken ice. Master Baffin told vs the shore to the eastward was much pestered with ice, and he had set vp the Kings armes at the entrance of a faire sound, about four leagues distant from Cape Barren. *We met with ice and stood to the northward. Our shallop came to vs.*

Now the weather being faire and calme, Master Sherwin, Master Baffin, and J, went in the shallop to the place where the Kings armes were set vp, purposing (because the ayre was very cleere) to goe vpon some high mountaine, from whence we might see how the sea was pestered with ice, and what likelihood there was of further proceeding. According to this our intent, we ascended a very high hill, and from thence we saw the ice lye vpon the sea so farre as we could discerne, so that the sea seemed to be wholly toured with ice, saue onely to the eastwards; we thought that we saw the water beyond the ice, which put vs in some hope that we should ere long get passage with our shallops along the shore, if we could not passe with our shippe. Being thus satisfied, we returned abord our ship and plyed towards Faire-hauen, aduising amongst our selues of the best course we could to further the businesse committed to vs. *We returned towards Faire-hauen.*

We resolued to make our discouery along the shore with both our shallops, and to carry with vs our prouision for *We intended to discouer with our shallops.*

the whale-killing, conceiuing good hopes besides, of profit which the beaches would afford vs; therefore we intended, when our ship was brought safe into harbour againe, to goe from her with both our shallops, and to put in practice this our late resolution. But the weather falling calme, and a fogge succeeding, which continued three dayes, so that our ship came not into harbour till the twelfth of July. I went from her the eleuenth day, intending to search the beaches, till Master Baffin came to me with the other shallop, and then we to proceede both together; but before he came, I had gone so farre as that the ice would not suffer mee to passe a boates length further, and I had also searched a very faire beach, which was altogether fruitlesse.

<small>*I went forth in the one shallop.*</small>

Master Baffin came to me at a place appointed, the fourteenth of Julie, in the other shallop, and we proceeded both together to the eastwards againe, and found passage amongst the ice, that lay almost two miles from the shoare of Red-beach, vnbroken vp this yeare. Here wee haled vp our shallops out of the water, lest the broken ice, which is carried to and fro with the winde, might split them or bruise them. Then Master Baffin and I, with foure men more, walked ouer the firme ice, and went ashore on Red-beach, where we trauelled about the space of three miles by the shore side, but found no commodities, as we expected to haue done; for here had the Hull-men[1] been in 1612, as we might know, by the fires that they had made, and gathered the fruites that many yeares before had brought forth. Thus, as we could not finde that which wee desired to see, so did we behold that which we wished had not beene there to be seene, which was great abundance of ice, that lay close to the shore, and also off at sea, so farre as we could discerne; wherefore, being thus satisfied, and more wearie to know that we could passe no further then with trauelling so farre, we returned to our shallops, and

<small>*Master Baffin came to me in the other shallop.*</small>

<small>*Red-beach.*</small>

<small>*We hailed our shallop upon the ice.*</small>

<small>*We returned to our shallop.*</small>

[1] Hull men, under the command of Captain Marmaduke.

went aboord of our ship in Faire hauen on Sunday, the seuenteenth of July, passing the neerest way betwixt the islands and the maine land, for now the ice was broken betwixt the south harbour, where we rid, and the north harbour, where the Hollanders rid.

The next day we sent our shallop to the north-east side of Faire-hauen, there to lye for the comming of the whales ouer against the *Gamaliels* two shallops that lye on the other side for the same purpose.

The twentieth of July, wee were vnder saile to goe forth of Faire-hauen with the *Gamaliel*, purposing to haue taken two ships that rid at the entrance of Maudlen-Sound with John Mason, who first descried them, supposed to be one a Bask, and the other an English man; but the winde blew right into the harbour, so that we could not get forth, and therefore we came to an anchor againe where we rid before. *We were vnder saile and came to an anchor againe.*

On the one and twentieth of July our harponiers killed a whale, which split one of our shallops, and strucke the harponier that was in her ouerboord; but both hee and the rest of the men were relieued, and taken into another shallop; then we sent our carpenter to mend the shallop that was split; and on the fiue and twentieth day they helpt to kill another whale. *We killed a Whale.*

On the sixe and twentieth of July I drew the plat of Faire-hauen, as it is here proiected (but here too costly to insert).

When this scoale of whales were past, we went out of Faire-hauen the first of August with both our shallops, Master Baffin in one, and I in the other, with fiue men more in each shallop, thinking that now we should find the ice broken, and cleere gone from the shore, conceiuing some good hope to proceede, and make some new discouery, which was the chiefe occasion of our imployment. Wee passed ouer Red-cliff Sound, which we found cleare of ice; and from thence we proceeded to Red-beach, where *August.*

we also found great alteration since our last being there, notwithstanding the ice was not clearly voided from the shoare; for in some places it was firm and vnbroken off, for the space of almost halfe a mile; so we rowed alongst it, till wee came neere the north end of the beach, which lyeth furthest into the sea, and there we found an open way to the shore with our shallops, and went on land; but seeing in all places great abundance of broken ice, we lay close to the shoare; and doubting that although perhaps with much adoe we might get about the point of the beach, yet should we still be pestered with ice from proceeding any further, we resolued to walke ouer land to the other side of the beach, where we saw a hill about foure miles distant, from which we thought we should be satisfied how much further it was possible for vs to proceede; so thither we trauailed, where, when we came, wee saw a very faire sound on the east side of the beach which was open within; but there lay very much ice at the entrance of it, which, although it was extended more than halfe ouer [the] sound, yet we doubted not but if we could get our shallops about the beach, we should finde either one way or other to passe ouer the said sound, and from the high land on the other side we should receiue very good satisfaction, if the weather continued faire and cleare as now it was, therefore we intended to make triall what we might do; but before we returned we went down to the point of the beach, at the entrance of the sound, and there set vp a crosse, and nailed a sixepence thereon with the Kings armes. This being done, we returned to our shallops, and according to our late determination, we rowed about the point of Red-beach, and with many crooked windings amongst the ice, at length we got ouer Wiches Sound (for so it is now termed).

As soone as we were ouer on the other side, about two leagues from Red-beach, Master Baffin and I clambered vp a very high hill, from whence we saw a point of land, bearing east north-east by the ordinary compasse, eighteene or twentie leagues distant, as I supposed. We likewise saw another faire sound to the southwards of vs, which was much pestered with ice, but we could not see the end of it. Here, vpon the mountaine, wee set vp a warelocke, and then came downe againe with lesse labour but more danger then we had in getting vp, by reason of the steepinesse thereof. Then we walked to the shoare side, and there found many beach finnes, whereby I coniectured that Master Marmadukes men, in his first discouery, made in Anno 1612, had not beene vpon this land to search the beaches, for in all other places where we had beene heretofore we could finde nothing at all. Now, therefore, we resolued to make further search alongst this shoare, and to proceede with our shallops so farre as we possibly could; wherevpon wee returned to our men againe, whom we left with our shallops where we first landed. We found beach Fins.

Hauing stayed here a while, and obserued the latitude, which I found to be 79° 54', we saw a shallop come rowing towards the extreamest point of this shoare; therefore we hastened towards them, to see who were therein, and found them to be Master Marmadukes men, lately come from their ship, the *Harts-ease*, which they said they left at sea amongst the ice, about a league from Red Beach. Here they were setting vp a crosse, which they said that they found there fallen downe, and had beene formerly set vp, in the time of Master Marmadukes first discouery, by one Laurence Prestwood, whose name I saw thereon engrauen, with two or three names more, and it had the date of the seuenteenth of August 1612. Vpon this crosse they nailed the Kings armes. We met with the *Harts-ease* shallop. Note.

Here we parted from them, and, according to our former determination, we proceeded, some in the shallops amongst the ice, and others on shoare, till wee went about foure leagues further, in which space we found many more finnes, and one pair of morses teeth; but now we found the ice so close packt together, that wee could not proceede any further with our shallops; wherefore Master Baffin and I intended to walke ouer land vntill we should be better satisfied how farre this sound went in, for wee could as yet see no end of it, and it seemed to make a separation of the land; so, leauing our men here with the shallops, wee trauailed almost a league further, till we came to the point of a sandie beach that shot into the sound, which was wonderfully stored with drift wood in great abundance. From this point we receiued such satisfaction as we looked for, because we saw the end of the sound, which lies south in about ten leagues. It hath in it harbour that is landlockt; and, doubtlesse, it is a good place for the whale killing, if it be not euery yeare, as now it is, pestered with ice. Here I saw a more naturall earth and clay then any that I haue seene in all the countrie, but nothing growing thereupon more then in other places. This sound is that which formerly had, and still retaineth, the name of Sir Thomas Smiths Inlet.[1]

The end of Sir Thomas Smiths Inlet discouered.

Being thus satisfied, we came backe againe to our shallops, and, seeing no way but one, we returned to our ship; but before we could get to Red-beach, there arose a very great storme from the east north-east after we had entered among the ice in Wiches Sound, so that we were separated the one shallop from the other, whereby our danger was the greater; for whiles wee were both in company together, the one might have beene helpefull to the other when neede required, and more easie it seemed to saue them both then, being separated, to keepe either of them from wracke. But God (who, in his wonted mercie, is euer ready to relieue the faithfull distressed) did not onely so prouide that we met together againe—and, indeede, were helpefull the one to the other (otherwise, I doubt the one shallop had mis-

We returned towards our ship. A storme began when we were amongst the ice.

[1] Called Hinlopen Strait on the modern charts.

carried, for she was in great danger)—but also deliuered vs safely out from amongst these perillous rockes of ice, which it was very hard to shun, and at the length brought vs into an open sea, where, with as scant a saile as we could make, we past swiftly before the winde, the sea comming diuers times ouer the sternes of our shallops, which wet our skinnes, that had scarse any dry cloathes on before to keepe them warme, by reason of a drizeling snow which fell with the storme. Then we went aboord our ship, into the south harbour of Faire hauen, the fift of August, with one hundred and fiftie beach finnes, and one pair of morses teeth, giuing thanks to God for his blessing and mercifull deliuerance. *We came aboord our ship.*

The ninth of August, two ships of the Hollanders, that were appointed for Northern Discouery, were seene thwart of Faire Hauen, sayling to the southwards. *The Holland discouerers go homewards.*

The eleuenth of August we set sayle forth of Faire Hauen, the winde at south south-west, intending to make tryall if yet the ice would admit vs to haue passage to the northwards or the north-eastwards. We held our course from Cape Barren, north-east and by east, till seuen a clocke at night, at which time, hauing runne eight leagues from the shoare, wee met with the ice which lay east and by south, and west and by north, and bore vp alongst it to the eastwards, for the winde was now come to the north northwest; then wee tackt about to the westwards, and plyed off and on close by the ice till the thirteenth day at midnight, still expecting a change of the weather, that we might haue made some aduenture amongst the shatterd ice, for both on the twelfth and thirteenth day the winde blew hard at north, and the weather was cold, thicke, and very winter-like, with fall of snow; this winde being so contrarie, droue both the ice and our ship to leewards towards the shoare, so that wee were forced to put into harbour againe, and came to an anchor the fourteenth day in the north harbour of Faire Hauen, where the fleet of Hollanders *Our ship went forth to sea. We meet with ice eight leagues from shore. We plyed off and on the ice two dayes. Wee anchored againe in the North Harbour.*

lately rid, at which time the *Hartsease* was there at an anchor.

Now was the land, both mountaynes and plaines, wholly couered with snow, so that almost all mens mindes were possessed with a desire of returning for England. But to preuent a sudden resolution for a homeward voyage, without further satisfaction, I made mention that once againe we might goe forth with our shallops, to see what alteration there might bee found alongst the shoare. It fell out that I was to goe in one shallop for this purpose, so I tooke with me eight men, and went from our ship the fifteenth day of August.

<small>I went to the east-wards in a shallop.</small>

We rowed to Red-cliffe Sound, where we passed through much ice that was newly congealed, being thicker than an halfe crowne piece of siluer, notwithstanding we broke way through it, and being ouer the sound, we had a cleere sea againe; then we proceeded to Red-beach, where, finding the shoare cleere of ice (which, at my last being there, was wonderfully pestered), I conceiued good hope to finde passage to the furthest land from thence in sight, bearing east halfe a point southerly, nine or ten leaages distant; to this end we put off from the shoare of Red-beach, and rowed a league and more in an open sea, and then we met with ice, which lay dispersed abroad, and was no hinderance to our proceeding, so that we continued rowing the space of sixe houres, in which time we had gotten more then halfe way ouer; but then we found the ice to lye very thicke thronged together, so that it caused vs much to alter our course, sometimes southward, and sometimes northward; and euen in this time, when we thought wee stood in most need of cleere weather, it pleased God to send vs the contrary, for it beganne to snow very fast, which made the ayre so thicke that we could not see to make choice of the most likely way for vs to passe; therefore I thought good to stay here awhile, hoping that ere long the weather would

<small>Ice was newly frozen in Red-cliffe Sound.</small>

<small>I intended to goe once to Port Desire.</small>

<small>A great snow began.</small>

bee more agreeable to our purpose; so a grapnell being laid forth vpon an Iland off, to hold fast our shallop, a tent was made of the shallops sayle, to keepe the weather from vs, and we remayned here fiue houres; but finding no alteration in the constant weather, I willed the men to take downe the tent, and with faire tearmes perswaded them, that notwithstanding the wet weather it were good to be doing something, to get ouer to the desired shoare, where we might refresh our selues, and haue fire to dry our wet clothes: they seemed well content with this motion, and so we rowed the space of foure houres more, the ice still causing vs to hold a south and south south-east course, which carried vs further into Sir Thomas Smith's Inlet, and put vs from the place where we wished to be. I could not passe for ice.

The thicke snowie weather continued all this time, which was very vncomfortable to vs all, but especially to the men that rowed; and as the snow was noysome to their bodies, so did it also begin to astonish their mindes, as I well perceiued by their speeches which proceeded vpon this occasion. The snow hauing continued thus long, and falling vpon the smooth water, lay in some places an inch thicke, being alreadie in the nature of an ice compact, though not congealed, and hindred sometimes our shallops way; this, I say, caused some of them, not altogether without reason, to say that if it should now freeze as it did that night when we came ouer Red-cliffe Sound, we should be in danger here to be frozen vp. Howsoeuer, this search might bee a meanes to discourage the rest, that considered not of such a thing till they heard it spoken of: yet true it is, that I saw no likelihood, by reason of the ice, how to attayne my desire at this time, and therefore I bade them row toward the shoare of Red-beach againe, where I intended to stay till the weather might happily be more conuenient. So holding a west north-west course, so neere as the ice would suffer vs, wee came to the east side of Red-beach, The originall cause of ice at sea. I went back to Red-beach.

hauing been eighteene houres amongst the ice, during all which time the snow fell, and as yet ceased not. When we had been here about an houre it began to cleere vp, and the wind to blow hard at east, which rather packt the ice close together in this place then disperst it, so that I was now out of hope to get any than I had done alreadie; wherefore I returned toward our ship, intending as I went to make a more particular discouery of Broad-bay and Red-cliffe Sound, hoping that one place or other would afford some thing worthy of the time and labour. When we were come to the west side of Red-beach it began to blow much wind, where withall the sea growing to be great, all men aduised to passe ouer Broad-bay, whilst the winde and weather would serue vs to sayle, for they said it was like to be very foule weather: so seeing that it was no conuenient time for coasting, we came ouer the bay to Point Welcome (which I so named because it is a place where wee oftentimes rested when wee went forth in our shallops), it is about foure leagues distant from the north end of Red-beach.

I returned toward our ship.

Point Welcome.

At this point the Hollanders had set vp Prince Maurice his armes, neere vnto a crosse which I had caused to bee set vp aboue a month before, and had nayled a sixe pence thereon with the Kings armes, but the men that were with me went (without any such direction from mee) and pulled downe the said Princes armes, whilst I was gone vp a mountayne to looke into the sea, if I could see any ice; and when I came downe againe they told me that the sixe pence was taken from the crosse I had set vp, and there was another post set by it, with the Hollanders armes made fast thereon, which they had pulled downe; so, because the sixe pence was taken away, I caused one to nayle the Kings armes, cast in lead, vpon the crosse; which, being done, we rowed to the bottome of Red-cliffe Sound, and as we coasted along the shoare, we searched two little beaches

The King's armes are set vp againe at Point Welcome. I went into Redcliffe Sound.

which had some wood on them, but nothing we found of better value.

About two leagues within the sound, on the east side, there is an harbour, where shippes may ride in good ground land-lockt; but if other yeeres be like this, I cannot say that this is an harbour fitting for ships, because it is late ere the Sound breake vp; for euen now there lay much ice at the bottome of it, insomuch that I was forced to leaue the shallop, because I could not passe with her for ice, and walke two miles ouer stonie mountaynes, with another man in my company, to bee satisfied concerning a point of land that shot into the Sound, whether it were an Iland or no, as by all likelihood it seemed to bee: but when I came to the farthest part of it, I saw it joyne to the mayne land, wherefore I called it Point Deceit, because it deceiued mee so much. From hence wee proceeded toward our shippe, and came aboord of her in the north harbour of Faire Hauen, on Friday night, being the nineteenth of August, where she rid alone, for Master Marmaduke was gone forth to sea that day. *Point Deceit.* *I come aboord our ship.*

The two and twentieth of August, John Mason, master of the *Gamaliell*, came ouer from the south harbour for helpe to hayle vp a whale which had beene sunke fourteene dayes, in one hundred and twentie fathome depth, or else to pull the wharpe and harping iron out of her, for now it was time to take her or forsake her. Master Sherwin, our master, caused our long boate to be manned, and went with him; when they came where the whale was sunke they haled, and shee presently rose, bolting suddenly vp with a thundring cracke, made with the bursting of her bodie; and notwithstanding she had layen so long, yet had shee all her finnes fast. Whilst this was in doing, the *Hartsease* was comming into the harbour from the northward, and anchored by our ship an houre after. *A whale lay sunken fourteene days.*

Here wee stayed till the seuen and twentieth of August,

and since my last returne hither in the shallop from the eastwards, the weather hath beene commonly warme, and the mountaynes were now more cleere of snow then they had beene any time this yeere, notwithstanding there had much snowe fallen since the beginning of this moneth, but it was quite consumed, and a greater signe of warmth and thaw was now to bee obserued then any time of the yeere heretofore; namely, by the often falling of the ice into the sea from the huge snowie bankes, making a noyse like thunder, so that the time was very hopefull, but thus wee made vse of occasion offered.

Warme weather in the end of August.

The seuen and twentieth of August, it was faire and warme weather, calme till noone, then had wee a gale of winde from the south south west, wherewithall wee set sayle out of Faire-hauen in the company of the *Hartsease*, with whom wee had beene in termes of consortship, but nothing was concluded. About sixe a clocke at night wee were sixe leagues from Cape Barren, which bore from vs south-west and by south.

We set sayle to the Eastward.

Wee proceeded still to the north-eastward, and on the eight and twentieth day in the morning wee had runne about twentie leagues from Cape Barren, in an east northeast way by the ordinary compasse, being open of Sir Thomas Smith's Inlet nine or tenne leagues from the shoare, at which time wee were come to the ice that trended east south-east, and west north-west, but the sea being very rough, wee stood off againe from the ice; in the afternoone it fell calme, and at night we had a gale of winde at east, and the ship was steered west, and then south-west homewards.

The Thomasine returnes for England.

The nine and twentieth day, the winde easterly, an easie gale. At foure a clocke in the afternoone, Hackluyts Headland bore from vs, south-east by east, foure leagues distant. This euening was very warme.

The thirtieth day, the winde at north-east, an easie gale.

At foure a clocke in the afternoone, Maudlen Point bore east north-east, halfe a point easterly, about three leagues distant. Towards the euening it fell calme; the weather not cold.

The thirtieth (?) day, faire sunne-shine weather, and calme till noone, and then we had a good gale of winde from the north-east, being fiue leagues distant from the foreland, which bore south-east. Now we altered our course, and stood to the west-ward; therefore, to keepe vs still in the parallel that now wee were in, which was 79° 8', a west north-west course was directed, in respect of the variation, to make good a true west way. We stood to the westwards.

This course wee held till wee had runne about twentie leagues, and then wee ranne twentie leagues more in a west and by north course till one a clocke on Friday morning, at which time it fell calme; and wee heard the sea make a great noyse, as if wee had beene neere land, but wee rather iudged it to bee ice, as, indeed, it proued to bee; for in the morning, when it was light and cleere, wee saw the ice, about a league from vs, which trended southerly. Hauing now a gale at east north-east, wee steered away south and south-east, but in the afternoone we were embayed with a long banke of ice, which wee could not weather; therefore wee were faine to tacke about, and, the winde having come more southerly then it was in the morning, wee stood off from the ice north-east and north-east and by north, and then to the southwards againe, making sundrie boardes to get forth to wind-wards of the ice. Wee met with ice.

The third day, befoore noone, wee had sight againe of ice to westwards of vs, and at noone were vnder the parallel of 78° 27', according to my obseruation. Then wee stood away south, to keepe cleere of ice; for wee had a great homing sea, although but little winde, and therefore durst not be to bold to edge too neere it, especially the winde being easterly, as then it was.

On the fourth day our men saw the ice againe from the mayne top-mast head, and therefore wee still maintayned a southerly course. The next day it began to be foggie, and continued close weather and hazie for three dayes, so that we had no more sight of the ice, neyther could we at this time receiue any further satisfaction concerning the same; therefroe [*sic*—therefore?] wee kept a southerly course, so neere as wee could, although wee had but little winde, and the same very variable, till the ninth day, but then wee had a good gale of winde at west north-west.

We left the ice and came for England.

On the tenth, beeing Saturday, we were, by my reckoning, fiftie leagues distant from Low-foot, which bore from vs east south-east, halfe a point southerly. This day the wind shifted to the south-west, and at night came to the south with much raine, then came backe againe to the west north-west, and began a great storme.

A storme beganne.

This night the master and others saw a light vpon the fore-bonnet, which the saylers call a Corpo Santo. It appeared like the flame of a candle, and (as sea-men obserue) it alwayes presageth an ensuing storme; which to verifie, this foule weather continued the next day, and grew to be so vehement on Sunday night that the sea oftentimes ouer-raked our ship, and wee were faine to lye atry with our fore course onely, and our mayne top-mast also strucke, which last thing (as sea-men say) is seldome done at sea; then, about one a clocke, we were forced to take in our fore course, and to lye a-hull for fiue houres.

A Corpo Santo. It is often seen at the end of stormes.

The fourth of October the shippe came to Wapping, with the whole number of men she carried forth (my selfe excepted, that was come before), being sixe and twentie, all in perfect health.

THE FOURTH RECORDED VOYAGE
OF
WILLIAM BAFFIN.
1615.

TO THE
RIGHT WORSHIPFVL AND TRVLYE HONORABLE *Sir* THOMAS SMITH:
knight. Sir DUDLY DIGGES: *kt.* Mr. JOHN WOLSTENHOLME:[1]
esquire. and the rest of the worthy ADUANCERS *and*
ADUENTURERS *for the* FINDINGE OF A PASSAGE
by the NORTH WEST.

THE AUNTIENTE (*Right Worshipfull*) had so much regard to the worthies of those tymes, that any waye sought the good and preferment of theare countrye and common wealth wheare they lyued, That ingratytude was so far from them, they honoured, yea with diuine honoure, those to whome theire countrye was in any way obleeged. But wee which liue in an age, whome the poets tearme an jron age, are so far from honouringe our worthies with due prayse, that many had rather seek occation of slander then otherwise, although not agaynst theare persons, yet agaynst theare acctions.

You are the worthyes of our tyme, whose many fould aduentures are such, but espetiall this of the north-west, which are not discouraged with spendinge and loss of many hundreth poundes, ney rather many thousand pounds; reapinge no other profitt butt onlye bare reports, and those little anaylable to the purpose. But I feare if I should take on me to sett forth your due prayse, I should come so far short of the marke I aymed at; that it weare better for me to

[1] See the Introduction for notices of Sir Thomas Smith, Sir Dudley Digges, and Sir John Wolstenholme.

leaue it undoone, then badlye doone: knowinge that who so seeketh to amend APELLES pictture had need be some good artist, and who so seeketh to sett forth the worthie prayse of our LONDON MARCHANTS, had need bee more than a good rethoritian. But what neede I spende tyme hearin, when neuer dyinge fame hath, and will, enroule your names in TYMES CHEEFEST CHRONICLE OF ETERNYTIE: where no ENUIOUS MOMUS shall have power to rase out the smallest tythe thereof.

And seinge I haue beene imployed, and haue reaped some profitt from your purses, I might be counted a uery bad seruant if I gaue not in some accounte howe we spent our tyme. Such as it is, I present it to your worshipps vewe: whearin I haue indeuoured to set doune our proceedinges in so short a methode as conueniently I coulde, referringe our pertyculer courses, latytudes, longitudes, windes, leagues we run, and variatyon of the compas, to the breefe table or Jurnall in the beginninge of the booke, wheare euery of these is sett in their seuerall collombes, with the tytles at the heade.

And whereas in the collombe tytle TRUCOURSE, in many places is sett a number betweene the letters, as on the last day of *Aprill*, is N. 20 E, which is north 20 degrees eastward, or allmost north north east: the tru waye that the shipp had room that 24 houers, the variatyon of the compas, and other accidentes alowed. Also there is a collombe wheare is sett downe the longitude, wheare we weare ech day at noone (although not usual in Jarnales) that theareby ech seuerall uariatyon of the compas, and any other accidente may be the more redylie found without protractinge all or parte of the voyage: in which variatyons I hope I haue not much erred from the truth, comminge nearer then some which haue beene imployed that way heretofore.

And because your worships may more redylie see and perseue howe far we haue beene, I haue heare following placed a small mapp, and it is to be noted that within the

Ile of Resolutyon wee sawe no more land then that I haue colored with greene, besides ilands. And heare is traced out our ships waye, with the red prickle lyne, notynge euery place wheare we came on shore (to make tryall of the tyde) with a red crosse, and for the tyme of high water at those places they are on the next page.

Thus bouldly haue I presumed on your worships clemencie in two respectes, the one in consideration of your selues, beinge so well acquaynted with these matters (as hauinge payde so deare for them) would in respect (not of the writer) but of the accion, vouchsafe the readinge thereof; the other, that beinge in duty bounde to be at your worships pleasure, I knowe not howe to shewe my selfe more dutyfull affected, then by giuinge in an accounte how we haue spent, or mis-spent our tyme; beseechinge your worships to accept them, not as my worke, but as my will and affection. And so with my daylie prayers to God for your health and prosperous successe in all your accions, I rest,

Your worships, most dutyfullie to be commanded to his best endeuoures, William Baffin.

The LONGITUDE and LATYTUDE of SUCH PLACES wheare we haue beene on shore within RESOLUTION ILAND & what Moone doth make a full sea, or the TYME OF HIGH WATER on the CHAINGE DAYE. And allso there distance from RESOLUTION ILAND.

	[1]*	[2]*	[3]*	[4]*	[5]*
	° ′	° ′			
Resolution Iland.	66.26	61.30	E.S.E.	7¼	legues.
Saluage iland	72.00	62.30	S.E. 4 E.	8¾	58
nine legues ½ beyond	73.00	62.40	S.E.	9	67½
Broken ilands	74.30	63.46	S.E. by S	9¾	87
North Shore	80.30	64.40	S.S.E.	10½	142
6 leagues short of Cape Comfort	85.20'	64.45	S. 5 E.	11¼	180
At Cape Comfort	85.22	65.00	S. 5 E.	11¼	186
Sea Horse Poynt	82.30	63.44	S. by E.	11¼	154
Sir Dudly Diggs iland	79.40	62.45	S.S.E.	10½	123
Nottyngam iland	80.50	63.32	S.S.E.	10½	13†

* Blank in the original. ? 1, *Long.*: 2, *Lat.*: 3, *Bearing*: 4, *Time*: 5, *Distance*.   † This corner of the page is torn.

II. THE BREEFE IOURNALL.

Dayes.	THE Tru course.	Leagues.	windes by the compass.	Latytude.	Longitude from London.	Variatyon.	
APRIL				° ′	° ′	° ′	
7	...	...	...	...	...	... E.	This morne wee sett sayle from Silly.
8	...	...	...	...	...	...	We came to anchor this eveninge att Padstowe.
18	...	...	S.E.	50 . 30	7 . 00	7 . 00	This morning wee sett sayle from Padstowe.
19	...	...	S.E.	50 . 30	7 . 00	...	
20	W. ⅓ N.	41	E.S.E.	50 . 38	10 . 15	...	
21	W. by N ¾ N.	37	E.S.E. : S.S.E.	51 . 12	13 . 00	6 . 50	
22	N.W. ⅓ N.	45	E.S.E. : E.N.E.	52 . 44	15 . 20	...	
23	N.W. by W.	50	E.N.E.	54 . 05	19 . 20	...	
24	W.N.W. ⅜ N.	44	E.N.E.	54 . 50	22 . 40	...	
25	W.N.W. ⅜ N.	24	N.N.E.	55 . 25	24 . 35	5 . 30	
26	N.W. by W.	36	E.N.E.	56 . 28	27 . 24	1 . 16	
27	N.W. by N.	13	E.N.E. : N.W.	57 . 00	28 . 00	...	
28	N.W. by W. ⅓ W.	10	N.W. : E.N.E.	57 . 28	28 . 15	...	
29	N. 29 W.	24	E.N.E. : W.	58 . 30	28 . 25	...	
30	N. 20 E.	10	variable but W. ward.	59 . 00	29 . 00	...	
MAYE							
1	N. by W.	17½	W N.W.	59 . 50	29 . 26	1 . 30 w.	This afternoone a storme att south-east.
2	W N.W. ¼ W.	24½	W N.W. : S.E.	60 . 24	31 . 40	...	We suppose a currante sett to the south-west.
3	W. by N.	35¼	S.E. : 8.W.	60 . 43	35 . 15	...	This forenoone wee sawe land.
4	W. 3 S.	25¼	S.S.E.	60 . 40	38 . 00	...	This night a storme.
5	W. 26 S.	25¼	S S.E.	60 . 04	40 . 24	9 . 24	
6	W. 12 S.	28	S.S.E. : S.E. : N.E.	59 . 45	43 . 00	10 . 30	
7	S.W. by S.	21	N.N.W. : N. : W.	58 . 56	44 . 15	...	

8	W. 13 S.	13	W. by N.	58	46	45	20	
9	W. 25 S.	7	N. by W.	58	32	46	00	
10	W. 15 N.	15	N.N.E.	58	40	47	30	
11	W. 20 N.	38	E.S.E. : S.E.	59	16	51	00	
12	W. 20 N.	39	S.S.E : S. by E.	59	48	54	40	
13	W. 18 N.	45	S. : S. by E.	60	30	58	50	
14	N.W.	9	N.W. : N. by E.	60	50	59	30	
15	W.N.W.	15	N.N.E.	60	55	61	00	
16	W.N.W.	4½	E.	60	58	61	15	
17	W.N.W.	26	E.N.E.	61	27	63	40	Cape Farewell bore north 15 leg. east at noone.
18	...	...	S.S.E.	...	...	...	...	
19	...	...	S.S.E.	...	...	...	...	
20	...	...	S. by E.	...	...	...	...	
21	...	...	W.S.W.	61	20	64	33	At noone we put into the ice.
22	...	...	W.N.W.	61	18	64	26	
23	...	13	W.N.W.	61	50	63	30	
24	N.E. by N.	12½	N.N.W.	62	20	62	40	
25	N.E. by N.	21	N. by W.	62	21	64	40	
26	W.	...	N.E. : E.	62	12	65	20	This eveninge at 8 a clock we weare forth of the ice.
27	...	...	E. : E.N.E.	61	40	66	30	
28	...	...	W. by N.	...	...	...	...	At 5 a clock this afternoone, we saw the iland of Resolution.
29	...	...	W. by N.	...	...	...	...	
30	...	...	S.S.E.	61	18	66	50	This morne we weare sett within the entraunce of the Strayts.
31	...	...	N.N.W.	61	20	66	50	Wee came to anchor on the west side of Resolution ile. Att noone we sett sayle.
IVNE								
1	...	...	W.N.W.	61	35	67	56	
2	...	...	E. : N.N.W.	61	58	68	04	
3	...	...	N.W.	...	...	...	...	
4	W. 4 N.	10½	W.S.W.	62	10	69	34	
5	N.W. 6 W.	17	S.S.E. : W.S.W.	62	32	71	30	
6	W.N.W. 4 N.	19	W.S.W.	62	21	71	40	
7	S.W. by S.	4	W.N.W. : N.W.					

Dayes.	THE Tru course.	Leagues.	windes by the compas.	La-ty-tude.	Longitude from London.	Variaty on.	
8	N. 40 w.	5	N.W.	62 . 27	72 . 00		We came to anchor at Saluage iles, at 8 a clock this night.
9	N.W.	1½	N.N.W.	62 . 30	72 . 06	27 . 20	
10	W.N.W.	9½	E. : N.W.	62 . 40	73 . 04		This morne we set saile, and in the afternoone came to anchor agayne 9 leagues W.N.W. of
11	...	...	N.W.	62 . 40	73 . 04		
12	...	...	W.N.W.	62 . 40	73 . 04		
13	W.N.W.	9	variable.	62 . 48	74 . 00		This eueninge we sett sayle.
14	...	...	N. : N.N.W.	...	...		
15	...	...	S.S.E.	...	...		
16	...	...	S.S.E. : W.N.W.	63 . 22	74 . 05	27 . 45	This eueninge we anchored among diuers iles.
17	...	...	N.W. by W.	63 . 26	74 . 45		
18	...	...	variable,	63 . 26	74 . 45		At eleuen a clock we sett sayle.
19	W.N.W.	12½	S.E.	63 . 40	76 . 14	28 . 30	We made fast to a piece of ice wheare we stayed 8 dayes.
22	...	...	...	...	...		This daye I obserued the moones comminge to the meri-dian and found the longitude 74° 5' west from Lon-don, and 91° 35' from Wittenberg.
24	...	...	N.N.W.	63 . 28	76 . 18		
25	...	...	N.W. by N.	63 . 28	76 . 20		
26	...	...	N.W. by N.	63 . 18	...		
27	...	...	S.E.	63 . 30	76 . 32		This eueninge we set sayle; hauinge had calme whether since the 19 daye.
28	...	...	S.E.	63 . 30	77 . 32		
29	W.N.W.	13	S.E.	63 . 42	78 . 30	28 . 34	Att noone we sawe Salisburie island.
30	W. 3 s.	5	variable.	63 . 40			
IvLy							
1	W.	11½	S.S.E.	63 . 40	79 . 45	28 . 10	This morne we weare by a smale iland, we called it Mill ile. At night our ship was in great distress with ice.
2	N. 31 w.	6½	N.N.W.	63 . 55	80 . 10	28 . 28	
3	W. 24 N.	10	W.s.W.	64 . 05	81 . 13		
4	N.W.	28	S.W.	64 . 54	82 . 45		
5	N.W. by N.	5	N. : N.N.W.	65 . 00	83 . 00		
6	N.E.	5	N.N.E.	65 . 10	82 . 40	... w.	

7	S.E. by E.	11	N.W.	64 . 48	81 . 28	28 . 20	This eueninge we anchored near the north shore.
8	S.	3½	W.	64 . 46	81 . 28	...	
9	S.E.	3	W. : N.W.	64 . 36	80 . 40	...	
10	S.W.	5	S.W.	64 . 24	81 . 04	...	
11	W. 6 N.	18	W.S.W. : N.N.W.	64 . 30	83 . 08	...	We sent our bote ashore 6 leagues south of Cape Comfort: att 6 a clock this eueninge we returned.
12	W. 3 N.	12	W. : W.S.W.	64 . 33	84 . 48	...	
13	N. 36 W.	17½	S.W.	65 . 18	85 . 56	...	
[14]	...	...	S.E.	65 . 02	85 . 22	...	We anchored neare Cape Comfort. At night wayed anchor.
[15]	...	...	S.E.	65 . 54	82 . 50	...	We came to anchor at Sea Horse Point this eueninge.
[16]	...	...	Variable.	63 . 38	82 . 00	...	This morne we wayed anchor and stood for Nottinghams
17	W.S.W.	6½	N.W. by W.	63 . 36	81 . 00	...	ile, wheare this night we anchored.
18	W.S.W.	8½	N. : N. by E.				
19	...	...	N.W.			...	
20	...	...	S.W. by S.	...	...	...	
21	...	...	W.N.W.	...	...	...	
22	...	...	N.N.W.	...	...	...	
23	...	...	N.N.W.	...	...	...	
24	...	...	Southward.	...	...	...	
25	...	...	W.S.W. : W. by S.	...	...	...	We passed betweene Nottinghame and Salisburies ile.
26	...	...	N.N.W.:N.:N.N.E.	63 . 30	80 . 00	...	At night we came to anchor.
27	E.N.E.	2	E. : E.N.E. : N.E.	...	...	...	This day stood ouer for Sea Horse Point agayne.
28	E.N.E.	13	N.E.	62 . 44	80 . 05	...	This morne we returned for Digges ile.
29	...	...	N.E. by N.	62 . 44	80 . 05	...	We came to anchor at Digges ile, foule wether.
30	...	...	S.	62 . 56	75 . 45	...	We wayed and sett sayle for homewards.
31	E. 8 N.	18					
Avg.							
1	E. by S.	15	S.S.W. : S.W.	62 . 46	76 . 5	...	This afternoone we came to anchor on the north shore
2	E. 19 S.	38	S.W.:N.W. by W.	62 . 16	72 . 6	...	among diuers ilands, 30 leagues within Resolution ile.
3	E. 17 S.	19	N.W. : S.E.	62 . 20	70 . 15	...	This day we sett sayle.
4	...	...	...	...	...	...	

Dayes.	THE Tru course.	Leagues	windes by the compas.	Latytude.	Longitude from London.	Variatyon.	
5	E. 32 S.	45	N.W.	61 . 00	65 . 30		We past by the ile of Resolution, but sawe it nott.
6	E. 20 S.	46	N.W.	60 . 20	61 . 00	19 . 30	
7	E. 18 S.	43	N.W.	59 . 36	57 . 00		
8	E. 13 S.	29	N.W. : S. by W.	59 . 14	54 . 14		
9	E.	26	S.S.W. : S.	59 . 15	51 . 40		We came through som smale ice, of Cape Farewell, but saw no land.
10	E. 7 S.	32	N.N.W.	59 . 4	48 . 52		
11	E. 34 S.	46	N.W.	57 . 32	45 . 40		
12	E. 7 S.	40	W.S.W.	57 . 18	42 . 00		
13	E. 8 S.	38	W.S.W. S. by E.	57 . 6	38 . 25		
14	E. 40 N.	20	S.E. by E.	57 . 42	36 . 56		
15	N. 22 E.	11	E. by S.	58 . 15	36 . 35		
16	S.S.E.	7		58 . 5	36 . 15		
17	E.N.E.	8	S.E.	58 . 20	35 . 35		
18	N. 30 E.	22	S.E.	59 . 20	34 . 30		
19	S. 25 E.	9	E.S.E. : E.	58 . 52	34 . 8		
20	S. 40 E.	14	N.N.E.	58 . 18	33 . 15		
21	S. 20 E.	20	E. : E.S.E.	57 . 22	32 . 30		
22	S.	4	E.	57 . 8	32 . 30		
23	S.S.E.	14	N.E.	56 . 30	32 . 6		
24	E. 25 S.	21	N.N.E.	56 . 5	30 . 20		
25	E. 30 S.	36	N. by E.	55 . 10	27 . 35	2 . 00	
26	E. 35 S.	38	N.N.E.	54 . 00	24 . 52		
27	S. 29 E.	39	N.E.	52 . 40	23 . 42		
28	S. 30 E.	18	N.E. by E.	52 . 18	23 . 5		
29	S. 30 W.	10	E.N.E.	51 . 25	23 . 30		
30	N. 30 E.	3	E.S.E.	51 . 32	23 . 25		A sore storme.
31	S.E.	20	N.E.	50 . 46	22 . 15		[*Note.* Here the journal ends, at the bottom of a reverse page. Whether left incomplete, or whether the concluding portion be lost, must be left to conjecture.]

A Tru Relatyon of such thinges as happened in *fourth voyage for the discouery of a passage to the north west, performed in the yeare* 1615.

After so many sundrye voyages to the north westward, to the greate charge of the aduenturers, The last being under the command of *Captaine* Gibbins, in which by som sinister accident, was little or nothinge performed. Yett the right worshipfull, *Sir* Tho. Smith, *knight;* Sir Dudly Digges, *knight; Mr.* John Wostenholme, *esquire; Mr.* Alderman Jones, with others, beinge not theare with discouraged, this yeare 1615 sett forth agayne the good shipp called the Discouerare, beinge of the burthen of 55 tonn or theare aboute, (which ship had beene the three former voyages on the accion).

March.

The cheefe mr. and commander, vnder God, *was* Robert Byleth, *a man well experienced that wayes, (hauinge beene imployed the three former voyages) my selfe beinge his mate and assotiate, with fourteene other men and 2 boyes. This ship being in redines, vpon the* 15*th daye*

15 *of March came abourd Mr.* John Wostenholme, *esquire, one of the cheefe aduenturers, and with him Mr.* Allwin Carye (*husband for the voyage*). *Who hauinge deliuered our mr. his commission, and reade certayne orders to be obserued by vs in the voyage, giuing vs good exortations, and large promyses of reward, as treble wages to all, if the accion weare performed, they departed, charginge vs to make what speede we could away. So the next day,*

16 *beeing thursdaye, we wayed anchor at* St. Katherins,
17 *and that tyde came to* Black wall, *and the next day to*
18 Graues ende; *and the morrow after to* Lee.

- 19 *Sondaye the* 19 *it blu hard at south west and by south, yet this daye we came to anchor neare the* BOOY *on the* NOURE ENDE. *The* 20 *daye the winde variable, but by* 2 *a clock this afternoone we came to the* NORTH FORLAND,
- 22 *wheare we stayed all the* 22 *daye, which day we wayed and*
- 23 *that night anchored in the* DOUNES. *The* 23 *in the morne we wayed anchor, the winde att east, and east and by south:*
- 26 *thus with indifferent windes and wether we came to anchor in* SILLY *the* 26 *daye.*

APRILL.

- 7 *Heare we stayed for a fayre winde till the* 7 *day of Aprill, being Good Frydaye, which day we wayed anchor in the morne, the winde south south east. We had not stoode on our course aboue* 10 *or* 12 *leagues, but the wind came to south, then to south south west and blu extreme hard, which encreased so sore, that we weare not able to beare any sayle at all.*
- 8 *The next morning we stood for* PADSTOW *in* CORNEWALL, *because we could not fetch Silly agayne, and about* 10 *a clocke we came to anchor in the entrance of the harbour,*
- 9 *and the next daye, being Easter Sonday, in the forenoone we moored our ship in the harboure. Heare we stayed till the* 19 *daye, hauinge had much foule wether and contrary windes. While heare we stayed we found much kindness at the handes of Mr.* RICHARD PENKEWILL, *who, beinge willinge to further vs with what things we wanted, or that place could afford, as with beefe and porke, and also with a capstand which we wanted, haueing broke ours in the storme when we came from Silly. And also he was desirous his eldest sonn should goe alonge with vs, to which our mr. and the rest of the company agreed, because he*
- 19 *layd in all prouition fitt for the voyage. So the* 19 *of Aprill in the morne we wayed anchor, the winde south east a good gale, we keepinge our courses as in the breefe Jarnall*

you may more conueniently see. And seinge fewe thinges of note happened in our outward bound voyage, I refer all other thinges to that table before noted.[1]

MAYE.

6 We haueing had an indifferent good passage, vpon the 6 of Maye we sawe land on the coste of GROYNLAND on the east side of CAPE FAREWELL; and that night we had a storme. So keeping a southwardly course to gett about the ice which lay on that coste, we kept on our course tyll the 17 daye of Maye: all which forenoone we sayled through many greate ilands of ice. Som of them were 200 foot aboue water, as I proued by on shortly after, which I found to be 240 foote high aboue water. And if reporte of some men be tru which affirme that there is but on seuenth part of it aboue water, then the height of that peece of ice I oberued was 140 [? 280] fathoms, or 1680 foote, from the top to the bottome. This proportion doth hould I knowe in much ice, but whether in all, or no, I know nott.

17 This 17 of May aboute noone, wee weare come to the firme ice as it shewed to sight, *although in deede it was many peeces drauen together*: wheare our mr. asked my opinion conserninge the puttinge into the ice. My judgment was it would be best for vs to stand somwhat more north ward, to se if we could find any more likley place, for heare we could not disserne wheare to put in the ships head. Hee answered we weare as for [far] to the north ward as the south end of RESOLUTION ILAND, and now had all the south channell southward of vs; and through much ice we must goe. Supposinge that, if

---

[1] The British Museum manuscript was very carefully collated with the narrative in Purchas, by Mr. Randall, and the foot-notes pointing out the differences are by him. The italic print denotes the matter *omitted* by Purchas. *Material alterations* or *additions*, in the version given by Purchas, are noticed in the foot-notes.

we could gett som 3 or 4 leagues within the ice, at euery tyde it would open and we should gett somthinge on our waye, it being now fayre wether, and if it should chance to blo hard, we should then be forced to enter in. *I could not much say agaynst his opynion, beinge indeede in the latitude of 61 deg. 26', and hee knew the manner of this ice better then my selfe, so presently we resolued to put into the ice. (This first entrance I liked not uery well, the ice being so uery thick, and by all our accounte and reconinge we were 30 leagues from shore, which after we found to be tru).*

After we weare entred a little into the ice, it was not longe before we weare fast sett vp, but sometymes of the tyde the ice would a little open, then we made our way as much to the north-west as we could, yet we playnlie found that we weare sett to the southward, *although the wind weare southwardly.*

22 Nowe vpon the 22 daye the wind came to north north-west, then we determined to gett forth agayne, fearinge the wind should com to the north-east, for then it would be hard for vs to fetch any part of the Straytes mouth: seinge this aboundance of ice and knowing that it must haue some time to dissolue, our mr. was determyned to run up DAUIS STRAYTES and to spend some 20 dayes therein, to trye what hopes that wayes would afford, supposinge by that tyme we myght come near RESOLUTION ILE. This purpose of our mr. contynued no longer but tyll we weare forth of the ice, which by God's assist-

23 ance was the 23d daye about 8 a clock att night, the wind at N.W. and by W. When we weare cleare of the ice, we stood to the northwarde, as much as the ice and winde would suffer vs, running about 13 leg. north east and by north; by the next day at noone, beinge in the latytude of 61° 50' and fayre weather.

25 The 25 daye we made our waye and course weare as

we did the daye before, namely N.E. and by N., 13 legues.[1]

26 The 26 daye all the forenoone fayre wether and could, but in the afternoone it blew uery hard, and close haysey wether, that about 2 a clock we weare forced to take in our sayles. All the tyme that we sayled this daye we passed through much ice, lyinge in longe driftes and ledges, hauing made a west way about [?] leagues.[2]

27 The 27 daye aboute 4 in the morninge we sett sayle. Most parte of the day proued close and foggy, with much snowe, freesinge on our shroudes and tackle, that the like we haue not had this yeare; but toward 5 a clock in the afternoone it cleared vp and we sawe the ILAND OF RESOLUTION, it bearinge west from vs about 13 or 14 leagues, and at night moored our ship to a peece of ice.[3]

28 The 28 daye, beinge Whitsondaye, it was fayre wether, but the winde at west and west by north, that we weare forced all this daye to make our shipp fast to a peece of ice, yet we playnlie perceued that we sett more into the straytes with one tyde of floud, then we sett forth in 2 ebbs, although the wind blu contrary.

29 The 29 the winde variable and fayre wether. About eleuen a clock we sett sayle and tacked too and fro
30 along the iland. And the next morne, about two a clocke, the winde came to the south south-east, but we hauinge so much ice we could doe but little good nowe we had a faire wind.[4] This night (or rather eueninge, because it was not darke), we were sett *within the*

---

[1] [About twelve leagues and an halfe, our latitude at noone 62 degrees 20 minutes. At sixe a clocke the winde was north north east. P.]

[2] [Havinge runne about twenty one leagues true vppon a west course. And note when I put this word true, I meane the true course, the variation of the compasse and other accidents considered. P.]

[3] [The winde being at west. P.]

[4] [The wind continued all this day and night a stiffe gale. P.]

poynt of the iland, so that nowe we weare within the straytes, playnly prouinge what is sayd before, namely, that one tyde of floud setteth more in then two tydes of ebb will sett forth.

31 The last daye of Maye also faire weather, the wind for the most part north north-west. The afternoone being cleare, we saw the point of the South shoare[1] bearing from vs south by the compas, which is indeed south south-east, somewhat eastward, because here the compas is varied to the west 24 degrees.

Ivne.

1 The first day of June some snowe in the forenoone, but afterward it proued very faire, the wind west north-west; and perceiuing the ice to be more open neare to the shore we made the best waye we could to get in, and to com to anchor if the place weare conueniente; seeinge the wind was contrary and also to make tryall of the tyde. And by seuen a clock we weare at anchor in a good harbour, on the west side of RESOLUTION ILAND, wheare an east south-east moone maketh a full sea, or halfe an houer past seuen on the chainge day, as seamen acounte. At this place the water doth rise and fall about 22 or 23 foote; the compas doth vary 24...6' west, and it is in longitude west from LONDON 66 degrees 35'. The latytude of the north ende of the iland is 61...36', *and the latytude of the south end is* 61...26'. The bredth of the south channell, or the distance betweene the iland and the south shore is 16 leagues, and the bredth of the north channell is aboute 8 miles in the narrowest place.

Vpon this iland we went on shore, but found no certaine signe of inhabitants, but only the tracke of beares and

---

[1] [Called *Button's Iles*. P.]

foxes. The soyle is only rocks and stonie ground, hardly any thinge growinge thearon which is greene. It is indifferent high land to the north, hauinge one high hill or hummocke to the north east side, but toward the southward it falleth away uery low.

2 The 2 June in the forenoone the wind came to east south east with snowe and foule wether. About noone we wayed and stood vp along by the iland[1] to the north ward. This afternoone it proued foule wether, but toward eueninge it cleared vp and we saw the north shore. But heare to wright of our often mooringe to ice, takinge in sayles, and fast inclosinge, would prooue but tedious to the reader, as it was troublesom to vs; so therefore I referre it: but our course, and waye we made from noone may be seene else wheare.

We continuing our courses so neare to the north shore as conueniently we could, with much variable wether and
8 windes, but stedfast in contynuance among ice, till the 8 daye. Then hauinge the winde contrary to vs, being somewhat neare a poynt of land (or rather a company of ilandes),[2] we determyned to come to anchor[3] among them *if possible we could. About 6 a clock we weare come to anchor,* and as we weare busy *in makinge vp our sayles and fittinge our ship,* we hard a great houlinge and noyse, as we supposed of doggs vpon the ilande neare to vs.

So soon as the ship was moored, we sent our bote somewhat nearer the shore, to see if they could perceue any people, who returninge, they tould vs they sawe tentes and botes, with a number of doggs, but people they sawe none.

---

[1] [So well as the ice would giue vs leaue to gett. P.]

[2] [Which after we called *Savag Isles*, hauing a great sound, or indraught betweene the north shoare and them. P.

[3] [Neere one of them, being the eastermost saving one. P.]

Then by and bye we went to prayer, and after our men had supt, we fitted our bote and selues with things conuenient; then my selfe and seuen other landed, and went to the tents, wheare findinge no people, we went to the top of the hill (being about a flite shot of) wheare we sawe one great cannoo, or bote, hauinge aboute fourteene personns in it; they being on the furthest, or north-west side theareof, beinge from vs somewhat aboue a musket shott of. Then I called vnto them (using some words of *Groynlandish* speeche), makinge signes of friendship. They did the like to vs; but seeing them *to be* fearefull of vs, and we not willinge to trust them, I made another signe to them, shewinge them a knife and other small thinges, which I left on the top of the hill, and returned doune to their tents agayne.

Beinge returned to theare tents, we found some whale finnes to the number of 14 or 15,[1] which I tooke aboard, leauinge kniues, bedes, and counters insteede thereof. And among other of theare househould, I found in a smale lether bagg a company of little images of men; and one the image of a woman with a child at hir backe: all the which I brought awaye.

Among there tents (being fiue in number) all couered with seale skinnes, weare runninge up and done, about 35 or 40 dogs, most of them mussled. They are most of them about the bigness of our mungrell mastives, being a brinded black culler, lookinge almost like wolues. These doggs they vse instede of horses, or rather as the *Lappians* doe theare deare, to draw theare sledes from place to place ouer the ice. Theare sleds beinge shod, or lined, with bones of great fishes to keepe them [from] wearinge, and the doggs have collers and furniture uery fittinge.

These people haue their apparell, botes,[2] tentes, with

---

[1] [Fortie or fiftie with a few seale-skinnes. P.]
[2] [Boots. P.]

other necesaryes, muche like to the inhabitaunte of Groyneland, sauing that they are not so neate and artefitiall, seminge to bee more rude and vnciuill, raynginge vp and doune as theare fishinge is in season. For in most places wheare we went ashore, we sawe wheare people had beene, although not this yeare, but wheare theare dwellinge or abode in winter is, I cannot well
9 coniecture. The next morninge we fetcht 2 botes ladinge of stones aboard, because our ship was very light, keepinge a good watch on shore, for feare the people should come doune vpon vs while we weare busie. By noone our ship was fitted. Then afterward we marched aboute the island, but could see no people.

This iland lyeth in the latytude of 62...30', and in longitude west from *London* aboute 72 degrees,[1] being 60 leagues within the entrance of the straytes. Here the compas doth varye 27.30', and a south-east 4 degrees east moone maketh a full sea. It doth ebb and flowe almost as much water as it doth at RESOLUTION ILE; and heare the floud commeth from the eastward, although our Master was confidente to the contrary.

10 The 10 daye,[2] in the morninge, we set sayle, the winde north, which contynued not longe, but was very variable tyll noone, and then it came to north-west, we hauinge sayled along by the shore, about 9½ leagues north northwest, the ice lyinge so thicke in the offen that we could not gett of. Then perceuinge a good harbour betweene the mayne and 2 smale ilandes, we went in with the ship, wheare we moored her, and stayed till the 12 day at night.

---

[1] By the observations made on board the *Fury* and *Hecla* (July 24, 1821), this anchorage was made 2¼ miles to the northward, and 1° 52' to the eastward of the position assigned to it by Baffin. Variation 52° 37'. —*Voyage of the Fury and Hecla (Parry)*, 1821, etc. P. 16. (*Chart.*) London: 1824.   [2] [At sixe a clocke. P.]

In this place it is high water on the chaunge day, at 9 a clock, or a south-east moone maketh a full sea.[1] Here the floud commeth from the south-east, as it did at SALVAGE ILAND,[2] *and because our Mr. was conceued otherwise, I tooke our surgeon (a man of good iudgment) to the top of the ile, where most apparently we saw the tru sett of the tyde by the ice dryvinge in the offen. For all the tyme the water doth rise by the shore, the ice did sett in to the straytes; aad as soon as the water fell it returned. But the truth of this was made more apparent by other places after ward.*[3]

12 The 12 day after we had doone som busines in our ship, as cleared our pumps and such lyke, seinge the ice to driue in more then vsuall it did before, about 8 a clock we set sayle, it being almost calme. Shortly after the winde came to south west and by south, which contynued but till 12 a clock; then it came to west with snowe and foule wether.

13 The 13 aboute noone we tooke in our sayles, and made the ship fast to a peece of ice, beinge some 9 leagues
14 from our last harbour. All this daye and the next the wind was contrarye, and foule wether, we driuinge too and fro with the wind and tide.

15 The 15 in the morne, the wind came to the south south east; then we set sayle, and made the best waye we could through the ice, and in the afternoone it blu uery much winde, and was foule wether, so that at 8 a clocke we weare forced to take in our sayles and to make the ship fast to ice agayne, it beinge a storme and amounge much ice.

16 The 16 day, lying still in the ice, the wether close and hasye (as it hath beene these six dayes) we being neare

---

[1] [The latitude of the place is 62° 40′. P.]
[2] [Although our master was perswaded otherwise. P.]
[3] [In this place is no sign of people, as we could perceive. P.]

a greate company of ilandes, and the wind at north north west, this afternoone wee stood towards these ilandes: and at night came to anchor neare one of them, in a small coue, the better to defend the ship from danger of
17 the ice. In this place we stayed all the next day: but
18 vpon the 18 being Sonday, at eleuen a clocke we set sayle, it beinge allmost calme, we makinge the best way we could gett from a monge those ilands, being more safe further *of* then neare them: for these iles lye in a bay (as it weare), being many of them, and euery one hath his seuerall sett and eddy, carryinge the ice to and fro, that a ship is allwaye in danger of some hurte. The latytude of the place is 63...26'; and west from *London*, neare 74...[1] 25': the compas doth vary 27...40';[2] and a south east and by south moone[3] maketh a full sea.

19 *This evening and the next forenoone we had a fine gale of wind at south east, we standinge alonge the lande, it being all broken ground and ilandes to the sea ward. By noone we weare come to the poynt of those ilandes, and being not past a league or 4 miles distant, we weare fast sett vp with ice, the wether very fayre and allmost calme. This poynt of ilands I after called Fair Ness,[4] by reason of the fayre wether we had at this place, for from this 19 daye till the 27 daye (yea till the 30) the wether was so faire, cleare and calme, that it was more then extraordinary in this place, and we so fast closed vp with ice, that many tymes one could not well dip a payle of water.*

[1] [72. P.]   [2] [46. P.]
[3] [And a quarter of an houre after nine on the chainge day. P.]
[4] [This evening, and the next morning, we had a faire steering gale of winde at south east, wee standing along by the land, it being all small broken ilands, to a point of land about twelve leagues in distance from the ile wee put last from: which point I called BROKEN POINT, it being indeede a point of broken iles. On the nineteenth day, by twelue a clocke at noone, wee were about foure miles from the point before named, fast inclosed with ice, very faire weather; and well might wee have called this point FAIRNESSE, or, POINT. P.]

And some dayes while heare we stayed we shott at butts with bowe and arrows, at other tymes at stoole ball, and some tymes at foote ball. And seinge I haue begun to speake of exercise, I think it not amiss to relate one dayes exercise of my owne.

While we weare thus fast inclosed with ice, and the wether fayre and cleare (as is sayd before) vpon the 21 daye I sawe both the sonn and moone very cleare. Then thinkinge it a fit tyme to be doinge of somthinge to imploy myself vpon, I fitted my instruments to take both the Almycanter and Azimuth of the sonn and also of the moone: fearinge I should not see them so well agayne. Which obseruations I think it not much unfitt heare to sett doune (although I neuer wrought it, because I had another the next daye, better to my contentment, otherwise I would have spent some tyme in this), as heare they followe:

		deg.				deg.
The	Sonns Almycanter ...	25.5		The	Moones Almycanter	32.5
	Sonns magne. Azimuth	29.00			Mones Azimuth ...	43.00
	w. of N.				s. of w.	

butt heare is to be noted that the moones Almycanter and Azimuth weare taken 4 minites 30 seconds of tyme after the sonns.[1]

---

[1] Baffin took every opportunity of taking astronomical observations, and especially of testing theoretical methods of finding longitude. His first recorded observation for longitude was taken in Cockin Sound, on the coast of Greenland, and is explained by him in his journal (see page 20). The first part of this Greenland observation is that for finding the time and place from the altitude of a heavenly body, the latitude and declination being known. But the method of finding the longitude by lunar culmination is unsuited to purposes of navigation, owing to the great error in longitude caused by a small error in the time of the moon's culmination.

The observation which Baffin describes in the text, at page 122, is a complete lunar observation. I have been favoured with the following interesting note upon it by Mr. John Coles, R.N., the Instructor in Practical Astronomy and Surveying to the Royal Geographical Society.

"This, in a very rough way, is a complete lunar observation. Baffin

22 The next morne being fayre and cleare, and allmost as stedy as on shore, it was no neede to bid me haue my instrument of uariation in redynes to take the time of [the] moone's comming to the meridian, hauinge my quadrant redy to take the sonnes Almicanter, it being indifferent large, as of 4 foote semydiameter. I hauinge[1]

appears to have chosen the method of measuring the distance by the difference of Azimuth, because, in all probability, he did not possess an instrument with which he could measure so large an angle as 104°, that being the computed distance from the Azimuths given; this distance would, however, be greatly in error unless the declinations of both heavenly bodies were the same. The Almicanters here mentioned are small circles, parallel to and, in this case, above the rational horizon; they are therefore the observed altitudes. Thus we have the following lunar observation:

Obs. Alt. of ☉	Angular Distance.	Obs. Alt. of the ☾
25° 5'.	104° 0'.	32° 5'.

which observation, cleared from the effects of parallax and refraction, would give the true distance, and the longitude could be found by using the right ascensions of the moon and sun, without the aid of such tables as are now given (of lunar distances) in the *Nautical Almanac*.

"Speaking of this observation, Baffin says, 'I never wrought it'; and, indeed, had he computed this observation, it is not possible that he could have got any satisfactory results. This will be the more clear when we consider that an error of 1' in this very roughly observed distance would, under the most favourable circumstances, produce an error of 25' in the longitude.

"Judging from this record, it seems quite certain that Baffin was acquainted with the theory of obtaining the longitude by observing the altitudes of the moon and some other heavenly body, and measuring the angular distance between them, this method of finding the longitude having been proposed as early as 1514 by John Werner of Nuremberg, and again, in 1545, by Gemma Frisius of Antwerp; but this observation of Baffin's is, so far as I am aware, the first recorded attempt to put it into actual practice at sea; and any one who will inspect Baffin's observations can scarcely fail to come to the conclusion that it is highly improbable that a man, so far in advance of his time as a navigator, and so intimately acquainted with the practical part of astronomy, would, in his studies, have overlooked so important an observation, or that he would have failed, when a favourable opportunity presented itself, to make an attempt to put it into practice." [1] [Haue. P.]

taken the uariation of my needle this forenoone and dyuers tymes before, which was 28...30′ W. Nowe hauinge all things in redynes (for I had tyme jnough) for it would be after foure in the afternoone before any thinge could be doone; so hauing wayted till the moone was precisely on the meridian, and that instant tooke the height of the sonn,[1] which was 26° 40′. *The latytude of the place is* 63...40′, and the sonns declination for that tyme 23 degrees 6 minites. By which three things giuen I haue found the houre to be fiue a clocke 4′...52″ ...1‴...4⁗ or 76 degrees 13′...16″ of the equinoctiall afternoone. Nowe according to *Searle's Ephemeris*,[2] the moone came to the meridian at LONDON at 4 a clocke 54′...30″: and after *Origanus*,[3] the moone came to the meridian at WITTENBERGE at 4 a clocke 52′.5″, the same day. Nowe hauinge this knowne, it is no hard matter to finde the longitude of the place sought for. For according to the moones ordinary meane motion, which is 12 degrees ech day, which is in tyme 48 minites: and [?] to this account, if the moone be on the meridian at 12 a clock this day, tomorrowe it will be 48 minites past 12.[4]

[1] [The sunnes Almicanter, at the instant when the moone was on the meridian, was 26°. P.]

[2] John Searle received his licence to practise chirurgery in 1607, and published, in 1609, *An Ephemeris from* 1609 *to* 1617, *whereunto is annexed three succinct Treatises of the use of an Ephemeris of the fixed Starres, and foure Sections of Astrologie* (4to., London). The book contains, among other tables, a correction of time in respect of difference of meridians; a list of places, with latitude and longitude in time; a table for converting degrees and minutes into time; eclipses; and a table of the inequality of days, and the equation or correction of them.

The copy of Searle's *Ephemeris* at the British Museum wants the title page; that at the Bodleian Library is a perfect copy.

[3] David Origanus was the author of an *Ephemeris* for the years 1595 to 1650. His meridian was Wittenberg. (Frankfort, 1599, 4to.)

[4] This is the same method he adopted in Cockin Sound for finding the longitude (see page 20), namely, by lunar culmination. Mr. Coles ob-

Nowe I hauinge the time at this place found by obseruation, which was 5 a clocke 4′...52″...1‴...4⁗ (but in this I neede not be so precise): and at LONDON 4 a clocke 54′...30″: which, substracted from the former, leaueth 10′...22″...1‴...4⁗; and the moone's motyon for that 24 houers was 12^1...38: which conuerted into tyme is 50′...25″...20‴. This beinge knowne, the proportion is as follows: If 50′...25″...20‴ giue 360, what shall 10′...22″...1‴.. 4⁗ giue? The fourth proportionall will be 74 degrees 5′, which is the longitude of this place west from LONDON: because the moone was later on the meridian at this place by 10′...22″.

And by the same forme of working by Origanus Ephemerides, the distance is 91 degrees 35 minites west from the place Origanus Ephemerides is supputated for, but for to decide which is the truer I leaue to others: but neyther of them is much different from my supposed longitude according to my iurnall which was 74...30′.[2] And seeing

serves:—"It is most surprising that Baffin should have obtained even such an approximation as he did, and his method of observing with two plumb lines set in the meridian, is both original and ingenious."

[1] [22. P.]

[2] [And by the same working of *Origanus Ephemerides*, the distance is 91 degrees, 35 minutes west of west. But whether be the truer, I leaue to others to iudge:—and in these workings may some errour be committed, if it be not carefully looked vnto: as in the obseruation, and also in finding what time the moone commeth to the meridian at the place where the ephemerides is supputated for, and perchance in the ephemerides themselves: in all which the best iudicious may erre; yet if observations of this kinde, or some other, were made at places far remote, as at the *Cape Bonasperanza, Bantam, Japan, Noua Albion,* and *Magellan Strayts*, I suppose wee should haue a truer Geography than wee haue. P.]

Alluding to Broken Point, Captain Parry remarks: "On the 29th we were off a point of land having several islands near it, and exactly answering the description of that called by Baffin, in the year 1615, Broken Point, it being indeed a point of broken islands. This headland is memorable on account of a lunar observation made off it by this able and indefatigable navigator, giving the long. 74 05′ which is not a degree to the westward of the truth." Parry had only seen Purchas. But

I am entred to speake of celestiall obseruations, I will note another which I made at sea the twenty six of April, by the moones comminge in a right, or strayte line with two[1] starres; the one was the *Lyons heart*, a starre of the first magnitude; the other a starre in the *Lyons rumpe*, being of the second bignes. *These 2 stars makinge a right line with the outward* edge, or circumference of the moone, at the instante I tooke the height of one of them, namely the *Lyons harte*, because I would haue the houer of tyme:[2] but in this obseruation it is good to attend for a fit tyme: as to haue the moone in a right line with two starres not far distante and those not to be much different in longitude, because then the moone will soone alter the angle or position, and such a tyme would also be taken when the moone is in or neare the 90 degree of the eclipticke aboue the horizon, for then there is no paralax[3] of longitude, but only of latytude: but who is so paynfull in these busines shall soone see what is needefull, and what is not: but the notes I tooke are as followeth:—

		°	′	″
Lyons heart ♌	Right assention	146[4]	28	30
	Declination	13	57	30
	Longitude	24	29	45
	Latytude	00	26	30
	Almycanter	33	40	00
Lyons rumpe ♍	Right assention	163	23	00
	Declination	12	38	00
	Longitude	5	53	45
	Latytude	14	20	00

Baffin's manuscript gives 74° 30′ for the longitude, which is still more correct.—See *Voyage of the Fury and Hecla*, 1821-23. P. 21. London: 1824.   [1] [Fixed. P.]

[2] [The circumference, or outward edge, of the moone, being in a right or straight line with these two starres before named: at the instant I tooke the altitude of the south ballance, which was 2° 38′, because I would haue the time. P.]

[3] [Paralell. P.]   [4] [46. P.]

		°	′	″
The Moone	{ Paralax	00	47	46
	{ Latytude	03	20	00
	{ Almycanter	37	00	00

Latytude of the Place, 56° 43′ 00″. *After Tycho Brahe.*

These notes I haue set doune, that if any other be desirous to spend a little tyme therein they maye; my selfe haue spent some therein, and more I would haue spent, if other busines had not letted. I haue not heare set downe the pertyculer worke, because I found it not altogither to my mynde. The working of this proposition I receued from Master *Rudston*.

But if it had pleased God that we had performed the accion we intended, I would not feare but to haue brought so good contentment to the aduenturars, concerning the tru scituation of notable places, that smale doubt should haue beene thereof: but seeing so smale hopes are in this place, I haue not set doune so many obseruations as otherwise I would.

27 28 29 We lying heare inclosed with ice, hauing fayre and calme wether (as before is said) till the 27 day at eueninge; which tyme we sett sayle, the winde at south east an easie gale. All the 28 and 29 dayes, we made the best waye we could[1] through the ice. At noone this day we sawe SALISBURY ILAND.[2]

30 *The last of June the wind variable; but our daylie object was still ice. All this day we stood toward the foresaid iland.*

IVLY.

1 The first of *July* close, haysie, wether, with much raine, the winde at south south east. By noone this daye we weare some 3 leagues from SALISBURY ISLAND; but

---

[1] [But the nine and twentieth day the ice was more open then it had been these ten dayes before, and at noone...... P.]

[2] [It bearing due west from vs. P.]

hauinge much ice by the shore stood alonge to the northward; and the next morninge we weare fayre by another smale ile (or rather a many of small ilandes), which we afterward called MILL ILAND by reason of the greate extremetye and grindinge of the ice, as this night we had proofe thereof. At noone beinge close by this ile we took the latytude thereof, which is near to 64 .. 00′, *but how it lyeth may be better seene in the mapp then heare nominated with writinge.* Heare driuinge to and fro with the ice most parte of this daye till 7 or 8 a clocke, at which time the ice began somewhat to open and separate. Then we set sayle and hauinge not stood[1] past an houer: but the ice came driuinge with the tyde of floud from the south east with such swiftnesse, that it ouerwent our shippe, hauinge all our sayles abroad and a good gale of winde, and forced her out of the streame into the eddy of these iles.

The ilande or iles, lying in the middle of the channell, hauinge many sounds runninge through them, with dyuers points and headlands, encountering the force of the tyde, caused such a rebounde of water and ice,[2] *that vnto them that saw it not is almost incredible. But our ship being thus in the pertition, between the eddy which runne on waye, and the streame which runne another, endured so great extremytie, that vnless the Lord himselfe had beene on our side we had shurely perished; for sometymes the ship was hoysed aloft; and at other tymes shee hauinge, as it were, got the vpper hand, would force greate mighty peeces of ice to sinke'doune on the on side of hir,*

---

[1] [Along by the ile, on the east side thereof. P.]

[2] [(Which ran one way and the stream another) our ship hauing met the ice with the first of the floud, which put her so neere the shoare, that she was in the partition betweene the ice, which the eddy caused to runne one way and the streame the other, where she endured great distresse; but God, which is still stronger than either ice or streame, preserued vs and our shippe from any harme at all. P.]

and rise on the other. But GOD, which is still stronger then either *rocks,* ice, *eddy,* or streame, preserued vs and our shippe from any harme at all. *And I trust will still contynue his love to vs, that we may performe some more acceptable seruis to his glory, and to the good of our common welth.*

This continued till towards high water, which was aboute one a clocke. Then with no smale trouble we got into the channell and stood away to the *north ward.*[1] When we had passt some distance from the ilande we had the sea more cleare of ice then it was since we came into

3 these straights; and sayled all the next day through an indifferent cleare sea, with the winde at south west: but towards 8 a clocke at night, we weare come agayne into much ice, it being thicker and bigger than any we came amonge yet. This place[2] is distant from Mill ilande som 26 leagues, and the tru course north west and by west.[3]

4 The next morne we sounded, and had ground at 120 fathoms, soft osey ground. Then standinge more north-
5 erly, the fifth day in the forenoone we had ground at 80 fathoms, which day the winde came to the north, and we settinge som thinge more southward, had ground at 110 fathoms. Thus seeing this great aboundance of ice in this place, and notinge that the more we get to the *northward,*[4] the more shoalder the water was, the ice also beinge foule and durtye, as not bred far from shore, our mr. determined to stand to the eastward, to be certainely informed of the tyde.

6 The sixth day in the forenoone (as we stood to the eastward) we broke in a planke and two tymbers in the ships

---

[1] [North-*west*-ward. P.]

[2] [Where we began to be inclosed againe. P.]

[3] [After wee were fast in the ice, we made but smale way, yet we perceiued a great tyde to set to and fro. P.]

[4] [North-*west*-ward. P.]

bow, which after we had mended we proceeded[1] forward.

7 The next forenoone, we saw the shore, it being but low land *(in respect of the other)* and *toward this side* the sea is *more* shoald *then at other places:* but excellent good channell ground, as smale stones and shels;[2] and also heare is a very great tide both of ebb and floud. But no other floud then that which commeth from Resolution ilande; for about 7 a clocke, we beinge neare the shore, hoysed forth our bote, then 5 other and myselfe wente on shore found it ebbinge water. We staied on shore about an houer and a halfe, in which time the water fell about 3½ foote, *all the ice in the offen settinge to the southward.* A south south east moone maketh a full sea, or halfe an houre past tenne[3] *on the chainge day.* Here we sawe no signe of people to be this yeare, but in yeares heretofore they have beene, as we might well see by dyuers things, as wheare their tents had stood, *and such like;* perchance theare tyme of fishing was not yet come, theare being so great aboundance of ice.

8. 9. The 8 day the winde was at west, and the next almost calme, we *keepinge*[4] not far from the shore, our mr. determined to stand over for NOTTYNGAM ILAND, to make triall of the tyde theare; but the winde being at south west we weare forced all this day to[5] *tack to and fro, whereby we had more proofe of the settynge of the tyde.* Towards the night the winde came to the north north west; then we stood away to the westward (leauing the search of Nottyngam ile) hauing a great swellinge sea out of the west with the winde which had blowne: which put vs in some hope.

---

[1] [For to get to the east side, which we called the north shore, because it is the land stretching from *Resolution*, on the north side of the straits. P.]

[2] [Some twelue or fourteene leagues from shore but the further off more osey. P.]   [3] [As the seamen account. P.]

[4] [Reeking. P.]   [5] [Turne. P.]

11 The eleuenth day, in the forenoone, we sawe land west
from vs, but no ground at 130 fathoms: so standinge
alonge by the land which here lay about north-west and
12 by north. And by the next morne we weare thwart of
a bay, *or sound runninge into the land. In the bottom
thereof the ice was not yet broke vp.* Then standing ouer[1]
that bay towards a faire cape, or headland, in the afternoone it was almost calme, and we beinge almost a league
from shore hoysed forth our bote, and sent six of our
men to see howe the tyde was by the shore.[2] They went
from the ship at 5 a clocke and came aboord agayne at
8, who brought vs word that it was falling water, and
that it had ebbd while they weare on shore somewhat
about 2 foote. Also they affirmed that the floud came
from the northward in this place, the which we also
sawe by the ship driuinge to the northward, and it being
calme (the cause thereof I suppose to be the indraft of
the bay) but this put vs in great hope of a passage this
waye, wherefore our Mr. named the poynte of land that
was some 6 leagues to the northward of vs CAPE COMFORT.
It lyeth in the latytude of 65de. 00'[3] and is 85de. 20'[4]
west from LONDON, and heare we had 140 fathoms water
13 not a league from shore. There our sudden hopes weare
as soon quayld, for the next morninge hauinge dubbled
the cape, when we supposed (by the account of the tyde)
we should be sett to the northward, it beinge little or
no winde, we weare sett to the contrary, and that day
hauinge a good gale of winde we had not proceeded on
our course past 10 or 12 leagues, but we sawe the land
trendinge from the cape, round aboute by the west tyll
it bore north-east and by east, and very thick pestred

---

[1] [To the northwards. P.]   [2] [And from whence it came. P.]
[3] [26'. P.] According to *Parry*, lat. "64° 54'".—*Voyage of the Fury and Hecla*, 1821-23, p. 33. London: 1824.
[4] [86°. P.] According to *Parry*, long. "82° 57'".—*Ibid.*

with ice, and the further we proceeded the more ice and shoalder water, with smale showe of any tyde.[1] We seeing this, our mr. soone resolued theare could be no passadge in this place, and presently we bore vpp the healme and turned the ships head to the southward. *This was about 6 a clock. The land which we sawe beare north and north-east was about 9 or 10 leagues from vs, and shurely without any question this is the bottom of the baye, on the west side; but howe far it runneth more eastward is yet uncertayne.*

14 The 14, the winde was for the most parte at south east, so that we could make but small waye backe agayne;

15 and the next morninge very foule wether, we comming to anchor in a smale coue near Cape Comfort, on the north west side thereof. Heare we found (as on the

---

[1] [At sixe a clocke this afternoone we sounded and had ground in 130 fathoms, soft osey, hauing had at noone 150 fathoms. P.]

In this vicinity, at 7 P.M. on the 5th of August 1821 (lat. 65° 22' 50" N., long. 81° 24' 00" W., var. 55° 05' 30"), Captain Parry found the tide set E. by S. at the rate of half a mile an hour; and by observation, he ascertained and confirmed the truth of Baffin's remark respecting "the small show of any tide".

The following day, the *Fury* and *Hecla* were two miles and a quarter (lat. 65° 28' 15" N.) to the northward of the locality in which Bylot and Baffin left off their search for the North-west passage. Parry says "the reasons which induced Baffin to relinquish the enterprise at this place were the increased quantity of ice, the water becoming less deep, and his seeing land bearing N.E. by E. from him: circumstances which led him to conclude that he was at the mouth of a large bay." "The same land," Captain Parry continues, "which we had now in sight, proved to be one of several islands, and I gave it the name of BAFFIN ISLAND, out of respect to the memory of that able and enterprising navigator". On the 15th of the same month, the expedition was within a league of a remarkable headland on Southampton Island, which was named by Captain Parry, CAPE BYLOT, as being "probably. the westernmost land seen by that navigator".—*Vogage of the Fury and Hecla*, 1821, etc., pp. 31-33-37. London: 1824. Baffin Island and Cape Bylot, named by Parry, are on each side of the entrance to Frozen Strait; the latter on Southampton Island.

other side) a south ½ east moone maketh a full sea, *or halfe an houre past* 11 *on the chainge daye:* but howe the floud doth set we could not well see, it beinge so foule wether at sea, *and so fogge.* In the afternoone the wind came to north by west, then we wayed anchor, and stood along by the land to the southward, with a stiffe

16 gale of winde and very hasey. By the 16 at noone we met with a great quantitie of ice lying som 7 or 8 leagues within the point of the land. Among this ice we saw som store of MORSE, *som vppon the ice and other in the water, but all so fearefull that I thinke little good would be expected in hope of killinge them. They are so beaten with the* SALUAGES *they will not suffer nether ship nor bote to com neare them.* By eight a clocke we were com to this southern point, which I called SEA HORSE POINT, wheare we anchored open in the sea, the better to proue the sett of the tyde.

Heare we found, most apparently to all our companies sight, that in this place the tyde of floud doth come from the south east, and the ebb from the north west, *being the certaynest sett of tyde we haue yet made proofe of; playnelie perceuing the sett of the ships ridinge at anchor, and also by the setting of the ice. And for our better assurance, our mr. went himselfe on shore to make proofe thereof. The tyme of high water on the chainge daye is about eleuen a clocke, something past: keping a proportion of tyme in all places as we haue beene at since we came into the strayts, all concurringe of the floud to come from the south east, and no place else, sauinge 6 leagues short of Cape Comfort, but the cause thereof I suppose to be nothing but the indraft of the baye.*

17 *The next morning our mr. asked our opinion whether it weare better for vs to seeke out some harboure heareaboute to see if we could kill any of those* MORSE *we sawe, or presently to go for* NOTTYNGAMS ILANDE *to make proofe of the*

tyde of floud theare, which was the place wheare formerly was affirmed the floud to come from the north west.

My answear and most of the companies was, that seeinge we are bound for discouery, it could not be our best waye to spend any tyme in search for these morse, they being so fearefull and beaten with the saluages. And yf we should kill some fewe of them they would not be worth the tyme we should spend. Seeinge we knewe not wheare to harboure our ship, and when shee is in harboure, we haue no other bote but our ships bote, which we dare not send far from the ship. And those morse we sawe weare in the sea, and what tyme or wheare they would com on shore was vncertayne.

These thinges considered I thought it better to go for NOTTYNGAM ILANDE, *and so to prosecute our voyage as theare we shoulde find occation, and if theare our hope of passadge was voyde, and the weather prooue fayre, we might soon com back to this place agayne, it beinge nott past 16 leagues distante.*

When I had spoke, our mr. sayd he was also of that minde, and so we wayed *anchor presently* and stood ouer with a stiffe gale of winde, which continued; and toward night a very foule wether, and a sore storme. By tenne a clocke we weare com to anchor on the north west side of NOTTYNGAM ILE, where are 2 or 3 smale iles lye off from the greater, which make very good sounds and harbours. About this ile we found some store of ice, but nothing in comparison of that which heretofore we haue had.

We staied about this island till the 27 day, hauinge much foule wether, many stormes, often foggs and vncertaine windes. Dyuers tymes we set sayle to goe to that side of the ile where the ship rode when CAPTAINE BUTTON was in her: findinge in other places of this iland the floud to com from the south eastward, and the tyme of high water on the chainge day to be at half an houer past ten, and not at halfe an houer past seuen, as some supposed. In these ten dayes we staied about this ile, we fitted our ship with ballast, and other necessaries we had neede of; and then proceeded as followeth.

26 The 26 daye, being indifferent faire wether, we passed between NOTTYNGAM ILE and SALISBURYS ILANDE at the south point thereof (I mean of Nottyngam Ile), wheare are many small, low, *broken* iles, without the which had beene a fit place for vs to haue anchord, to haue found out the tru sett of the tyde. But our mr. desirous to com to the same place wheare they had rode before, stood along by this ile to the westward, and came to an anchor in the eddy of these broken groundes, wheare the ship rode at no certaintie of tyde at all.

27 The next morning the wether proued very foule and much rayne and winde, so that our *kedger*[1] would not hold the ship,[2] but was driuen into deepe water, that we weare forced to set sayle, the winde beinge at east, and then east-north-east, and at noone at north-east, still foule weather. Being vnder sayle, we stood away towards SEA HORSE POINT. Our mr. (as I suppose) was perswaded that there might be som passadge between SEA HORSE POINT and that land which they called SWAN ILANDE: so this afternoone we saw both SEA HORSE POINT and NOTTYNGAM ILE. The distance is about 15 leagues, bearinge the one from the other north west and south east.

28 The 28 in the morninge we weare neare the former point, *being somwhat southward of it*, trendinge away west south west so farre as we sawe; and very much pestred with ice. At seuen a clocke we tacked about and stood south east and by south.

[1] [Reger. P.]   [2] [At eightie fathoms' scope. P.]

29 The next day at eleuen a clocke we came to anchor at DIGGES ILE, hauinge very foule weather. At this place wheare we rode, it lyeth open to the west, hauinge two of the greatest iles which breake off the force of the floud till the tyde be well bent; for after the water beinge risen by the shore about an houer and a halfe, then the ship *doth wind vpp and* ride truly on the tyde of floud all the tyde after. Now the tyme of high water on the chainge daye is halfe an houer past ten,[1] *nearest eleuen, whom hearetofore was taken to be halfe an houer past seuen, or an east south east moone, by which mistake I suppose hath growne the erroure at Nottyngam iland, afferminge the floud to com from the north west, makinge account that it would be high water at both places alike (as indeede it is), but the mistakinge of the tyme was all, for it is an easey thinge to make a man beleeue that which he desireth.*

30 The 30, being fayre weather, about noone we set sayle,[2] wheare we presently perceued the saluages to be close hid on the top of the rockes; but when they see we had espyed them, dyuers of them came runninge downe to the water side, calling *and weauinge* vs to com to anchor, which we would haue done if conueniently we could. But heare the water is so deepe, that it is hard to find a place to ride in, which we seeinge, lay to and fro with our ship, while som of our men in the bote killed 70 fowle, for in this place is the greatest quantitie of these fowle (whom we call WILLOCKS), that in few places else the like is to be seen: for if neade were we might haue killed many thousands, almost incredible to those which haue not seene it. Heare also we had sufficient proofe of the tyde, as we lay to and fro with the ship, but when our men weare com aboord agayne, we

---

[1] [Or neerest thereabout. P.]
[2] [And stood along close by Digges Ile. P.]

set all our sayles for homeward, makinge the best expedition we could.

AVGVST.

3 But on the third of August we were forced to com to anchor agayne about thirtie leagues within RESOLUTION
4,5 ILAND, on the north shore. The next day we set sayle, and the 5th in the forenoone we past by RESOLUTION ILAND, without sight thereof: thus continuing our course (as in the breefe iournall may be seene) with much contrarie windes and foule wether.

SEPTEMBER.

6 We had sight of CAPE CLEERE in Ireland the sixt of September. The next morninge by daylight we were faire by SILLY, and that night, at two a clocke the next morne, we came to anchor in PLYMOUTH SOUND, *without the loss of one man. For these and all other blessings the Lord make us thankfull.*[1]

And now it may be that som expect I should give my opynion conserninge the passadge. To those my answere must be, that doubtles theare is a passadge. But within this strayte, whome is called Hudson's Straytes, I am doubtfull, supposinge the contrarye. But whether there be, or no, I will not affirme. But this I will affirme, that we haue not beene in any tyde then that from Resolutyon Iland, and the greatest indraft of that commeth from Dauis Straytes; and my judgment is, if any passadge within Resolution Iland, it is but som creeke or in lett, but the mayne will be vpp fretum Dauis; but if any be desirous to knowe my opynion in pertyculler, I will at any tyme be redy to showe the best resons I cann, eyther by word of mouth, or otherwise.

[1] [With all our men liuing, hauing onely three or four sicke, which soone recouered. P.]

THE FIFTH RECORDED VOYAGE

OF

WILLIAM BAFFIN.[1]

A briefe and true Relation or Journall, contayning such accidents as happened in the fift voyage, for the discouerie of a passage to the North-west, set forth at the charges of the Right Worshipfull SIR THO. SMITH, Knight; SIR DUDLEY DIGGES, Knight; MASTER JOHN WOSTENHOLME, Esquire; MASTER ALDERMAN JONES, with others, in the good ship called the *Discouerie*, of London; ROBERT BILETH, Master; and myselfe Pilot, performed in the yeere of our Lord, 1616.

[March 26.] IN the name of God, Amen. The forenamed ship being in full readinesse vpon the twentie sixe of March, we set saile at Grauesend, being in number seuenteene persons, hauing very faire weather, which continued till the second of Aprill: by that time we were off Portland, then the winde comming westward, with foule weather, we kept sea till the fourth day, then being not able to fetch Plimouth, bore roome for Dartmouth, where wee stayed eleuen dayes, in which time was much foule weather and westerly windes.

The fifteenth day of Aprill, being cleere of Dartmouth, we were forced the next day to put into Plimouth. The nineteenth day we set saile from thence, and the twentieth, in the morning, we past betweene the Lands end and Silly, with a faire winde. Continuing our course, as in the briefe Table or Journall is set dow   th euery particular from noone to noone, that here I need not make a

[1] From *Purchas*, Part III, lib. IV, cap. xix, p. 844.

tedious repetition, nothing worthy of note hapning, but that we had a good passage, and the first land we saw was in Fretum Dauis, on the coast of Groinland, in the latitude of 65° 20'.[1] On the fourteenth of May, in the forenoone, then sixe of the people, being a fishing, came to vs, to whom we gaue small pieces of iron, they keeping vs companie, being uery ioyfull, supposing wee had intended to come to anchor; but when they saw vs stand off from shoare, they followed vs a while, and then went away discontented, to our seeming.

<small>Groinland.</small>

We prosecuting our voyage, were loth to come to an anchor as yet, although the winde was contrarie, but still plyed to the northward, vntill we came into 70° 20'; then wee came to an anchor in a faire sound (neere the place Master Dauis called London Coast).[2] The twentieth of May at euening, the people espying vs, fled away in their boates, getting on rocks, wondring and gasing at vs, but after this night we saw them no more, leauing many dogs running to and fro on the iland.[3]

<small>Men and dogs</small>

At this place we stayed two dayes, in which time wee tooke in fresh water and other necessaries; here we had some dislike of the passage, because the tydes are so small as not arising aboue eight or nine foot, and keepe no certaine course; but the neerest time of high water, on the change day, is at a quarter of an houre past nine, and the flood commeth from the south.

The two and twentieth day, at a north sunne, wee set saile and plyed still northward, the winde being right against vs as we stood off and on. Vpon the sixe and twentieth day, in the afternoone, we found a dead whale,

<small>Dead Whale.</small>

[1] This would be Sukkertoppen, or the Cockin Sound visited by Baffin during his first voyage. See page 16.

[2] The north point of Disco Island is in 70° 20' N. Hare Island, north of Disco, is in 70° 26' N. Baffin may have anchored on the north shore of the Waigat, in this latitude, near Noursak.

[3] Probably Hare Island.

about sixe and twentie leagues from shoare, hauing all her finnes.[1] Then making our ship fast, wee vsed the best means wee could to get them, and with much toile got a hundred and sixtie that euening. The next morning the sea went uery high, and the winde arising, the whale broke from vs, and we were forced to leaue her and set saile, and hauing not stood past three or foure leagues north-westward, came to the ice, then wee tacked and stood to the shoare-ward, a sore storme ensued.

By the thirtieth day, in the afternoone, wee came faire by Hope Sanderson, the farthest land Master Dauis was at,[2] lying betweene 72 and 73°; and that euening, by a north sunne, we came to much ice, which we put into, plying all the next day to get through it.

<small>Hope Sanderson.</small>

The first of June, we were cleere of the ice before named, and not farre from shoare, the winde blowing very hard at north north-east, then we put in among diuers ilands; the people seeing vs, fled away in all haste, leauing their tents behinde, and vpon a small rocke they hid two young maides, or women. Our ship riding not farre off, we espyed them, to whom our master, with some other of our companie, went in the boate, they making signes to be carried to the iland, where their tents were close adioyning. When they came thither they found two old women more, the one uery old, to our estimation little lesse than fourscore, the other not so old. The next time we went on shoare, there was another woman with a child at her back, who had hid herselfe among the rocks, till the other had told her how wee had vsed them, in giuing them pieces of iron and such like, which they highly esteeme; in change thereof they gaue vs seales skinnes; other riches they had

<small>Tents, men and women.</small>

---

[1] That is, whale-bone.

[2] On the 30th of June 1587. See *Voyages of John Davis* (Hakluyt Society, 1880), pp. xxx, and 44. Davis gives the latitude of Hope Sanderson at 72° 12′ N.

none, saue dead seales, and fat of seales, some of which fat or blubber afterward we carried aboord. The poore women were very diligent to carry it to the water side, to put into our caske, making shew that the men were ouer at the mayne, and at another small iland something more eastward. Then making signes to them that wee would shew them our ship, and set them where the men were, the foure youngest came into our boate; when they were aboord, they much wondred to see our ship and furniture; we gaue them of our meat, which they tasting, would not eate. Then two of them were set on the iland, where they supposed the men to be; the other two were carried to their tents againe. Those that went to seeke the men could not finde them, but came as neere the ship as they could, and at euening wee set them ouer to the other.

This place wee called Womens Ilands; it lyeth in the latitude of 72° 45';[1] here the flood commeth from the southward at nep tydes; the water ariseth but sixe or seuen foote, and a south south-east moone maketh a full sea. The inhabitants very poore, liuing chiefly on the flesh of seales, dryed, which they eate raw; with the skinnes they cloathe themselues, and also make couerings for their tents and boats, which they dresse very well. The women, in their apparell, are different from the men, and are marked in the face with diuers blacke strokes or lines, the skin being rased with some sharpe instrument when they are young, and black colour put therein, that by no means it will be gotten forth.

Womens Ilands.

The people described.

Concerning their religion I can little say; onely they haue a kinde of worship or adoration to the sunne, which continually they will point vnto, and strike their hand on

Religion.

---

[1] These islands are Upernivik, now a Danish settlement, and the surrounding islets and rocks. Upernivik is in 72° 48' N. The most northern Danish station is at Kingitok, in 72° 55' N.; where a very interesting runic stone was found in 1824. See *R. G. S. J.*, viii, p. 127.

Buriall of Men and Dogs.

their breast, crying "Ilyout"; their dead they burie on the side of the hils, where they live (which is commonly on small ilands), making a pile of stones ouer them, yet not so close but that wee might see the dead body, the aire being so piersing that it keepeth them from much stinking sauour. So likewise I haue seene their dogs buried in the same manner.

Vpon the fourth day wee set sayle from thence, hauing very faire weather, although the winde were contrary, and plyed to and fro betweene the ice and the land, being as it were a channell of seuen or eight leagues broad: then on the ninth day, being in the latitude of 74° 4',[1] and much pestered with ice, neere vnto three small ilands, lying eight miles from the shore, we came to anchor neere one of them.

These ilands are vsed to be frequented with people in the latter part of the yeare, as it seemed by the houses and places where the tents had stood; but this yeare, as yet, they were not come. Here the tides are very small, especially the floud, which ariseth not aboue fiue or sixe foot, yet the ebbe runneth with an indifferent streame, the cause thereof (in mine opinion) is the great abundance of snow melting on the land all this part of the yeare.

The tenth day wee set sayle from thence, and stood through much ice to the westward, to try if that further from the shoare, we might proceede; but this attempt was soone quailed, for the more ice we went through, the thicker it was, till wee could see no place to put in the ships head.[2]

Seeing that as yet we could not proceede, we determined

---

[1] Probably those now known as the Baffin Islands, north of Cape Shackleton. They are in 73° 54' N.

[2] This attempt to take the middle pack is very perilous. Parry succeeded in 1819, and Nares in 1875. But it is always safer to stick to the land-floe in passing through Melville Bay.

to stand in for the shoare, there to abide some few dayes, till such time as the ice were more wasted and gone (for we plainely saw that it consumed very fast; with this resolution we stood in, and came to anchor among many ilands, in the latitude of 73° 45',[1] on the twelfth day, at night. Here wee continued two dayes without shew or signe of any people; till, on the fifteenth day in the morning, about one a clocke, there came two and fortie of the inhabitants in their boates or canoas, and gaue vs seale skinnes, and many peeces of the bone or horne of the sea vnicorne, and shewed vs diuers peeces of sea mors teeth, making signes that to the northward were many of them; in exchange thereof we gaue them small peeces of iron, glasse beads, and such like. At foure seuerall times the people came to vs, and at each time brought vs of the aforesaid commodities, by reason thereof we called this place Horne Sound.[2] *42 Inhabitants. Vnicornes hornes. Horne Sound.*

Here we stayed six dayes, and on the eighteenth day, at night, we set sayle, hauing very little winde; and being at sea, made the best way we could to the northward, although the winde had beene contrary for the most part of this moneth; but it was strange to see the ice so much consumed in so little space, for now we might come to the three ilands before named, and stand off to the westward almost twenty leagues, without let of ice, vntill we were more north (as to 74° 30'), then we put among much scattered ice, yet euery day we got something on our way, nothing worthy of note happening, but that at diuers times we saw of the fishes with long hornes, many and often, which we call the sea vnicorne: and here, to write particularly of the weather, it would be superfluous or needelesse, *They see many Sea Vnicornes.*

---

[1] Islands off Cape Shackleton, which is 1400 feet high, and nearly perpendicular.

[2] The name is not retained on modern maps. It should be placed just north of Cape Shackleton, where there is a loomery.

because it was so variable, few dayes without snow, and often freezing, in so much that on Midsummer day, our shrowds, roapes, and sailes were so frozen that we could scarce handle them; yet the cold is not so extreame, but it may well be endured.

<small>Sharp frost on Mid-Summer Day.</small>

The first of July we were come into an open sea, in the latitude of 75° 40′, which anew reuiued our hope of a passage; and because the winde was contrary, wee stood off twenty leagues from the shoare before we met the ice; then standing in againe; when we were neare the land, we let fall an anchor to see what tyde went, but in that we found small comfort. Shortly after the winde came to the southeast, and blew very hard, with foule weather, thicke and foggie; then we set sayle, and ran along by the land; this was on the second day, at night. The next morning we past by a faire cape or headland, which we called Sir Dudley Digges Cape; it is in the latitude of 76° 35′, and hath a small iland close adioyning to it;[1] the winde still increasing, we past by a faire Sound twelue leagues distant from the former cape, hauing an iland in the midst, which maketh two entrances.[2] Vnder this iland we came to anchor, and had not rid past two houres but our ship droue, although we had two anchors at the ground; then were we forced to set sayle and stand forth. This Sound wee called Wostenholme Sound; it hath many inlets or smaller sounds in it, and is a fit place for the killing of whales.[3]

<small>Sir Dudly Digs his Cape.</small>

<small>Wostenholme Sound.</small>

The fourth day, at one a clocke in the morning, the

---

[1] The cape with the small island off it, now called Cape Dudley Digges, and probably the one Baffin alludes to, is only in 76° 8′ N. Saunders Island, off the entrance of Wolstenholme Sound, is in 76° 35′ N.

[2] Saunders Island.

[3] Here H.M. ship *North Star*, commanded by Mr. Saunders (Master, R.N.), wintered in 1849-50. She was sent out with stores for the expedition of Sir James Ross, but was unable to get through the ice of Melville Bay until late in the season, and eventually wintered in Wolstenholme Sound.

storme began againe at west and by south, so vehement, that it blew away our forecourse, and being not able to beare any sayle, wee lay a drift till about eight a clocke, then it cleared vp a little, and we saw our selues imbayed in a great Sound; then we set sayle, and stood ouer to the south-east side, where, in a little cove or bay we let fall an anchor, which we lost with cable and all, the winde blowing so extreamely from the tops of the hils, that we could get no place to anchor in, but were forced to stand to and fro in the Sound, the bottome being all frozen ouer; toward two a clocke it began to be lesse winde, then we stood forth.

In this Sound we saw great numbers of whales, therefore we called it Whale Sound, and doubtlesse, if we had beene prouided for killing of them, we might haue strooke very many. It lyeth in the latitude 77° 30′. All the fift day it was very faire weather, and wee kept along by the land till eight a clock in the euening, by which time we were come to a great banke of ice, it being backed with land, which we seeing, determined to stand backe some eight leagues to an iland we called Hakluits Ile—it lyeth betweene two great Sounds, the one Whale Sound, and the other Sir Thomas Smith's Sound; this last runneth to the north of 78°, and is admirable in one respect, because in it is the greatest variation of the compasse of any part of the world known; for by diuers good obseruations I found it to be aboue fiue points, or fifty-six degrees varied to the westward,[1] so that a north-east and by east is true north, and so of the rest. Also, this Sound seemeth to bee good for the killing of whales, it being the greatest and largest in all this bay. The cause, wherefore we minded to stand to this iland, was to see if we could find any finnes or such like on the shore,

Sir Thomas Smith's Sound, in 78°. Variation of the compasse 56° to the West, which may make questionable D. Gilberts rule, tom. I, l. 2, c. i, that where more earth is more attraction of the compasse happeneth by variation toward it. Now the known continents of Asia, &c., must be unspeakably

[1] The variation at Port Foulke in Smith Sound (lat. 78° 19′ N.) was 110°W., on July 28th, 1875; as observed by Captain A. H. Markham, R.N. See note at page 154.

146   THE FIFTH RECORDED VOYAGE OF

<small>more than here there can be, and yet here is more variation then about Jepan or Brasil, Peru, &c.[1]</small>

and so, indeed, this night wee came to anchor, but with foule weather, that our boat could not land. The next day wee were forced to set sayle, the sea was growne so high, and the wind came more outward. Two dayes wee spent and could get no good place to anchor in; then, on the eight day it cleered vp, and wee seeing a company of ilands lye off from the shoare twelue or thirteene leagues, wee minded to goe to them to see if there we could anchor. When wee were something neere, the winde took vs short, and being loth to spend more time, we tooke opportunitie of the wind, and left the searching of these ilands, which

<small>Caries Ilands.</small>

wee called Carys Ilands,[2] all which Sounds and ilands the map[3] doth truly describe.

So we stood to the westward in an open sea, with a stiffe gale of wind, all the next day and till the tenth day at one or two a'clocke in the morning, at which time it fell calme and very foggie, and wee neere the land in the en-

<small>Alderman Jones Sound.</small>

trance of a faire Sound, which wee called Alderman Jones[4] Sound. This afternoone, being faire and cleere, we sent our boat to the shoare, the ship being vnder sayle, and, as soone as they were on shoare, the winde began to blow; then they returned againe, declaring that they saw many sea morses by the shoare among the ice, and as farre as they were they saw no signe of people, nor any good place

---

[1] See note at page 154.

[2] Probably named after Mr. Alwyn Cary, the ship's husband, for this and the former voyage.

[3] "This map of the authour for this and the former voyage, with the tables of his iournall and sayling, were somewhat troublesome and too costly to insert." So says Master Purchas. His want of funds and of discernment resulted in an irremediable loss to posterity. The map of the "former voyage" has, fortunately, been preserved in manuscript, and a facsimile is given in the present volume. But that illustrating the important discoveries made in the voyage of 1616 is gone, without, it is to be feared, a hope of its ever now being found.

[4] For an account of Alderman Jones, see Introduction.

to anchor in along the shoare. Then hauing an easie gale of wind at east north-east, we ranne along by the shoare, which now trendeth much south, and beginneth to shew like a bay.

On the twelfth day we were open of another great Sound, lying in the latitude of 74° 20', and we called it Sir James Lancaster's Sound;[1] here our hope of passage began to be lesse euery day then other, for from this Sound to the southward wee had a ledge of ice betweene the shoare and vs, but cleare to the seaward, we kept close by this ledge of ice till the fourteenth day in the afternoone, by which time wee were in the latitude of 71° 16', and plainely perceiued the land to the southward of 70° 30'; then wee hauing so much ice round about vs, were forced to stand more eastward, supposing to have beene soone cleare, and to haue kept on the off side of the ice vntill we had come into 70°, then to haue stood in againe. But this proued quite contrary to our expectation, for wee were forced to runne aboue threescore leagues through very much ice, many times so fast that wee could goe no wayes, although we kept our course due east; and when wee had gotten into the open sea, wee kept so neere the ice that many times wee had much adoe to get cleare, yet could not come neere the land till we came about 68°, where indeede we saw the shoare, but could not come to it by eight or nine leagues, for the great abundance of ice. This was on the foure and twentieth day of July; then spent we three dayes more to see if conueniently wee could come to anchor to make triall of the tides; but the ice led vs into the latitude of 65° 40'. Then wee left off seeking to the west shoare, because wee were in the indraft of Cumberland

Sir James Lancasters Sound.

They see Land, and find themselues embraced.

Cumberland Iles.

---

[1] Sir John Ross remarks upon the accuracy of Baffin's latitude of Lancaster Sound. See page 3 for some account of Sir James Lancaster.

Iles, and should know no certaintie, and hope of passage could be none.

Now seeing that wee had made an end of our discouery, and the yeare being too farre spent to goe for the bottome of the bay to search for drest finnes; therefore wee determined to goe for the coast of Groineland to see if we could get some refreshing for our men; Master Herbert and two more hauing kept their cabins aboue eight dayes (besides our cooke, Richard Waynam, which died the day before, being the twenty-six of July), and diuers more of our company so weake, that they could doe but little labour. So the winde fauouring vs, we came to anchor in the latitude of 65° 45', at six a clocke in the euening, the eight and twentieth day, in a place called Cockin Sound.[1]

<small>Cockin Sound.</small>

<small>Scuruy Grasse.</small>

The next day, going on shoare on a little iland, we found great abundance of the herbe called scuruie grasse, which we boyled in beere, and so dranke thereof, vsing it also in sallets, with sorrell and orpen, which here groweth in abundance; by meanes hereof, and the blessing of God, all our men within eight or nine dayes space were in perfect health, and so continued till our arriuall in England.

<small>Six men.</small>

Wee rode in this place three dayes before any of the people came to vs; then, on the first of August, six of the inhabitants in their canoas brought us salmon peele, and such like, which was a great refreshment to our men; the next day following, the same six came againe, but after that we saw them no more vntill the sixt day, when we had wayed anchor, and were almost cleere of the harbour; then the same six and one more brought vs of the like commodities, for which we gaue them glasse beads, counters, and small peeces of iron, which they doe as much esteeme as we Christians do gold and siluer.

---

[1] See note at page 16. Baffin, at page 16, gives the latitude of Cockin Sound at 65° 20' N. Perhaps this 65° 45' is a misprint for 65° 25'.

In this Sound we saw such great scoles of salmon swim- <small>Plenty of Salmon.</small>
ming to and fro that it is much to be admired; here it
floweth about eighteene foote water, and is at the highest
on the change day at seuen a clocke : it is a uery good harbour, and easie to be knowne, hauing three round high hils
like piramides close adioyning to the mouth of it, and that
in the middest is lowest, and along all this coast are many
good harbours to be found, by reason that so many ilands
lye off from the maine.

The sixt of August, by three a clocke in the afternoone,
wee were cleere of this place, hauing a north north
west winde, and faire weather, and the Lord sent vs a
speedy and good passage homeward as could be wished;
for, in nineteene dayes after, wee saw land on the coast of
Ireland, it being on the fiue and twentieth day; the seuen
and twentieth at noone we were two leagues from Silly,
and the thirtieth day, in the morning, wee anchored at
Douer in the roade, for the which and all other His blessings the Lord make vs thankfull.

Master BAFFIN *his Letter to the right Worshippfull Sir* JOHN
WOLSTENHOLME, *one of the chiefe Adventurers*
for the discovery of a passage to
the North-west.

Worthy Sir, there needs no filling a Journall or short
Discourse with preamble, circumstance, or complement;
and therefore I will onely tell I am proud of my remembrance, when I expresse your worth to my conceit; and
glad of my good fortune, when I can auoid the imputation
of ingratitude, by acknowledgeing your many favours; and
seeing it is not vnknowne to your worship in what estate
the businesse concerning the North-West hath beene heretofore; and how the only hope was in searching Fretum

Davis; which if your selfe had not beene the more forward, the action had wel-nigh beene left of. Now it remayneth for your worship to know what hath beene performed this yeere; wherefore I intreat you to admit of my custome, and pardon me if I take the plaine highway in relating the particulars, without vsing any refined phrases, or eloquent speeches.

Therefore briefly thus, and as it were in the fore-front, I entend to shew the whole proceeding of the voyage in a word: as namely, there is no passage nor hope of passage in the north of Davis Straights. We hauing coasted all, or neere all the circumference thereof, and finde it to be no other then a great bay, as the voyage doth truely shew. Wherefore I cannot but much admire the worke of the Almightie, when I consider how vaine the best and chiefest hopes of men are in thinges vncertaine; and to speake of no other then of the hopeful passage to the North-West. How many of the best sort of men haue set their whole endeauoures to prooue a passage that wayes? not onely in conference, but also in writing and publishing to the world. Yea, what great summes of money haue been spent about that action, as your worship hath costly experience of. Neither would the vain-glorious Spaniard haue scattered abroad so many false maps and journals, if they had not beene confident of a passage this way; that if it had pleased God a passage had beene found, they might haue eclipsed the worthy prayse of the adventurers and true discouerers. And for my owne part I would hardly haue beleeued the contrary vntill my eyes became witnesse of what I desired not to haue found; still taking occasion of hope on euery likelihood, till such time as we had coasted almost all the circumference of this great bay. Neither was Master Davis to be blamed in his report and great hopes, if hee had anchored about Hope Sanderson,[1] to haue taken notice

[1] See page 140 and note.

of the tydes. For to that place, which is 72° 12', the sea is open, and of an vnsearchable depth, and of a good colour : onely the tydes keepe a certaine course, nor rise but a small height, as eight or nine foote ; and the flood commeth from the southward ; and in all the bay beyond that place the tyde is so small, and not much to be regarded. Yet by reason of snow melting on the land, the ebb is stronger then the floud; by meanes whereof, and the windes holding northerly the fore part of the yeere, the great iles of ice are set to the southward, som into Fretum Hudson, and other into Newfoundland : for in all the channell where the sea is open, are greate quantities of them driuing vp and downe; and till this yeere not well knowne where they were bred.

Now that the worst is knowne (concerning the passage) it is necessarie and requisite your worship should vnderstand what probabilitie and hope of profit might here be made hereafter, if the voyage might bee attempted by fitting men. And first, for the killing of whales ; certaine it is, that in this bay are great numbers of them, which the Biscayners call the Grand Bay whales, of the same kind as are killed at Greeneland, and as it seemeth to me, easie to be strooke, because they are not vsed to be chased or beaten. For we being but one day in Whale Sound (so called for the number of whales we saw there sleeping, and lying aloft on the water, not fearing our ship, or ought else); that if we had beene fitted with men and things necessarie, it had beene no hard matter to haue strooke more then would have made three ships a sauing voyage; and that it is of that sort of whale theare is no feare. I being twise at Greeneland[1] tooke sufficient notice to know them againe; besides a dead whale we found at sea, hauing all her finnes (or rather all the rough of her mouth),[2] of which with much labour we got one hundred and sixtie the same evening we found her : and if that foule wether and a

[1] Spitzbergen.   [2] Whale bone.

storme the next day had not followed, we had no doubt but to haue had all, or the most part of them: but the winde and sea rising, shee broke from vs, and we were forced to leaue her ther. Neither are they onely to be looked for in Whale Sound, but also in Smith's Sound, Wolstenholme's Sound, and others, etca.

For the killing of sea-morse I can give no certaintie, but onely this: that our bote being but once a shore in all the north part of this bay, which was in the entrance of Alderman Jones his Sound; at their returne our men told vs they saw many morses alonge by the shore on the ice; but our ship being under sayle, and the winde comming faire, they presently came aboord without further search: besides, the people inhabiting about 74°, tould vs by diuers signes, that toward the north were many of those beasts, having two long teeth; and shewed vs diuers peeces of the same.

As for the sea-unicorne, it being a great fish, hauing a long horne or bone growing forth of his forehead or nostrils (such as Sir Martin Frobisher, in his second voyage, found one), in diuers places we saw of them: which, if the horne be of any good value, no doubt but many of them may be killed.

As concerning what the shore will yeeld, as beach-finnes, morse-teeth, and such like, I can say little, because we came not on shore in any of the places where hope was of findinge them.

But here som may obiect why we sought that coast no better? To this I answere, that while we were thereabout, the wether was so exceeding foule, we could not; for first we anchored in Wolstenholme Sound, where presently we droue with two anchors a head; then were we forced to stand forth with a low saile. The next day, in Whale Sound, we lost an anchor and cable, and could fetch the place no more; then we came to anchor neere a small iland, lying between Sir Thomas Smith's Sound and Whale

Sound: but the winde came more outward, that we were forced to weigh againe. Neuerthelesse, if we had bene in a good harbor, hauing but our ship's bote, we durst not send her farre from the ship, having so few men (as seventeen in all), and som of them very weake: but the chiefe cause we spent so little time to seeke a harbor, was our great desire to performe the discouery; having the sea open in all that part, and still likelihood of a passage; but when we had coasted the land so farre to the southward, that hope of passage was none, then the yeere was too farre spent, and many of our men very weake, and withall we hauing some beliefe that ships the next yeere would be sent for the killing of whales, which might doe better than we.

And seeing I have briefly set doune what hope there is of making a profitable voyage, it is not vnfit your worship should know what let or hindrance might be to the same. The chiefest and greatest cause is, that som yeere it may happen by reason of the ice lying betweene 72 and a halfe and 76 degrees, no minutes, that the ships cannot com into those places till toward the middest of July, so that want of time to stay in the countrey may be some let: yet they may well tarry till the last of August, in which space much businesse may be done, and good store of oile made. Neuertheless, if store of whales come in (as no feare to the contrarie) what cannot be made in oyle, may be brought home in blubber, and the finnes will arise to good profit. Another hinderance will be, because the bottome of the sounds will not be so soone cleere as would bee wished; by meanes whereof, now and then a whale may be lost. (The same case sometimes chanceth in Greeneland.) Yet I am perswaded those sounds before named will all be cleere before the twentieth of July: for we, this yeere, were in Whale Sound the fourth day, amongst many whales, and might have strooke them without let of ice.

Furthermore, there is little wood to be expected either

for fire, or other necessaries; therefore coales and other such thinges must be prouided at home; they will be so much the readier there.

This much I thought good to certifie your worship, wherein I trust you will conceiue that much time hath not beene spent in vaine, or the businesse ouer carelessly neglected; and although we haue not performed what we desired (that is, to have found the passage), yet what we have promised (as to bring certaintie and a true description), truth will make manifest that I haue not much erred.

And I dare boldly say (without boasting) that more good discouerie hath not in shorter time (to my remembrance) beene done since the action was attempted, considering how much ice we have passed, and the difficultie of sayling so neere the pole (vpon a trauerse). And above all, the variation of the compasse, whose wonderfull operation is such in this bay, increasing and decreasing so suddenly, and swift, being in some part, as in Wolstenholme Sound and in Sir Thomas Smith's Sound, varied aboue fiue points or 56°, a thing almost incredible and matchlesse in all the world beside;[1] so that without great care and good obseruations, a true description could not have beene had.

[1] On the subject of Baffin's observations for variation see also page 145, and the marginal note there, referring to the work of Dr. Gilbert.

Baffin evidently paid much attention to questions relating to terrestrial magnetism and to phenomena connected with the magnetic needle. The variation had been observed in London since 1580, and in 1581 William Borough published his *Discourse of the Compass or Magnetical Needle*. A second edition appeared in 1596. This was followed in 1585 by a work entitled "*The newe Attractive*, containing a short discourse of the magnet, or loadstone, and among other his Vertues of a new discovered Secret and subtil propertie, concerning the declining of the needle touche, and therewith under the plaine of the horizon, now first found out by Robert Norman, Hydrographer". New editions of the *New Attractive* appeared in 1596 and 1604. The great work of Dr. Gilbert, of Colchester, referred to in the marginal note at page 145, was published in 1600. The title was, *De magnete, magneticisque corporibus, et de magno magnete tellure; Physiologia nova, plurimis et argu-*

In fine, whatsoeuer my labours are, or shall be, I esteeme them too little to expresse my thankfull minde for your many fauours, wherein I shall be ever studious to supply my other wants by my best endeauours, and euer rest at your worship's command,

WILLIAM BAFFIN.

A briefe Discourse of the probabilitie of a passage to the Westerne or South Sea, illustrated with testimonies: and a briefe Treatise and Mappe by MASTER BRIGGES.

I thought good to adde somewhat to this relation of Master Baffin, that learned-vnlearned mariner and mathematician, who, wanting art of words, so really employed himselfe to those industries, whereof here you see so euident fruits. His mappes and tables would haue much

mentis et experimentis demonstrata. Dr. Gilbert pointed out, for the first time, the magnetic properties of the earth, and showed that the earth, by its directive force, performed, relating to the compass needle, the office of a real magnet.

Baffin must have studied the works of Borough, Norman, and Gilbert; and he strove diligently, by his own observations, to furnish new materials for the study of magnetic phenomena. Thus the scientific results of Baffin's voyages are still valuable, for the changes in the magnetic inclination and declination of places in the earth's surface make the comparison of observations taken at different periods a most important element in the study of terrestrial magnetism. In 1580, the variation at London was $11\frac{1}{4}$ E.; in 1818, it was $24\frac{3}{4}$ W.; and in 1878, it was $18\frac{1}{2}$ W. At the Cape of Good Hope there was no variation in 1608; in 1840, it was 29 W.; and in 1878, it was 30 W. It is due to the first observers, such as Baffin, that these changes are known to us. Without Baffin's observations, Professor Hansteen, of Christiania, could not have constructed the first of his series of magnetic maps. It is a variation map for 1600. *Abweichungskarte für das Jahr* 1600, the second for 1700, the third for 1756, and the fourth for 1770. See *Magnetischer Atlas gehörig zum Magnetismus der Erde, von Chr. Hansteen, Professor, Christiania*, 1819 (folio).

illustrated his voyages, if trouble, and cost, and his owne despaire of passage that way, had not made vs willing to content our selues with that mappe following of that thrice learned (and, in this argument, three times thrice industrious) mathematician, Master Brigges,[1] famous for his readings in both vniuersities and this honourable citie, that I make no further voyage of discouery to finde and follow the remote passage and extent of his name. Master Baffin told mee, that they supposed the tyde from the north-west, about Digges Iland, was misreported, by mistaking the houre, eight for eleuen, and that hee would, if hee might get employment, search the passage from Japan, by the coast of Asia (*qua data porta*) any way he could. But in the Indies he dyed, in the late Ormus businesse, slaine in fight with a shot, as hee was trying his mathematicall proiects and conclusions.

Baffins death.

Now for that discouery of Sir Thomas Button, I haue solicited him for his noates, and receiued of him gentle entertainment and kinde promises: but being then forced to stay in the citie vpon necessary and vrgent affaires, he would at his returne home seeke and impart them. Since I heare that weightie occasions haue detained him out of England, and I cannot communicate that which I could not receiue: which if I doe receiue, I purpose rather to give thee out of due place, then not at all. Once he was uery confident in conference with me of a passage that way, and said that he had therein satisfied his Maiestie, who from

---

[1] Henry Briggs, a Yorkshireman, was born in 1556, and became professor of geometry at Oxford in 1596. He promoted the use of logarithms first explained by Lord Napier in 1614, and made a journey to Edinburgh on purpose to confer with the discoverer. In 1629 Briggs printed his *Arithmetica Logarithmica*. He also published the first six books of Euclid. He was a promoter of the voyage of N. W. Fox, but did not live to see its departure. The great mathematician died at Oxford on January 26th, 1630. Fox, who sailed in 1631, named a group of islands in Hudson's Bay " Brigges his Mathematickes".

his discourse in private inferred the necessitie thereof.
And the maine argument was the course of the tyde : for
wintering in Port Nelson (see the following mappe) hee
found the tyde rising euery twelue houres fifteene foote,
(whereas in the bottome of Hudsons Bay it was but two
foote, and in the bottome of Fretum Davis, discouered by
Baffin, but one); yea, and a west winde equalled the nep
tydes to the spring tydes : plainely arguing the neighbourhood of the sea, which is on the west side of America. The
summer following, he found, about the latitude of 60°, a strong
race of a tide, running sometimes eastward, sometimes
westward; whereupon Josias Hubbard in his plat called
that place Hubbarts Hope, as in the map appeareth. Now Hubberts Hope.
if any make scruple because this discouery was not persued
by Sir Thomas Button, let him consider that, being Prince
Henries seruant, and partly by him employed (whence I
thinke he named the country New Wales), the vntimely
death of that prince put all out of ioint; nor was hee so
open that others should haue the glory of his discouerie.[1]

[1] There was, for some unexplained reason, a good deal of obstruction placed in the way of those who sought for information respecting Sir Thomas Button's voyage. The instructions were drawn up by Henry, Prince of Wales, in 1612. Button was ordered to make the best of his way up Hudson's Strait to Digges Island, carefully observing the tides and currents, the elevation and variation of the compass, and the latitude, as well as the distance of the moon from any fixed stars of note. All observations were to be entered in a book, to be delivered to the Prince on the return of the expedition. Digges Island was appointed as the rendezvous for the two ships.

The two ships were the *Resolution* (commanded by Sir Thomas Button) and the *Discovery* (Captain Ingram). After a stay of eight days at Digges Island, the expedition steered N.W., and fell in with land which Button named " Cary's Swan's Nest", on August 13th, 1612. They then anchored at the mouth of a river which was named Port Nelson, after the Master of the *Resolution*, who died there. Button was thus the first navigator who reached the western side of Hudson's Bay. Here the expedition wintered. The men suffered severely from sickness, although they seem to have obtained great numbers of ptarmigan. Josias Hubart was the pilot of the *Resolution*, and, on the breaking up of the ice, he

And if any man thinke that the passage is so farre, as the maps vse to expresse America, running out into the west, it is easily answered, that either of negligence, or ouer-bisie diligence, maps by Portugals in the east, and Spaniards in the west, haue beene falsely proiected. Hence, that fabulous strait of Anian, as before by Francis Gaule's testimonie and navigation is euident.[1] And hence the Portugals, to bring in the Moluccas to that moity of the world, agreed vpon betwixt the Spaniards and them, are thought to haue much curtailed Asia and the longitude of those ilands, giuing fewer degrees to them then in iust longitude is requisite. So the older maps of America make the land from the Magelane Straits to the South Sea runne much west, when as they rather are contracted somewhat easterly from the north. The like is iustly supposed of their false placing Quinira,[2] and I know not (nor they neither) what countries they make in America to run so farre north-westward, which Sir Francis Drake's voyage in that sea (his Nova[3] Albion being little further westward than Aquatulco)[4] plainely euince to be otherwise. Yea, the late map of California, found to be an iland, the sauages discourses in all the countries northwards and westwards from Virginia, fame

advised that a north-westerly course should be steered. They got as far north as 65° on July 29th, 1613, and then turned southwards, discovering Mansel's Islands on August 4th. The return of Sir Thomas Button did not discourage the adventurers, who considered that his discoveries gave fresh hopes for a north-west passage.

[1] This is Francisco de Gali, a Spanish pilot, who made a voyage from Acapulco to Manilla, in 1583, returning so as to strike the coast of California in 37° 30' N. His narrative is given in Linschoten (1598) and Hakluyt. He proved that there was no Strait of Anian where it had been placed in 38° N., but a wide ocean between Japan and California. The question is discussed by Davis in his *Worlde's Hydrographical Description* (p. 211).

[2] On the coast of Drake's "New Albion", near Cape Mendocino.

[3] "This easily appeareth in obseruing his voiage, and comparing that before of Fr. Gaul therewith."

[4] On the coast of Mexico.

whereof filled my friend Master Dermer with so much confidence, that hearing of strange ships which came thither for a kind of yre or earth, the men vsing forkes in their diet, with caldrons to dresse their meate, etc., things nothing sutable to any parts of America, hee supposed them to come from the east, neere to China or Japan, and, therefore, he made a voyage purposely to discouer, but, crossed with diuers disasters, he returned to Virginia, frustrate of accomplishment that yeare, but fuller of confidence, as in a letter from Virginia he signified to me, where death ended that his designe soon after. But how often are the vsuall charts reiected by experience in nauigations in this worke recorded? Painters and poets are not alwayes the best oracles. For further proofes of a passage about those parts into the West Sea (or South, as it is called from the first discouery thereof to the south, from the parts of New Spain, whence it was first descried by the Spaniards), there is mention of a Portugall (and taken in a carricke in Queene Elizabeth's dayes, of glorious memory) confirming this opinion. Sir Martin Frobisher, also from a Portugall in Guinie, receiued intelligence of such a passage, he saying he had past it. The pilots of Lisbone are said generally to acknowledge such a thing, and the Admirall of *D. Garcia Geoffroy Loaisa*, of Cite-Real, in the time of Charles the Fifth, is reported by the coast of Baccalaos and Labrador to haue gone to the Moluccas. Vasco di Coronado writ to the emperour that at Cibola he was one hundred and fiftie leagues from the South Sea, and a little more from the North.[1] Antonio de Herera, the king's choronista maior (part of whose worke followeth) maketh with vs also in the distances of places by him described. But to produce some authority more full, I haue here presented Thomas Cowles, a marriner, and Master

---

[1] All this is discussed in the *Worlde's Hydrographical Description* by Davis. (See *Voyages of Davis*, p. 212 and note.)

Michael Locke, merchant, and after them a little treatise ascribed to Master Brigges, together with his map. And if any thinke that the Spaniard or Portugall would soone haue discouered such a passage, these will answere that it was not for their profit to expose their East or West Indies to English, Dutch, or others, whom they would not haue sharers in those remote treasures by so neere a passage. First, Thomas Cowles auerreth thus much :—

"I, Thomas Cowles, of Bedmester, in the countie of Somerset, marriner, doe acknowledge that six years past, at my being at Lisbon, in the kingdome of Portugall, I did heare one Martin Chacke, a Portugall of Lisbon, reade a booke of his owne making, which he had set out six yeares before that time, in print, in the Portugale tongue, declaring that the said Martin Chacke had found, twelue yeares now past, a way from the Portugall Indies through a gulf of the Newfound Land, which he thought to be in 59° of the eleuation of the North Pole. By meanes that hee, being in the said Indies, with foure other shippes of great burden, and he himselfe in a small shippe of fourscore tunnes, was driuen from the company of the other four shippes with a westerly winde, after which hee past alongst by a great number of ilands, which were in the gulfe of the said Newfound Land. And after hee ouershot the gulfe, he set no more sight of any other land vntill he fell with the north-west part of Ireland; and from thence he took his course homewards, and by that meanes hee came to Lisbone foure or fiue weekes before the other foure ships of his company that he was separated from, as before said. And since the same time, I could neuer see any of those books, because the king commanded them to be called in, and no more of them to be printed, lest in time it would be to their hindrance. In witnesse whereof I set to my hand and marke, the ninth of April Anno 1579.

A Note made by me, Michael Lok the elder, touching
the Strait of Sea, commonly called Fretum Anian, in the
South Sea, through the North-west passage of
Meta Incognita.

WHEN I was at Venice, in Aprill 1596, happily arriued there an old man, about threescore yeares of age, called commonly Juan de Fuca, but named properly Apostolos Valerianos, of nation a Greeke, borne in the Iland Cefalonia, of profession a mariner, and an ancient pilot of shippes. This man being come lately out of Spaine, arriued first at Ligorno,[1] and went thence to Florence, in Italie, where he found one John Dowglas, an Englishman, a famous mariner, ready comming from Venice, to be pilot of a Venetian ship, named *Ragasona*, for England, in whose company they came both together to Venice. And John Dowglas being well acquainted with me before, he gaue me knowledge of this Greeke pilot, and brought him to my speech; and in long talke and conference betweene vs, in presence of John Dowglas, this Greeke pilot declared, in the Italian and Spanish languages, thus much in effect, as followeth :—

First he said, that he had bin in the West Indies of Spaine by the space of fortie yeeres, and had sailed to and from many places thereof, as mariner and pilot, in the seruice of the Spaniards.

Also he said, that he was in the Spanish shippe, which, in returning from the Ilands, Philippinas and China, towards Noua Spania, was robbed and taken at the Cape California,

---

[1] Here we see the commencement of the gradual process of corrupting Livorno into Leghorn.

by Captaine Candish, Englishman, whereby he lost sixtie thousand duckets, of his owne goods.[1]

<small>Captaine Candish.</small>

Also he said, that he was pilot of three small ships, which the Vizeroy of Mexico sent from Mexico, armed with one hundred men, souldiers, vnder a captaine, Spaniards, to discouer the Straits of Anian, along the coast of the South Sea, and to fortifie in that strait, to resist the passege and proceedings of the English nation, which were feared to passe through those straits into the South Sea. And that by reason of a mutinie, which happened among the souldiers, for the sodomie of their captaine, that voyage was ouerthrowne, and the ships returned backe from California coast to Noua Spania, without any effect of thing done in that voyage: and that after their returne, the captaine was, at Mexico, punished by iustice.

Also he said, that shortly after the said voyage was so ill ended, the said Vizeroy of Mexico sent him out againe, Anno 1592, with a small carauela, and a pinnace, armed with mariners onely, to follow the said voyage, for discouery of the same Straits of Anian, and the passage thereof, into the sea which they call the North Sea, which is our northwest sea. And that he followed his course in that voyage, west and north-west, in the South Sea, all alongst the coast of Noua Spania and California, and the Indies, now called North America (all which voyage hee signified to me in a great map, and a sea-card of mine owne, which I laied before him) untill hee came to the latitude of forty-seuen degrees, and that there finding that the land trended north and north-east, with a broad inlet of sea, betweene forty-seuen and forty-eight degrees of latitude, hee entred thereinto, sayling there in more then twentie dayes, and found that land trending still sometime north-west, and north-east and north, and also east and south-eastward, and very much

<small>Land trending in 47°.</small>

---

[1] Cavendish captured this prize off Cape San Lucas, on November 14th, 1587.

broader sea then was at the said entrance, and that hee passed by diuers Islands in that sayling. And that, at the entrance of this said strait, there is, on the north-west coast thereof, a great hedland or iland, with an exceeding high pinacle, or spired rocke, like a piller thereupon.

Also he said, that he went on land in diuers places, and that he saw some people on land clad in beasts skins; and that the land is very fruitfull, and rich of gold, siluer, pearle, and other things, like Noua Spania.

And also he said that he being entred thus farre into the said strait, and being come into the North Sea already, and finding the sea wide enough euery where, and to be about thirtie or fortie leagues wide in the mouth of the Straits, where he entred, hee thought he had now well discharged his office, and done the thing which he was sent to doe; and that hee not being armed to resist the force of the saluage people that might happen, hee therefore set sayle, and returned homewards againe towards Noua Spania, where hee arriued at Acapulco, Anno 1592, hoping to be rewarded greatly of the Viceroy, for this seruice done in this said voyage. *The mouth of the Straight where he entred 30 or 40 leagues broad.*

Also he said, that after his comming to Mexico, hee was greatly welcommed by the Viceroy, and had great promises of great reward, but that hauing sued there two yeares time, and obtained nothing to his content, the Viceroy told him that he should be rewarded in Spaine of the king himselfe very greatly, and willed him, therefore, to goe into Spaine, which voyage he did performe.

Also he said, that when he was come into Spaine, he was greatly welcommed there at the Kings Court, in wordes after the Spanish manner; but after long time of suite there also, hee could not get any reward there neither, to his content. And that, therefore, at the length he stole away out of Spaine, and came into Italie, to go home againe and liue among his owne kindred and countrimen, he being very old.

Also he said, that hee thought the cause of his ill reward, had of the Spaniards, to bee for that they did not vnderstand very well, that the English nation had now giuen ouer all their voyages for discouerie of the North-West Passage, wherefore they need not feare them any more to come that way into the South Sea, and therefore they needed not his seruice therein any more.

Also he said, that in regard of this ill reward had of the Spaniards, and vnderstondinge of the noble minde of the Queene of England, and of her warres maintayned so valiantly against the Spaniards, and hoping that her Maiestie would doe him iustice for his goods lost by Captaine Candish, he would bee content to goe into England, and serue her Maiestie in that voyage, for the discouerie, perfectly, of the North-West Passage into the South Sea, and would put his life into her Maiesties hands to performe the same, if shee would furnish him with onely one ship of fortie tunnes burden, and a pinnasse, and that he would performe it in thirtie days time, from one end to the other of the Streights, and he willed me so to write into England.

The straight to be discouered in 30 dayes.

And vpon this conference had twise with the said Greeke pilot, I did write thereof accordingly into England, vnto the right honourable the old Lord Treasurer Cecill, and to Sir Walter Raleigh, and to Master Richard Hakluyt, that famous cosmographer, certifying them hereof by my letters. And in the behalfe of the said Greeke pilot, I prayed them to disburse one hundred pounds of money, to bring him into England with my selfe, for that my owne purse would not stretch so wide at that time. And I had answere hereof by letters of friends, that this action was very well liked, and greatly desired in England to bee effected; but the money was not readie, and therefore this action dyed at that time, though the said Greeke pilot perchance liueth still this day at home, in his owne countrie in Cefalonia, towards the which place he went from me within a fortnight after this conference had at Venice.

And in the meane time, while I followed my owne businesse in Venice, being in law-suit against the Companie of Merchants of Turkie, and Sir John Spencer, their Gouernour, in London, to recouer my pension due for my office of being their Consull at Aleppo, in Turkie, which they held from me wrongfully. And when I was (as I thought) in a readinesse to returne home into England, for that it pleased the Lords of her Maiesties honourable Priuie Counsell in England to looke into this cause of my law-suit for my reliefe, I thought that I should be able, of my owne purse, to take with me into England the said Greeke pilot. And therefore I wrote vnto him from Venice a letter, dated in July 1596, which is copied here-vnder.

"*Al Mag$^{co.}$ Sig$^{or.}$ Capitan Ivan De Fvca Piloto de Indias amigo mio char$^{mo.}$ en Zefalonia.*

" Mvy honrado Sennor, siendo yo par a bueluerme en Inglatierra dentre de pocas mezes, y accuerdandome de lo trattado entre my y V. M. en Venesia, sobre el viagio de las Indias, me ha parescido bien de scriuir esta carta à V. M. par aque si tengais animo de andar con migo, puedais escribirme presto, en que maniera quereis consertaros. Y puedais embiarmi vuestra carta, con esta nao Ingles que sta al Zante (sino hallais otra coientur a meier) con el sobrescritto que diga, en casa del Sennor Eleazar Hycman Mercader Ingles, al tragetto de San Thomas en Venisia. Y Dios guarde la persona de V. M. Fecha en Venesia al primer dia de Julio, 1596, annos.

"Amigo de V. M. MICHAEL LOK, Ingles."

And I sent the said letter from Venice to Zante, in the ship *Cherubin.* And shortly after I sent a copie thereof in the ship *Mynyon.* And also a third copie thereof by Manea Orlando, Patron de Naue Venetian. And vnto my said letters he wrote mee answere to Venice by one letter which came not to my hands. And also by another letter which came to my hands, which is copied here-vnder.

"*Al Illmo. Sig^{or.}* Michal Lock, Ingles, *in casa del* Sig^{or.} Lasaro *Mercader Ingles, al tragetto de San Thomas en Venesia.*

"Mvy Illustre Seg^{or.} la carta de V. M. receui à 20 dias del Mese di Settembre, por loqual veo Loche V. M. me manda, io tengho animo de complir Loche tengo promettido à V. M. y no solo yo, mas tengo vinte hombres para lieuar con migo, porche son hombres vaglientes; y assi estoi esperando, por otra carta che avise à V. M. parache me embiais los dinieros che tengo escritto à V. M. Porche bien saue V. M. como io vine pouer, porche me glieuo Capitan Candis mas de sessanta mille ducados, come V. M. bien saue; embiandome lo dicho, ire à seruir à V. M. con todos mis compagneros. I no spero otra cossa mas de la voluntad è carta de V. M. I con tanto nostro Sig^{or.} Dios guarda la illustre persona de V. M. muchos annos. De Ceffalonia à 24 de Settembre del 1596.

"Amigo and seruitor de V. M.,

"Juan Fuca."

And the said letter came to my hands in Venice, the 16 day of Nouember, 1596; but my law suite with the Companie of Turkie was not yet ended, by reason of Sir John Spencers suite made in England at the Queenes Court to the contrarie, seeking onely to haue his money discharged which I had attached in Venice for my said pension, and thereby my owne purse was not yet readie for the Greeke Pilot.

And, neuerthelesse, hoping that my said suite would haue shortly a good end, I wrote another letter to this Greeke Pilot from Venice, dated the 20 of November, 1596, which came not to his hands, and also another letter dated the 24 of Januarie,

1596, which came to his hands. And thereof he wrote me answere, dated the 28 of May 1597, which I receiued the first of August 1597, by Thomas Norden an English merchant yet liuing in London, wherein he promised still to goe with me into England to performe the said voyage for discouerie of the north-west passage into the South Sea, if I would send him money for his charges according to his former writing, without the which money, he said he could not goe, for that he said he was vndone vtterly, when he was in the ship *Santa Anna*, which came from China, and was robbed at California. And yet againe afterward I wrote him another letter from Venice, whereunto he wrote me answere, by a letter written in his Greeke language, dated the 20 of October 1598, the which I haue still by me, wherein he promiseth still to goe with me into England, and performe the said voyage of discouerie of the north-west passage into the South Sea by the said streights, which he calleth the Streight of Noua Spania, which he saith is but thirtie daies voyage in the streights, if I will send him the money formerly written for his charges. The which money I could not yet send him, for that I had not yet recouered my pension owing mee by the Companie of Turkie aforesaid. And so of long time I stayed from any furder proceeding with him in this matter.

The Ship Santa Anna

The Streigh of Noua Spania thirtie dayes iourney in the Streight.

And yet, lastly, when I my selfe was at Zante, in the moneth of June 1602, minding to passe from thence for England by sea, for that I had then recouered a little money from the Companie of Turkie, by an order of the Lords of the Priuie Counsell of England, I wrote another letter to this Greeke Pilot to Cefalonia, and required him to come to me to Zante, and goe with mee into England, but I had none answere thereof from him, for that as I heard afterward at Zante, he was then dead, or very likely to die of great sicknesse. Whereupon I returned my selfe by sea from Zante to Venice, and from thence I went by land through France into England, where I arriued at Christmas, An. 1602, safely, I thanke God, after my absence from thence ten yeeres time; with great troubles had for the Company of Turkies businesse, which hath cost me a great summe of money, for the which I am not yet satisfied of them.

A Treatise of the North-west passage to the South
Sea, through the Continent of Virginia, and by Fretum
Hudson.

By Henry Briggs, the Mathematician.

The noble plantation of Virginia hath some very excellent prerogatiues aboue many other famous kingdomes, namely, the temperature of the aire, the fruitfulnesse of the soile, and the commodiousnesse of situation.

The aire is healthfull and free both from immoderate heate, and from extreme cold; so that both the inhabitants and their cattell doe prosper exceedingly in stature and strength, and all plants brought from any other remote climate, doe there grow and fructifie in as good or better manner, then in the soile from whence they came. Which though it doe manifestly prooue the fruitfulnesse of the soile, yelding all kindes of graine or plants committed vnto it, with a rich and plentifull increase; yet cannot the fatnesse of the earth alone produce such excellent effects vnlesse the temperature of the aire be likewise so fauourable, that those tender sprouts which the earth doth abundantly bring forth, may be cherished with moderate heate and seasonable moisture, and freed both from scourching drought, and nipping frost.

These blessings are so much the more to be esteemed, because they are bestowed vpon a place situated so conueniently, and at so good a distance, both from Europe and the West Indies, that for the mutuall commerce betwixt these great and most rich parts of the habitable world, there cannot bee deuised any place more conuenient for the succour and refreshing of those that trade from hence thither, whether they be of our owne nation, or of our neighbours and friends; the multitude of great and nauigable rivers, and of safe and spacious harbours, as it were inuiting all nations to entertaine mutuall friendship, and to participate of those blessings which God, out of the abundance of his rich treasures, hath so graciously bestowed some vpon those parts of Europe, and others no lesse desired vpon these poore people, which might still haue remayned in their old barbarous ignorance, without knowledge of their owne miserie, or of Gods infinite goodnesse and mercy, if it had not pleased God thus graciously, both to draw vs thither with desire of such wealth as those fruitfull countries afford, and also to grant vs, too, easie, certaine, and safe a meanes to goe vnto them, which passage is, in mine opinion, made much more secure and easie by the commodious harbours and refreshing which Virginia doth reach out unto vs. The coasts of Florida, to the west, being not so harberous; and of New England to the east, somewhat more out of the way, amongst so many flats and small ilands, not so safe. Neither is the commodiousnesse of Virginia's situation onely in respect of this West Atlanticke Ocean, but also in respect of the Indian Ocean, which we commonly call the South Sea, which lyeth on the west and north-west side of Virginia, on the other side of the mountaines beyond our Falls, and openeth a free and faire passage, not onely to China, Japan, and the Moluccaes; but also to New Spaine, Peru, Chili, and those rich countries of Terra Australis, not as yet fully discouered. For the sea wherein Master Hudson did winter, which was first discouered by him, and is, therefore, now called Fretum Hudson, doth stretch so farre towards the west, that it lyeth as farre westward as the Cape of Florida. So that, from the Falls aboue Henrico Citie, if we shape our iourney towards the north-west, following the riuers towards the head, wee shall, vndoubtedly, come to the mountaines, which, as they send diuers great riuers southward into our Bay of Chesepiock, so likewise doe they send others from their further side north-westward into that bay where Hudson did winter. For so wee see in our owne countrie, from the ridge of mountaines continued from Derbishire into Scotland, doe issue many great riuers on both sides into the East Germane Ocean, and into the Westerne Irish Seas; in like sort from the Alpes of Switzerland and the Grizons, doe runne the Danubie eastward into Pontus Euxinus, the Rhene into the North Germane Ocean, the Rhone west into the Mediterranean Sea, and the Po south into the Adriaticke Sea. This bay, where Hudson did winter, stretcheth itself southward into forty-nine degrees, and cannot be, in probabilitie, so farre distant from the Falls as two hundred leagues; part of the way lying by the riuers side towards the mountaines, from whence it springeth, and the other part on the other side cannot want riuers likewise, which will conduct us all the way, and I hope carry vs, and our prouisions, a good part of it. Besides that bay, it is not vnlikely that the Westerne Sea, in some other creeke or riuer, commeth much neerer then that place. For the place where Sir Thomas Button did winter, lying more westerly then Master Hudsons Bay, by one hundred and ninetie leagues in the same sea, doth extend it selfe very neere as farre towards the west as the Cape of California, which is now found to be an Iland stretching it selfe from twenty-two degrees to forty-two, and lying almost directly north and south; as may appeare in a map of that Iland, which I haue seene here in London, brought out of Holland; where the sea, vpon the north-west part, may very probably come much neerer then some doe imagine; who, giuing too much credit to our vsuall globes and maps, doe dreame of a large continent, extending it selfe farre westward to the imagined Streight of Anian, where are seated (as they fable) the large kingdomes of

Cebola and Quiuira, hauing great and populous cities of ciuill people; whose houses are said to bee fiue stories high, and to haue some pillars of Turquesses, which relations are cunningly set downe by some vpon set purpose, to put us out of the right way, and to discourage such as otherwise might be desirous to search a passage by the way aforesaid into these seas.

Gerardus Mercator, a very industrious and excellent geographer, was abused by a map sent vnto him, of foure Euripi meeting about the North Pole; which now are found to bee all turned into a mayne icie sea. One demonstration of the craftie falsehood of these vsuall maps is this, that Cape Mendocino is set in them west north-west, distant from the south Cape of California about seuenteene hundred leagues, whereas Francis Gaule, that was imployed in those discoueries by the Vice-roy of New Spaine, doth in Hugo Linschotten, his booke, set downe their distance to be onely fiue hundred leagues.

Besides this, in the place where Sir Thomas Button did winter in fifty-seven degrees of latitude, the constant great Tydes euery twelue houres, and the increase of those tydes whensoeuer any strong westerne winde did blow, doe strongly persuade vs that the maine westerne ocean is not farre from thence; which was much confirmed vnto them the summer following; when sayling directly north, from that place where they wintered, about the latitude of sixty degrees, they were crossed by a strong current, running sometimes eastward, sometimes westward. So that if we finde either Hudsons Bay, or any other sea more neere vnto the west, wee may assure our selues that from thence we may, with great ease, passe to any part of the East Indies. And that, as the world is very much beholding to that famous Columbus, for that he first discouered vnto vs the West Indies; and to the Portugal for the finding out the ordinarie, and as yet the best way that is knowne to the

East Indies, by Cape Bona Speranza, so may they and all the world be in this beholding to vs in opening a new and large passage, both much neerer, safer, and farre more wholesome and temperate through the Continent of Virginia, and by Fretum Hudson, to all those rich countries, bordering vpon the South Sea, in the East and West Indies. And this hope that the South Sea may easily from Virginia be discouered ouer land, is much confirmed by the constant report of the sauages, not onely of Virginia, but also of Florida and Canada; which, dwelling so remote one from another, and all agreeing in the report of a large sea to the westwards, where they describe great ships not vnlike to ours, with other circumstances, doe giue vs very great probabilitie (if not full assurance) that our endeavours this way shall, by God's blessing, haue a prosperous and happy successe, to the encrease of his kingdome and glorie amongst these poore ignorant Heathen people; the publique good of all the Christian world, the never-dying honour of our most gracious Soueraigne, the inestimable benefit of our nation, and the admirable and speedie increase and advancement of that most noble and hopefull plantation of Virginia; for the good successe whereof all good men with mee, I doubt not, will powre out their prayers to Almightie God. H. B.

INSTRUCTIONS

TO

WILLIAM BAFFIN,

A.D. 1616.

(*From Purchas, iii, p.* 842.)

"For your course you must make all possible haste to *Cape Desolation;* and from thence you, William Baffin, as pilot, keep along the coast of Greenland and up *Fretum Davis,* until you come toward the height of eighty degrees, if the land will give you leave. Then, for feare of inbaying, by keeping too northerly a course, shape your course west and southerly, so farre as you shall thinke it convenient, till you come to the latitude of sixtie degrees; then direct your course to fall in with the land of *Yedzo,* about that height, leaving your further sayling southward to your owne discretion, according as the time of the year and windes will give you leave; although our desires be, if your voyage prove so prosperous that you may have the year before you, that you goe so farre southerly as that you may touch the north part of *Japan,* from whence, or from *Yedzo,* if you can so compasse it without danger, we would have you bring home one of the men of the countrey; and so God blessing you, with all expedition to make your return home againe."

BAFFIN'S SHIPS.

I. 1612.—*Patience* (140 tons), forty men and boys.

James Hall (General).
WILLIAM BAFFIN (Pilot).
William Gordon (Master's Mate).
John Hemsley (Master's Mate).
William Huntriss (Master's Mate).
John Gatonby (Quarter Master).
Mr. Wilkinson (Merchant).
James Carlisle (Goldsmith).

II. 1613.—*Tiger* (260 tons).

Benjamin Joseph (General).
Thomas Sherwin (Master).
WILLIAM BAFFIN (Pilot).
Master Spencer (Master's Mate).

III. 1614.—*Thomasine*.

Thomas Sherwin (Master).
WILLIAM BAFFIN (Pilot).
Robert Fotherby (Master's Mate).
Robt. Hambleton (Master's Mate).

IV. 1615.—*Discovery* (55 tons), fourteen men and two boys.

Robert Bylot (Master).
WILLIAM BAFFIN (Pilot).

V. 1616.—*Discovery* (55 tons), fourteen men and two boys.

Robert Bylot (Master).
WILLIAM BAFFIN (Pilot).
Master Herbert.
Richard Waynam (Cook).

VI. 1617-19.—*Anne Royal* (1057 tons).

Andrew Shilling (Master).
WILLIAM BAFFIN (Master's Mate).
Edward Haynes (Merchant).
Joseph Salbanke (Merchant).
Richard Barber (Merchant).

VII. 1620-22.—*London*.

Andrew Shilling (General).
WILLIAM BAFFIN (Master).
Bartholomew Symonds (Surgeon).
Nicholas Crispe (Purser).
John Woolhouse (Chaplain).
Archibald Jennison (Master's Mate).
Edwyn Guy (Purser's Mate).
John Barker (Merchant).
Edward Monox (Merchant).
Robert Jefferies (Merchant).

INDEX.

CONTENTS OF THE INDEX.

I.—List of Persons mentioned in Baffin's Voyages - - 176
II.—Animals and Plants mentioned in Baffin's Voyages - 178
III.—List of Spitzbergen Names mentioned by Baffin and Fotherby - - - - - - 179
IV.—Names in Hudson's Strait mentioned by Baffin - - 180
V.—Greenland and Baffin Bay Names mentioned by Baffin - 181
VI.—General Index - - - - - 182

I.

LIST OF PERSONS MENTIONED IN BAFFIN'S VOYAGES.

Baffin, William, *passim*.
Ball, Richard, 3. A London merchant, adventurer in the Greenland voyage of 1612. Ball's river, a fiord opening on Godthaab harbour was named after him.
Barker, Andrew, 13, 24, 26. Master of the *Heart's Ease* in the Greenland voyage of 1612, and took chief command on the death of Hall. An old and experienced seaman. Warden of the Hull Trinity House, 1606, 1613, 1618.
Bonner, Thos., 44, 50, 52, 72. Master of an Amsterdam ship in Spitzbergen in 1613, which was captured by the English, and sent northward for discovery under Captain Marmaduke.
Button, Sir Thomas, 134. Commander of an expedition of discovery in Hudson's Bay in 1612-13, wintering to Nelson River. His ship was the *Discovery*, the same ship in which Baffin made his two voyages in 1614 and 1615.
Bylot, Robert, 111, 138. Master of the *Discovery* when Baffin was pilot in 1615 and 1616. He also served with Hudson in his last voyage, and with Button and Gibbons, always in the *Discovery*.

Carlisle, James, 25, 33. Goldsmith in Hall's Greenland expedition, 1612.
Cary, Allwyn, 111, 146. Ship's husband for the *Discovery* in the voyage of 1615 and 1616.
Cockayne, Sir William, 4. Adventurer for Hall's Greenland voyage of 1612. For a notice of him, see note at p. 4.
Cooper, Master, 49. In the Spitzbergen voyage of 1613. Complaint against him by the master of the French ship who had been allowed to fish.
Cudner, Master, 52. Merchant on board a ship of Alborough called the *Desire*, in Spitzbergen in 1613.
Davis, John, 8, 139, 140, 150. References to his discoveries of Cape Farewell, London Coast, and Hope Sanderson, and to his views respecting a passage.
Digges, Sir Dudley, 103, 111, 138. See his life in the Introduction, p. x to xvi.
Edge, Thomas, 49, 50. In 1611 he went to Spitzbergen in command of the *Mary Margaret*. The fleet of 1613 was under the joint command of Joseph and Edge. Edge made several other voyages to Spitzbergen down to 1616.

INDEX.

Fisher, Thos., 42. Gunner on board a French ship at Spitzbergen, 1613.

Fletcher, 52. Master of a ship from Alborough called the *Desire*, 1613.

Fopp, Captain, 40, 42, 43. Captain of a ship of Dunkirk, in Spitzbergen, 1613.

Fotherby, Robert, 54-79, 80-102. Author of the two narratives, 1613 and 1614, with Baffin, and of another, 1615. For a notice of him and his family, see note at p. 80.

Frobisher, Sir Martin, 152. Reference to his bringing home a narwhal's horn.

Gatonby, John, 1, 26, 27. Quartermaster of the *Patience*, in Hall's Greenland voyage of 1612, of which he wrote a narrative published in Churchill. He went home master's mate of the *Heart's Ease*.

Gibbons, Captain, 111. Sent out in command of an expedition in 1614, but did nothing. Bylot was with him in the *Discovery*.

Gordon, William, 26, 52. Master's mate of the *Patience* in Hall's Greenland voyage of 1612. He was afterwards employed in Spitzbergen voyages.

Green, Mr., 68. One of the master's mates of the *Mathew* in the Spitzbergen voyage of 1613, who died on the way home.

Hall, James, 3, 15, 22, 24, 25. Commander of the Greenland expedition of 1612, who was murdered by the Eskimo on July 22. For an account of his former services with the Danes, see Introduction, p. xviii.

Hambledon, Robert, 88. Master's mate of the *Thomasine*, with Baffin, in the Spitzbergen voyage of 1614.

Hemsley or Hemstay, John, 10, 26. Master's mate of the *Patience* in Hall's Greenland voyage of 1612. He displayed some insubordinate feeling when Andrew Barker succeeded to the chief command.

Herbert, 148. Master Herbert is mentioned as suffering from scurvy on board the *Discovery* in the voyage of 1616.

Hildyard, Sir Christopher, 1. Gatonby dedicated his narrative to Sir C. Hildyard of Winestead; for a notice of him, see note at p. 1.

Hubbard, Josiah, 157. With Hall in his third voyage with the Danes, and drew sketches of land. Afterwards he was pilot with Sir T. Button, and drew a chart, now lost.

Huntriss, William, 24, 27, 32. A Yorkshire lad of Scarborough, the faithful follower of Hall, both in the Danish voyages and in 1612. On Hall's death, he became master of the *Heart's Ease*.

Jones, Sir Francis, 111, 138, 146, 152. Adventurer in the voyages of 1615 and 1616. For an account of him, see Introduction, p. x.

Joseph, Benjamin, 38 (*n.*), 40, 55, 81, General of the Spitzbergen voyages of 1613 and 1614. For some account of him, see note at p. 39.

Lancaster, Sir James, 3, 13, 147. An adventurer in the expeditions of 1612, 1615, and 1616. See note at p. 3.

Marmaduke, Master, 50 (*n.*), 60, 61, 72, 93, 99. A captain from Hull, who made several voyages to Spitzbergen, and explored part of the north coast in 1612.

Martin, Clais, of Horn. In command of a pink from Dunkirk, 1613.

Mason, John, 49, 86, 88, 91, 99. In the Spitzbergen voyages of 1613 and 1614. Master of the *Gamaliel*.

Origanus, David, 124, 125. Reference to his *Ephemeris*, by Baffin.

Penkewill, Richard, 112. A gentleman from Padstow, who showed kindness to the crew of the *Discovery*, 1616.

Prestwood, Lawrence, 93. Served with Marmaduke in Spitzbergen in 1612, and set up a cross on Red Beach.

Pullay, James, 14, 15. One of the crew of the *Patience*, in Hall's Greenland voyage of 1612. Killed by the Eskimo at Godthaab.

Rudston, Master, 127. A mathematician, who worked out some of Baffin's observations.

Sallowes, Allen, 40, 42. (Allane Sallis.) An English pilot on board a French ship at Spitzbergen, 1613.

Searle, John, 124. His *Ephemeris* referred to by Baffin. For some account of him, see note at p. 124.

Sherin or Sherwin, Thomas, 45, 81, 89, 99. Master of the *Tiger* in Spitzbergen in 1613, and again in the *Thomasine* with Baffin in 1614

Silvator, Pierce de, 60. Captain of a Bordeaux ship, 1613, allowed to fish on conditions.

178   INDEX.

Spencer, Master, 45. Master's mate in the *Tiger* with Baffin in the Spitzbergen voyage of 1613.

Smith, Sir Thomas, 13, 54, 103, 111, 138. Adventurer in the voyages of 1612, 1615, and 1616. For his life, see Introduction, pp. ii to ix.

Waynam, Richard, 148. Cook of the *Discovery* in 1616. He died of scurvy on July 26th.

Wilkinson, Mr., 15, 26. Merchant on board the *Patience* in Hall's Greenland voyage of 1612.

Wilkinson, Thos., 62. Master's mate in the *Mathew* in the Spitzbergen voyage of 1613. He shot a bear.

Wilmote, John, 57. Master's mate in the *Mathew* in 1613.

Wolstenholme, Sir John, 103, 111, 138, 149. Adventurer in the voyages of 1612, 1615, and 1616. For his life, see Introduction, pp. xvi, xvii.

Woodcock, Nicholas, 46, 85. Pilot to Jonas Poole in 1610, and to a ship of San Sebastian in 1612. Master of the *Prosperous* in Spitzbergen in 1614. See note at p. 85.

II.

ANIMALS AND PLANTS MENTIONED IN BAFFIN'S VOYAGES.

MAMMALS.

Bear (*Ursus maritimus*), 35, 62, 65, 71.
Dog (*Canis familiaris*), 35, 118, 142.
Fox (*Vulpes lagopus*), 18, 35, 62, 71.
Grampus (*Orca gladiator*), 7.
Hare (*Lepus glacialis*), 35.
Morse (*Odobænus rosmarus*), 36, 47, 48, 61, 62, 71, 78, 133, 146, 152.
Reindeer (*Rangifer tarandus*), 35, 47, 57, 62, 70, 71.
Seal (*Phoca*), 35, 36, 61, 71.
Unicorn (*Monodon Monoceros*), 13, 17, 71, 143, 152.
Whale (*Balæna mysticetus*), 7, 46, 47, 49, 59, 71, 72, 73, 78, 88, 99, 139, 143, 144, 151, 152.
White Whale (*Beluga leucas*), 71.

BIRDS.

Culverdumes, 62; Cuelverduns, 71. Probably a corrupt form. *Culver* suggests a pigeon.
Geese (*Bernicla Brenta*), 62, 71.
Gulls (*Larus?*), 71.
Partridges (*Lagopus rupestris*, Ptarmigan), 17, 71.
Sea Pigeons (*Uria grylle*, Dovekeys), 71.
Sea Parrots (*Fratercula Arctica*, Puffins), 71.
Stints (*Tringa*, Sandpipers), 71.
Willocks (*Uria arra*, Guillemots), 62, 71, 136.

FISH.

But Fish, Halibut (*Pleuronecthes hippoglossus*) (Torbut? *Egede*, p. 91), 19.
Cod (*Gadus*), 19, 71.
Musk Fish (?), 19.
Salmon (*Salmo salar*), 36, 71.
Salmon Trout (*Salmo carpio*), 18, 19.
Salmon Peel, 148.

PLANTS.—GREENLAND.

Angelica (*Archangelica officinalis*, Quan), 34.
A little branch running along the ground, bearing a black berry (*Empetrum nigrum*, Crowberry), 34.
Grove of small wood, 6 or 7 feet high (*Betula alpestris*, dwarf birch), 34.
Scurvy Grass (*Cochlearia officinalis*), 148.
Sorrel (*Oxyria reniformis*), 148.
Orpen, 148. (A yellow flowered *sedum*.) Name from orpine (orpiment), gold pigment. There are three *sedums* (stonecrops), but all in South Greenland: *Sedum annuum, sedum rhodiola, sedum villosum*).

PLANTS.—SPITZBERGEN.

A white moss, 70.
Straggling grass, with a bluish flower, like young heath, 70. (*Silene acaulis?* a little purple flower, grows level with the moss, or, perhaps, *Saxifraga oppositifolia*).

III.
SPITZBERGEN NAMES MENTIONED BY BAFFIN AND FOTHERBY.

Barren, Cape, 86, 87, 95, 100. An island eastward of Hakluyt Headland, the Vogel-sang of Van Keulen and modern charts. On August 29th, 1613, Baffin and Fotherby sailed E.N.E. about 20 leagues from it. This would place their ship off the entrance of Hinlopen Strait, and about 25 miles from the shore.

Bell Sound, 49, 63. In 77° 35' N. (70 miles from south point of Spitzbergen on west coast). Retains the same name.

Black Point, 51. South point of Prince Charles Island. Van Keulen makes the south point "Zuydhoek", and places Swarte Hoek further north, on the west coast of the island.

Cold Cape, 52. On west coast of Prince Charles Island. On Swedish chart called Cape Sietoe.

Cross Road, 85. Inlet in Spitzbergen, opposite north end of Prince Charles Island. Now called Cross Bay. Van Keulen has Kruys-baay, 79° 10' N.

Deceit Point. 99. At the bottom of Red Cliffe Sound (now called Liefde Bay), on north coast of Spitzbergen. So named by Fotherby, because he mistook it for an island.

Fair Foreland, 40, 51, 59. North point of Prince Charles Island, 78° 53' N. Name preserved. This is probably the *Vogel Hoek* of Barents. Hudson was off it in June 1607.

Fair Haven, 50, 83, 86, 88, 91, 95. North coast, 8 miles east of Hakluyt Headland, protected by Cloven Cliff, and other islands, 79° 50' N. Name preserved.

Greene Harbour, 41, 45, 46, 48, 49, 59, 65, 71. On south side of Ice Sound, 78° 5' N. Name preserved. Van Keulen so places it.

Hakluyt Headland, 83, 86, 88, 100. North-west point of Spitzbergen, 79° 50' N. The name was given by Hudson in July 1607. On Amsterdam Island.

Horn Sound, 39, 43. The most southern sound on the west coast, 76° 55' to 77° N. It was discovered and so named by Jonas Poole, in 1610.

Ice Sound, 48, 60. Entrance in 78° 9' N. So named by Jonas Poole, in 1612. Van Keulen has Ys-sond.

Joseph's Bay, 63, 65. A bay in Bell Sound.

Lizets Islands, 48. Off the southern entrance of Ice Sound. They are not given on the Swedish chart.

Lord Ellesmere Bay, 65.

Low Ness, 43. Between Bell Sound and Ice Sound. A low point.

Low Sound, 43. A bay on the north side of Bell Sound. Not on modern charts.

Maudlin Sound, 83, 84. Magdalena Bay of modern charts, 79° 35' N. Fifteen miles south of Hakluyt Headland.

Niche's Cove, 41, 46. Another name for Pooppy Bay. It is on the west coast, facing the channel which separates Prince Charles Island from the main. It is probably a misprint for Wiche's Cove.

Pooppy Bay, 41, 46, 50. Same as Niche's Cove.

Prince Charles Island, 40 (*n.*), 57, 84. An island 50 miles long by 7 or 8, and about 10 miles from the mainland. Lat. 78° 18' to 78° 53' N. Now called Prince Charles Foreland. Hudson was off the island in June and July 1607. Van Keulen calls it "Het Voorland".

Red Beach, 90, 91, 92, 96, 97. On the north coast, at the western entrance of Liefde Bay. First reached by Captain Marmaduke and his Hull men in 1612. On the Swedish chart, Red Beach is placed at the western entrance of Liefde Bay.

Red Cliff Sound, 91, 96. Probably "Red Bay" of the Swedish chart, east of Fair Haven.

Saddle Island, 87. This is apparently Cloven Cliff of modern charts, which forms the northern protection to

Fair Haven, "Gansen Eyl" of Van Keulen.
Sea Horse Bay, 49.
Sir T. Smith's Bay, 51, 56, 59, 60, 85. The channel between Prince Charles Island and the main; now called Foreland Fiord.
Sir T. Smith's Inlet, 94, 97, 100. The Hinlopen Strait of modern charts; or, possibly, Wiide Bay. On the map of Porchas, it is certainly in the position of Hinlopen Strait. But Baffin and Fotherby say they saw the end of it, 30 miles distant, and this answers better to Wiide Bay.

Trinity Harbour, 86. In Magdalena Bay (or Maudlin Sound), so named by Fotherby, who took possession there, in the name of King James, on June 22nd, 1613.
Wiche's Sound, 92, 94. This appears to be the Wiide Bay of modern charts, on the north coast. Baffin and Fotherby crossed it, and climbed a high hill, whence they saw a point of land, E.N.E., 18 or 20 leagues. They would have been on a hill over Mossel Bay, whence 60 miles E.N.E. would just reach the North Cape of North-East Land.

IV.

NAMES IN HUDSON'S STRAIT MENTIONED BY BAFFIN.

Broken Islands, 105. Baffin's latitude, 63° 46' N.
Broken Point, 121, 125. So named by Baffin in 1614. On the north side of Hudson Strait. Sir Edward Parry (Second Voyage, p. 21) says the spot is memorable, because here Baffin took the first lunar ever observed at sea, giving his longitude 74° 30' W. Parry was there on July 29th, 1821.
Comfort, Cape, 104, 131, 132, 133. Baffin's latitude, 65° N. So named by Bylot. Parry gives the latitude 64° 54' N. He sighted it on August 6th, 1821. It is on Southampton Island.
Digges Island, 105, 136. Baffin's latitude, 62° 45' N. On the south side of the western entrance to Hudson Strait. It was here that the villains, Green and Jewett, who abandoned Hudson, were murdered by Eskimo, 1615.
Fair Ness, 121, named by Baffin in 1614.
Mill Island, 128. So named by Baffin from "the greate extremetye and grindinge of the ice". His latitude is 64° N. It is on the north side of the western entrance of Hudson Strait, west of Salisbury and Nottingham Islands.
Nottingham Island, 105, 130, 133, 134, 135. Baffin's latitude, 62° 45' N. Nottingham and Salisbury Islands are at the western end of Hudson Strait, on the north side.
Resolution Island, 105, 113, 114, 115, 116, 137. Baffin's latitude, 61° 30' N. He sighted it on May 27th, 1615. Parry sighted it on July 6th, 1821. This island is at the eastern entrance of Hudson Strait, on the north side. Discovered by Davis.
Salisbury Island, 127, 135. Sighted by Parry on July 31st, 1821. At the western end of Hudson Strait. So named by Hudson, who thought it was a cape on the main land.
Savage Islands, 105, 117, 120. Baffin's latitude, 62° 30' N. Named by Baffin in June 1614. Parry was off them on July 22nd, 1821 (p. 16). They are on the north side of the entrance to Hudson Strait.
Sea Horse Point, 105, 135. Baffin's latitude, 63° 44' N. The eastern point of Southampton Island.
Swan Island, 135.

V.

GREENLAND AND BAFFIN'S BAY NAMES MENTIONED BY BAFFIN.

Ball's River, 13, 34. So named by Hall in 1612. Baal's river of some old maps. Called after Richard Ball, for a notice of whom see note at p. 3.

Burnil Cape, 28. The Cape Burnitt of the Admiralty Chart. Name given by Hall in 1605, see note at p. 29.

Cary Islands, 111, 146. Named by Baffin after Alwyn Cary, ship's husband for the voyage. Baffin discovered them on July 8th, 1616. They were next seen by Captain Ross on August 20th, 1818, in 76° 45′ N.

Cockin Sound, 16, 20, 21, 22, 148, 149. Named by Hall in 1612, after Sir William Cockayne. Baffin gives the latitude at 65° 20′ N. This is nearly the latitude of the existing Danish settlement of Sukkertoppen in 65° 22′ N. *Coquin* Sound, wrongly spelt and wrongly placed on the Admiralty Chart in 65° 38′ N.

Comfort Land, 10. Part of the coast of Greenland north of Cape Desolation, so named by John Hemstay (or Hemsley) master's mate, and John Gatonby, quarter master of the *Patience*, 1612. Cape Comfort of the Admiralty Chart is in 61° 49′ N.

Cumberland Isles, 147. On the western side of Davis Strait.

Cunningham Fiord, 23. On the Greenland Coast, north of Cape Queen Sophia, so named by Hall in 1605, in 67° 15′ N.

Cunningham Mount, 18. A high peak south of the Danish settlement of Holsteinborg, so named by Hall, 1605. Called *Kærlinghætten* by the Danes, and *Nusasak* by the Eskimo.

Desolation, 9. Part of the west coast of Greenland, so named by Davis. Cape Desolation is in 60° 43′ N. *Nunarssuit* of the Eskimo.

Dudley Digges Cape, 144. Discovered by Baffin July 2nd, 1616, and named by him, in 76° 20′ N., *Jenna* of the Eskimo.

Farewell Cape, 8, 113. The southern extreme of Greenland, so named by Davis. *Herjulfnaes* of the old Normans. "Staten hook" of the Dutch, 59° 48′ N.

Gabriel Mount, 17. A hill on the Greenland Coast, north of Cape Queen Anne.

Hakluyt Island, 145. Between Whale and Smith Sound, discovered and named by Baffin on July 5th, 1616. *Aypagssuak* of the Eskimo.

Hatclife Mount, 12, 15. Probably a misprint for Huntcliff. A hill so named by Hall in 1612, over Godthaab.

Hope Harbour, 12. The Gilbert Sound of Davis, and Godthaab of the Danes, in 64° 8′ N.

Hope Sanderson, 140, 150. The most northern point of Davis, on June 30th, 1587. Sighted by Baffin on May 30th, 1616. It is 3,300 feet high, in 72° 12′ N.

Horne Sound, 143. So named by Baffin, just north of Cape Shackleton.

Jones Sound, 146, 152. Discovered and named by Baffin, on July 10th, 1616.

King's Fiord, 18, 26; or King Christian's Fiord, named by Hall in 1605.

Lancaster River, 13. A deep fiord opening on Godthaab harbour, named by Hall 1612.

Lancaster Sound, 147. Discovered and named by Baffin, in 74° 20′ N., on July 12th, 1616.

London Coast, 139. Part of the Greenland Coast, so named by Davis.

Queen Anne's Cape, 17. So named by Hall in 1605, after the wife of Christian IV. In 66° 24′ N.

Queen Sophia's Cape, 25. So named by Hall in 1605, after the mother of Christian IV, the Queen Dowager of Denmark. In 67° N.

Ramel's Fiord, 23, 25, 26. So named by Hall in 1605, "Henrick Rommels Fjord". It is the modern harbour of Holsteinborg. The settlement is in 66° 54′ N.

Smith's Sound, 145, 152. Discovered and named by Baffin in July 1616. The entrance is in 78° 12′ N. (Cape Alexander), 78° 22′ N. (Cape Isabella).

Throughgood Island, 18. On the

Greenland Coast, north of Cape Anne, so named by Hall in 1612. Whale Sound, 145, 151, 152. Discovered and named by Baffin in 1616. In 77° 5′ N. Wilkinson Islands, 12. Islands so named by Hall in 1612, off Godthaab.

Wolstenholme Sound, 144, 152. Discovered and named by Baffin on July 3rd, 1616. Women Islands, 141. Discovered and named by Baffin. He gives the latitude 72° 45′ N. They include Upernivik, which is in 72° 48′ N.

VI.

GENERAL INDEX.

Abbas the Great, Shah of Persia, joins with the English to drive the Portuguese out of Ormuz, xliii
Abbot, Archbishop, tutor and friend of Sir Dudley Digges, xii, xiii
Abbott, Sir Maurice. Son of Sir Dudley Digges married to a daughter of, xiv; Inspects Captain Pring's fleet, xxxvii
Adams, Robert, master of the *Bull*, xxxv
Albion, Nova, 158
Albuquerque, Viceroy, occupied Ormuz, xliii
Andrada, Ruy Frere de, commander of the Portuguese fleet, xli
Angelica, 34, 34 (*n.*)
Anian, Fabulous Strait of, 158, 162, 171
Anne, Cape (*see* Queen Anne Cape)
Anne Royal, Baffin, master's mate of, xxxiv; sent to the Red Sea, xxxviii; return home, xxxviii
Annula, ship of the Spitzbergen fleet, 38, 55; homeward bound, 51
Aquatulco, 158
Aristega, Michael de, 63
Ashford, Customer Smith buried at, ii
Assab, Gulf of, Baffin at, in the *Anne Royal*, xxxviii

Baffin, William, his attainments, i; first mention of, xxi; entries of the name in parish registers, xxii; probable origin, xxiii; chief pilot of Hall's ship, xxiii; narrative of the Greenland voyage by xxiv; his narrative of the Spitzbergen voyage, xxvii, 38-53; his second voyage to Spitzbergen, xxviii; takes service with N. W. Company, xxix; Pilot of *Discovery*, xxx; system of keeping logs, xxx; history of 1615 voyage written by, xxxi; facsimile of his map, xxxii; his fifth Arctic voyage, xxxii; loss of the journals and maps, xxxii, xxxiii, l, liv, 155; surveys in the Red Sea and Persian Gulf, xxxviii; return home, xxxviii; appointed master of the *London*, xxxix; reward for surveys, xxxix; in consultation as to route for the fleet, xl; witness to a certificate as to quarrel between two merchants in the *London*, xliii; *resumé* of his voyages, xlvii; his observations, xlviii to l; his geographical discoveries, li; vindication of, lvii; his place as a discoverer, lviii; death of, at Kishm fort, xlv; account of his death, 156

—— his observation for longitude by moon's culmination, 20, 21; his observation for refraction, 51; goes in a shallop to examine the ice off Hakluyt headland, 85; returns, 86; report on the ice, 89; lands on "Red Beach" with Fotherby, 90, 91; climbs a high hill near "Red Beach", 92; examines Sir T. Smith's Inlet, 94; his letter to his employers, 103; his relation of the 1615 voyage, 111; his lunar observations, 122, 123 (*n.*); reasons for relinquishing attempt by Hudson's Strait 132 (*n.*); his opinion concerning a passage, 137; his relation of the fifth voyage, 138-49; letter to Sir John Wolstenholme, 149; reports no passage by Davis Strait, 150; his remarks on tides, 130, 131, 151, 156; on a fishery in Baffin's Bay, 151, 152; on variation, 154; his achievements and qualifications in 1616, xxxiii; desire to attempt discovery from the side of Asia, xxxiv; enters the service of the East India Company, xxxiv; master's mate in the *Anne Royal*, xxxiv; permanent value of his magnetic observations, l; instructions to, in 1616, 174

INDEX.

Baffin, Mrs., her claim on the East India Company, xlvi, xlvii
Baffin Island, named by Parry, xxxii
Baffin's Bay, name of Sir D. Digges, immortalized on coast of, xvi ; discovery by Baffin, xxxiv, 138-155 ; maps of, liv to lvii
Ball, Richard, xvii : adventurer in Hall's Greenland voyage, xxi, 3 ; notice of, 3 (n.)
Ball's river, 13, 34
Bandar, Abbasi, xliv
Barber, Richard, merchant in the London, xxxviii
Barker, Andrew, master of the *Heart's Ease*, xxiv, 13 ; takes command on Hall's death, 24, 26 (n.); account of, 27 (n.)
——— John, merchant in the *London*, xl (n.)
Barrington, Hon. Daines, map of Baffin's Bay, lvi
Barren Cape, xxviii, reached by Baffin, 86, 87, 95, 100
Barrow, Sir John, omission of Baffin's Bay in map to illustrate work of, lvi
Basques. (*See* Biscayans.)
Bays, Assab, xxxviii ; Joseph's, 63, 65 ; Lord Ellesmere's, 65 ; Pooppy, 41, 46, 50 ; Saldanha, xxxvii, xl ; Sea Horse, 49 ; Sir T. Smith's, 51, 56, 59, 60, 85
Bears, 62, 65, 66, 71
Bee. (*See* Ship.)
Beer, scurvy grass boiled in, 148
Bel Sound, 49, 63
Bidborough Manor, inherited by Sir T. Smith, iii
Birds, cuelverduns, 62, 71 ; wild geese, 62, 71 ; partridges (ptarmigan), 17, 71 ; sea pigeons (doveykeys), 71 ; sea parrots (puffins), 71 ; stints, 71 ; willocks (looms), 62, 71, 136
Biscay, ships of, in Spitzbergen, xxvii, 42, 48. (*See* Ships.)
Biscayans (or Biscayners), whale fishers, account of xxv, xxvi, xxvii : rule as to striking a whale, 49 ; whales killed by, on board *Desire*, 49, 59 ; in English ships, 38 (n.), 54 ; "Our whale strikers," 71 ; they call whales of Greenland "Grand Bay Whales," 151
Black-point, 51
Blithe, Captain of the *Hart*, xxxix ; assumes command on death of captain Shilling, xlii ; fleet under, on coast of Arabia, xliii
Blythe. (*See* Blithe.)
Bonner, Thomas, 44, 50, 52, 72 (n).

Boralio, Joam, second in command of Portuguese fleet, xli
Borough, William, on the magnetic needle, 154 (n.)
Bourne, Robert, adviser of Mrs. Baffin, xlvi, xlvii
Bowen, Adam, to copy Baffin's charts, xxxix
Bowles, atlas, map of Baffin's Bay in, lvi
Brigges, Henry, notice of, 156 (n.) ; treatise on a North-west Passage, 160, 169 to 173
Broken Islands, position, 105
——— Point, named, 121 (n.) ; Baffin's lunar taken at, 125 (n.)
Brooke Place, the seat of Sir T. Smith, iii ; sold in 1699, x
Brown, Christopher, Captain of the *Eagle*, xxxix ; removed to the *Roebuck*, xlii
Brun, Hans, in the second Danish Greenland voyage, xix
Bull. (*See* Ship.)
Burnil, Cape, 28
But fish, 19
Button, Sir Thomas, vi ; his voyage, xxix, 134 ; discoveries, 156 ; notice of, 157 (n.), 171
Bylot, Robert, in command of *Discovery*, xxx, xxxii, 111, 138 ; with Hudson, Button, and Gibbons, xxix

Cabot, Sebastian, system of keeping log-books, inaugurated by, xxx
California, found to be an island, 158
Cape, Barren, 86, 87, 95, 100
——— Black Point, 51
——— Broken Point, 121, 125
——— Burnil, 28
——— Cold, 52
——— Comfort, 104, 131, 132, 133
——— Deceit, 99
——— Dudley Digges, xvi, 144
——— Fair Foreland, 40, 51, 59
——— Fair Ness, 121
——— Farewell, 8, 113
——— Hakluyt Headland, 83, 86, 88, 100
——— Hope Sanderson, 140, 150
——— Low Ness, 43
——— Queene Anne, 17
——— Queen Sophia, 28
——— Ras al Had, xliii
——— Sea Horse Point, 105, 135
Carleton, Sir Dudley, with Sir T. Smith, negotiating with Dutch Commissioners, vi
Carlisle, James, Goldsmith in Hall's voyage, 25, 33

INDEX.

Cary, Allwin, ship's husband, 111
—— Islands, liii, lv-lvi, 146
—— Swan's Nest, 157 (n.)
Cavendish, prize taken by, with Juan de Fuca on board, 162, 164
Chacke, Martin, a Portuguese, as to North-west Passage, 160
Chester, Colonel, aid from, in searching for name of Baffin, xxiii
Chichelay, Sir Robert, ancestor of Sir T. Smith, ii
Chilham, home of Sir Dudley Digges, xv, xvi ; subsequent owners of, xv
Christian IV of Denmark, his expeditions to Greenland, xviii, xix ; gives up the Greenland enterprise, xx
Churchill, "Voyages and Travels," Gatonby's narrative of Hall's Greenland voyage in, xxiv
Cibola, 139, 172
Coard, John, slain in action with Portuguese, xli
Cockayne, Sir William, vi, xvii ; notice of, and family, 4 (n.); adventurer in Hall's Greenland voyage, xxi
Cockin Sound, 16 (n.) ; Baffin's observations at, xlviii, 20, 21 ; named after Alderman Cockayne (Cockin), 22 ; *Discovery* in, liii, 148 ; salmon in, 149 ; Baffin's Greenland narrative commences at xxiv
Cod, 19, 71
Cold Cape, Spitzbergen, 52
Colebrookes, owners of Chilham, xv
Colepeppers of Leeds Castle, iii
Comfort, Land of, 10 (n.)
—————— Cape, position, 104 ; named, 131 ; at anchor near, 132, 133
Cooper, Master, 49
Coronado, Vasco de, 159
Corpo Santo seen, 102
Cove, Nicke's, 41, 46
Cowles, Thomas (mariner), evidence as to North-west Passage, 160
Crispe, Nicholas, power of the *London*, xl
Cromwell, family, kinship with Sir T. Smith, ii (n.)
Cross Road, Spitzbergen, 85
Cudner, Master, 52
Cuelverduns, birds in Spitzbergen, 62, 71
Cullen, Viscount, title of the Cockayne family, 4 (n.) See Cockayne
Cumberland Isles, 147
Cunningham, John, General of the Danish Greenland expedition, xviii
—————— Mount, xviii, 18
—————— Fiord, xx, 23

Danish voyages to Greenland, xviii, xix ; manuscript accounts of, first printed by Pingel, xix (n.)
D'Anville, map of Baffin Bay, lvi
David, Walter, slain in action with Portuguese, xlii
Davis, John, inlets seen by, xxix ; named Cape Farewell, 8 ; "London Coast" of, 139 ; his furthest at Hope Sanderson, 140 ; not to be blamed for believing in a passage, 150
—— Strait, 114, 137, 139 ; Baffin on a passage by, 150, 174
Deceit Point, named by Fotherby, 99
Declination of the needle (or Dip), 39, 44
Denmark Haven, 18
Deptford, house of Sir T. Smith at, iii ; burnt, vi
Dermer, Master, 159
Desire, ship in Spitzbergen fleet, 38, 41, 42, 45, 81, 82, 84 ; Basques on board, 49 ; homeward bound, 67
Desolation land sighted, 9, 174
De Wit, Atlas, map of Baffin's Bay in, lv
Digges, Sir Dudley, ancestry, x ; birth, xi ; embassies, xii, xiii ; parliamentary life, xiii ; marriage and children, xiv ; death, xiv ; home at Chilham, xv ; monument, xvi ; director of North-West Company, xxix ; Baffin's letter to, 109, xxxi ; Not discouraged by failure of Captain Gibbon's, 111 ; adventurer in expedition of, 1616, xxxii, 138
—— Cape, lii, lv, 144
—— Island, position, 105, 136 ; Button at, 157, (n.)
—— Leonard, his works, x, xi
—— Thomas, father of Sir Dudley, xi
—— West, xiv
Dip of the magnetic needle, xlviii, 39, 44
Discovery, Hudson's ship, xxix ; Ingram's ship in Button's expedition, 157, (n.) ; Bylot and Baffin in 1615 ; liii, 111 ; sails, 111 ; in 1616, xxxii, 138 ; illness on board, 148 ; return of, 149
Dogs, Eskimo, 35, 118, 142
Dolphin. (See Ships.)
Dovekeys, or sea pigeons, 71
Drake, Sir Francis, his discoveries do not show that America extends north-west, 158
Dunkirk ships in Greenland, 40, 42
Dutch ships at Spitzbergen, 41, 48, 64 ; two appointed for discovery, 95 ;

INDEX. 185

possession of land taken by, 98; homeward bound, 95

Eagle. (*See* Ships.)
East India Company. (*See* Sir. T. Smith.) Baffin enters service of, xxxiv; arrangements of fleet, xxxv
Edge, Master, in Bel Sound, 49, 50
Elizabeth, Princess, fleet returning from taking her to Holland, salute, 55
Ellesmere, Lord, bay of, 65
Ephemeris. (*See* Origanus, Searle)
Eskimo, seized by Danes, xx; intercourse with Hall's ships, 13; murder of one of Hall's men by, 14; murder of Hall by, 24; Baffin's account of, 35; in Hudson's Strait, 117, 118; description of dogs, 35, 118, 142; at Woman Islands, 140, 141; their religion, 36, 141; kayaks, 28 *n.*, 35; umiaks, 36; burials, 36

Fairfax, Lady, sister married John Wolstenholme, xvii
Fair Foreland, 40, 51, 59
—— Haven, 50, 83, 86, 88, 91, 95
—— Ness, 121
Fanshaw, Sir H. and J., married sisters of Sir T. Smith, iii
Farewell, Cape, 8, (*n.*); 113
Fiords, Cunningham, 23; King's, 18, 26; Ramel's, 23, 25, 26
Fish, But fish, 19; cod, 19, 71; musk fish, 19; salmon, 36, 71; salmon trout, 18, 19; salmon peel, 148
Fisher, Thomas, 42
Fleets, East India, officers, xxxv; inspection, xxxvii
Fopp, captain of a Dunkirker, 42, 43
Foreland. (*See* Fair Foreland.)
Fotherby, Robert, narrative of 1613 Spitzbergen voyage by, xxvii, 54, (*n.*), 54-79; narrative of 1614 Spitzbergen voyage by, xxviii, xlix, 80-102; account, of and family, 80, (*n.*); exploring north coast of Spitzbergen with Baffin, 90, 91, 92, 94, 96; rides from Yarmouth to London, 68
Fox, Luke, his circumpolar map, liv; notice of, liv (*n.*).
Fox, 18, 35, 62, 71
Friesland, 6 (*n.*)
Frobisher, Sir Martin, 152, 159
Fuca, Juan de, discoveries by, 161, 162; offer to discover the Northwest Passage, 164; correspondence with Michael Lok, 165; death, 167

Gabriel, Mount, 17
Gali, Francisco de, 158, 172
Gamaliel, ship of the Spitzbergen fleet, 38, 41, 42, 45, 51, 55, 86, 88, 91.
Gatonby, John, his dedication to Sir C. Hildyard, 1, 126 (*n.*), 27; quartermaster in the *Patience*, xxiv
Gatonby, Nicholas, 2 (*n.*)
Gaule, Francis. (*See* Gali.)
Gemma Frisius, on finding longitude by lunar distance, xlix
Gibbons, Captain, nothing performed by, xxx, 111
Gilbert Sound, 12 (*n.*)
Gilbert, Dr., on the magnetic needle, 145 (*marg. n.*), 154 (*n.*)
Gilliflower, a Scotch vessel in the Danish Greenland voyages, xix; Hall on board, xx
Glacier in Spitzbergen, description of, 66
Gombroon, xliv
Goose, wild, 62, 71
Gordon, William, master's mate in the *Patience*, 26 (*n.*), 52
Gracechurch Street, Sir T. Smith's house in, iii
Grampus, 7
Grand, Henry, slain in Portuguese action off Jáshak, xli
Green, Mr., master's mate of the *Mathew*, death of, 68
Green Harbour, Spitzbergen, 41, 45, 46, 49, 59, 65
Greenland, xxxiii; sighted, 5; Baffin's description of, 33; vegetation, 34; Angelica, found in, 34; scurvy grass, sorrel, and orpen, 148; animals, 35; inhabitants, 13, 14, 34, 35; 140, 141; sighted in 1615, 113; in 1616, 139. (*See* Eskimo.)
Greenland, Spitzbergen, so called by a mistake of Hudson, Pool, and others, 69, 38 (*n.*)
Guipuzcoa, whaling, ports in, xxvi. (*See* San Sebastian).
Guillemots. (*See* Willocks.)
Gulls, 71
Guy, Edwyn, purser's mate in the *London*, xl (*n.*)

Hakluyt, materials supplied to, by Sir T. Smith, vii
—— Headland, li; 83, 16, 100. Taken possession of for King James, 88
—— Island, liii; 145
Hall, James; in the Danish voyages to Greenland, xviii, xix, xx; returns to England, xx; his MS. report in

the British Museum, xxi (n.); commands the Hull Greenland expedition, xxi, 3; his rules for traffic with Eskimo, 15; goes on board the *Heart's Ease*, to explore, 22; murdered by Eskimo, 24; cause of his murder, xx; his burial, 25

Hambledon, Robert, master's mate; struck two whales, 88

Hansteen, Professor; use of Baffin's magnetic observations by, l, 155 (n.)

Harbours; Denmark Haven, 18; Green, 41, 45, 46, 48, 59, 65, 67; Hope, 12; Trinity, 86; Fair Haven, 50, 83, 86, 89, 91, 95

Hardy, Charles Stewart, owner of Chilham, xv

Hares, 35

Hart. (*See* Ships.)

Hatch, John, master of the *Bee*, xxxv; his journal of the voyage, xxxvii

Hatcliffe, Mount, 12, 15. (*See* Huntcliff)

Havens. (*See* Harbours.)

Haywood, Sir Rowland, Lord Mayor, married a sister of Sir T. Smith, iii

Heart's Ease, Vice Admiral; ship in Hall's Greenland voyage, xxi, 3; Hall goes on board to explore further N., 22; W. Huntriss made master of, 32 (n.); parts company with *Patience*, 32; arrives in the Thames, 32 (n.); in Spitzbergen, 93, 96, 99, 100

Hemsley, or Hemstay, John, master's mate in the *Patience*, 10, 26 (n.)

Henry. (*See* Prince Henry of Wales.)

Herbert, master in the *Discovery*, 1616; illness, 148

Herons, owners of Chilham, xv

Hexham; edition of *Hondius*; map of Baffin Bay in, lv

Heynes, Edward, merchant in the *London*, xxxviii; his journal of the voyage, xxxvii (n.)

Hildyard, Sir Christopher, of Winestead; dedication to, xxiv, i; notice of, i (n.)

Hinlopen Strait; same as Sir Thomas Smith's Inlet, xxviii, li

Hollanders. (*See* Dutch.)

Holstenborg, xviii

Hondius; his map of Baffin's Bay, lv

Hood, Dr.; lectures on navigation at Sir T. Smith's house, vii

Hope, harbour of; same as Godthaab, 12, 12 (n.)

Hope Sanderson, lii, 140, 150

Horne Sound, Spitzbergen, 39, 43

Horne Sound, Greenland, 143

Hubbard, Josiah; in third Danish Greenland voyage, xx, 157

Hubbert's Hope, 157

Hudson, Henry, vi; voyage to Spitzbergen, xxv; last voyage, xxix, 170, 171

Hudson's Bay, west side, discovered by Button, 157

Hudson's Strait, 137, 157 (n.); examined by Baffin, xxxi, xxxiii, xlix

Hull, Hall's Greenland expedition fitted out at, xxi; sails from, 4; return of the *Patience* to, 33; men of, on the north coast of Spitzbergen in 1612, 90, 93; James Hall, a native of, xviii; Gatonby and Barker, natives of, 2 (n.), 27 (n.). (*See* Marmaduke.)

Huntriss, William, Hall's boy, xxi, 24 (n.), 27; master's mate of the *Patience*, xxiv; account of, 27 (n.); commands the *Heart's Ease*, 32 (n.)

Ice Sound, Spitzbergen, 48, 60

Ice, along southern shore of Greenland, 12 (n.); Spitzbergen fleet beset in the, 81; Baffin and Fotherby in danger from, 94; Fotherby stopped by, 97; examination of, by Baffin, to the north of Spitzbergen, 85, 86, 89, 90, 91, 92; formation of at sea, 97; in Baffin's Bay, 153

Ingram, Captain of *Discovery*, under Sir T. Button, 157 (n.)

Inlet, Sir Thomas Smith's, 94, 97, 100

Islands, Cary, 146
—— Cumberland, 147
—— Digges, 105, 136
—— Hakluyt, 145
—— Lizet's, 48
—— Mansel's, 158 (n.)
—— Masirah, xliii
—— Mill, 128
—— Nottingham, 105, 130, 133, 134, 135
—— Prince Charles, 40 (n.), 57, 84
—— Resolution, 105, 113, 114, 115, 116, 137
—— Saddle, 87
—— Salisbury, 127, 135
—— Savage, 105, 117, 120
—— Swan, 135
—— Throughgood, 18
—— Wilkinson's, 12
—— Women, 141

Jacques, ship of Bordeaux, 60

James Island; on D'Anville's map, lvi

INDEX.   187

James I, King, knights Sir T. Smith, iv ; names the *Trade's Increase*, iv ; his special wish that Sir T. Smith should continue Governor of the East India Company, vi ; knights Sir John Wolstenholme, xvii ; Hall presents a report to, xxi ; knights Sir W. Cockayne, 4 (*n.*)

Jáshak, fight with Portuguese off, xl, xli ; burial of Captain Shilling at, xlii

Jefferies, Robert, merchant in the *London*, xl (*n.*); insulted by Mr. Monox, xliii

Jennison, Archibald, master mate of the *London*, his journal, xl (*n.*)

John and Francis, ship of Spitzbergen fleet, 38, 46, 55, 84 ; homeward bound, 51

Jonas. (*See* Ships.)

Jones, Alderman Sir Francis, i, v, vi ; account of, x ; not discouraged by failure of Captain Gibbons, 111 ; set forth Baffin's expedition, xxxii, 138

Jones Sound, liii, 146 ; morses in, 152

Joseph, Benjamin, general of two Spitzbergen voyages, xxvii, xxviii, 38 (*n.*), 40, 55, 81

Joseph Bay, 63, 65

Judd, Sir Andrew, godfather of Sir J. Smith, ii

Kathen, a pinnace commanded by John Knight in the Danish voyage to Greenland, xviii, xix

Kayak, descriptive of, 28 (*n.*), 35

Kempe, Mary, heiress of Chilham, wife of Sir Dudley Digges, xv

King James, his Newland, or Spitzbergen, possession taken of, 86, 88, 89, 92, 93

King's Fiord, 18, 26

Kishm Fort at, xliv ; death of Baffin at, xlv

Knight, John, in the Danish voyage to Greenland, xviii ; narrative of the expedition in which he perished, xix

Lancaster, Sir James, i, v, xvii ; notice of 3 (*n.*); adventurer in Hall's Greenland voyage, xxi

Lancaster River, 13

Lancaster Sound, liii, 147

Leeds Castle, owned by a brother of Sir T. Smith, whose heirs sold it to the Colepeppers, iii

Limejuice as a cure for scurvy, xxxvi

Lion. (*See* Ships.)

Lindenov, Godske, commander of the *Loven*, in the Danish voyage to Greenland, xviii ; in the *Trost*, xix

Lizet's Islands, Spitzbergen, 48

Loaysa, Don Garcia de, reported to have gone from Labrador to the Moluccas, 159

Lok Michael, as to a North-west Passage, 160 ; information obtained from Juan de Fuca by, 162 to 168

Log Books, system of keeping, xxx ; of East India voyages, xxxvii (*n.*), xl (*n.*)

London, Baffin, master of, xxxix ; sails from Gravesend, xl ; fight with the Portuguese, xli ; at London's Hope, xliii ; in the Ormuz business, xliv ; anchored in port of Súr, xliii

"London's Hope," the port of Súr, xliii

London Coast, of Davis, 139

Longitude, Baffin's observations by moon's culmination, xlviii, 20, 21, 124 ; by lunar observation, 122, 123

Lord Ellesmere's Bay, 65

Loven, ship in Danish Greenland voyages, xviii, xix

Low Ness, 43

Low Sound, 43

Lunar Observation of Baffin, xlix, 122, 123

Madagascar, consultation as to the route of the fleet round, xl

Magdalena Bay, Spitzbergen. (*See* Maudlin Sound.)

Magnetic Needle. (*See* Borough, Gilbert, Hansteen, Norman, Dip, Variation.)

Maltebrun Atlas, map of Baffin's Bay in, lvi

Mammalia, bears, 62, 65, 71 ; dogs, 35, 118, 142 ; foxes, 18, 35, 62, 71 ; grampus, 7 ; hares, 35 ; morses, 36, 47, 48, 61, 62, 71, 78, 133, 146, 152 ; reindeer, 35, 47, 57, 62, 70, 71 ; seals, 35, 36, 61, 71 ; unicorns, 17, 71, 143, 152 ; whales, 7, 46, 47, 49, 59, 71, 72, 73, 78, 88, 99, 139, 143, 144, 151, 152 ; white, 71

Mansel Isles, discovered by Baffin, 158 (*n.*)

Marmaduke, Captain, of Hull, 50 (*n.*), 60, 61, 72 (*n.*), 93, 99

Mary Ann Sarah, ship in Spitzbergen fleet, 82

Mary Margaret, 84

Mason, John, 49 ; master of *Gamaliel*, 86, 88, 91, 99

Marston Moor, Henry Wolstenholme slain at, xvii

188 INDEX.

Masirah Isle, East India Company's ships at, xliii

Mathew, vice-admiral, Spitzbergen fleet, 38, 48, 55, 62; freight of, 63; homeward bound, 67

Maudlin Sound, Spitzbergen, 83, 84; Trinity Harbour in, 86

Melville Bay, lii

Mendocino Cape, 172

Mercator, Gerardus, 172

Merchant Adventurers, notices of, i, ii to xvii

Mica, xx, 25

Michael de Aristega, ship of St. Jean de Luz, on Spitzbergen coast, 60

Mill Island, Hudson Strait, 128

Mináb in Persian Gulf, English fleet at, xliv

Mocha, Firman for English to trade at, obtained by Captain Shilling, xxxviii

Moll's Atlas, map of Baffin's Bay in, lv

Monox, Edward, merchant in the *London*, xl (*n.*); quarrel with Mr. Jefferies, xliii; his report on the Ormuz business, xlv (*n.*)

Morses, 36, 47, 48, 61; slaughter of, 62; in Spitzbergen, 71; account of, 78; in Hudson Strait, 133; in Jones Sound, 146, 152

Mountjoy, Lord, ix

Mounts, Cunningham, 18; Gabriel, 17; Hatclife, 12, 15

Muscovy Company, iii; Baffin serves under, xxv; voyages sent to the north by, xxv; system of keeping log-books, xxx

Muscovie Fludd, or mica, 25

Musk Fish, 19

Narwhals (or Unicorns), 13, 17, 71, 143, 152

Nelson, Port, in Hudson's Bay, xxx, 157; where Button wintered, 157 (*n.*)

New Year's Gift. (*See* Ships.)

Nicke's Cove, Spitzbergen, 41, 46

Nolk, Andres, in the second Danish Greenland expedition, xix

Norman, Robert, his "new attractive", 154

North-West Passage, Sir T. Smith's advocacy of search for, v; company for the discovery of, v, xxix; opinion of Baffin as to passage by Hudson Strait, 132 (*n.*), 137; Baffin's opinion as to passage by Davis Strait, 150; brief discourse on, 155-60; reported to have been made by a Spanish admiral, 159; Button's opinion, xxx. (*See* Cowles, Frobisher, Lok.)

Nostell Priory, owned by Sir J. Wolstenholme, xvii

Nottingham Island, position, 105; standing for, 130, 133, 134, 135

Nova Albion, 158

Observations. (*See* Longitude, Lunars, Dip, Tides, Variation, Refraction, Quadrant.)

Okely, Edmund, wounded in action with Portuguese, xli

Oman Coast, xliii

Ores, mica mistaken for, xx, 25

Origanus, Ephemeris of, 124, 125

Ormuz business, death of Baffin in, 156; combined Persian and English attack on, xliii, xlv (*n.*); English fleet anchored off, xliv; accounts of the operations at, xlv (*n.*).

Ornen, ship in second Danish Greenland voyage, xix

Orpen, plant in Greenland, cure for scurvy, 148

Padstow, *Discovery* puts into, 112

Parry, Sir Edward, notes on Baffin's work in Hudson's Strait, xxxi, lii, 125, 131, 132; names Baffin's Island, xxxii

Partridges (ptarmigan), 17, 71

Passe, Simon, the engraver, portrait of Sir T. Smith by, viii, ix

Patience, Captain Hall's ship in the Greenland voyage of 1612, xxi, 3, 23, 25, 26, 27; Return to Hull, 33

Penkewill, Mr. Richard, of Padstow, his kindness to the crew of the *Discovery*, 112

Persian Gulf, Baffin's surveys in, xxxviii. (*See* Kishm, Ormuz.)

Petermann, Dr., his error in supposing that Baffin sighted Franz Josef Land, li

Philpot Lane, Sir T. Smith's house in, iii

Pigeons, Sea. (*See* Dovekeys.)

Pinder, W., his letter on the taking of Ormuz in Purchas, xlv (*n.*)

Plants, angelica, 34; scurvy grass, 148; sorrel, 148; orpen (*sedum*), 148; white moss, 70; crowberry, 34; dwarf birch, 34; saxifrage, 70

Poole, Jonas, voyages to Spitzbergen, xxv, 39 (*n.*), 47 (*n.*); murder of, xxv

Pooppy Bay, Spitzbergen, 41, 46, 50

Portuguese off Jáshak, fight with, xli; Persians and English combine to drive them out of Ormuz, xliii; besieged at Kishm, xliv

INDEX. 189

Prestwood, Lawrence, 93
Pricket, Abacuk, his account of Hudson's last voyage, xxix
Prince Charles Island, Spitzbergen, 40 (*n.*), 57, 84
Prince Henry of Wales, his instructions to Sir T. Button, xxix ; death, xxix (*n.*)
Pring, Captain Martin, commands 7th Joint Stock East India Company's voyage, xxxiv ; sails and arrives at Saldanha Bay, xxxvii
Prosperous, ship in Spitzbergen fleet, 81, 82, 85
Ptarmigan, 17, 71
Puffins (*see* Parrots), 71
Pringel, C., accounts of Danish voyages to Greenland, published by, xix (*n.*)
Pullay, James, one of Hall's men murdered by Eskimo at Godthaab, 14, 15
Purchas, Rev. Samuel, materials supplied to by Sir T. Smith, vii ; neglect to print Hall's third Danish voyage, xx ; Baffin's Greenland narrative published by, xxiv ; Baffin's Spitzbergen narrative given by, xxviii ; collation of 1615 voyage published by, with MS. in British Museum, xxxi ; his conduct in not printing Baffin's journals and maps of the 1616 voyage, xxxii, xxxiii, l, liv

Quadrant, Baffin's, 44
Queen Anne's Cape, xviii, 17
Queen Sophia's Cape, xxiii, xx, 25
Queenborough, Spitzbergen, fleet sails from, 38, 55
Queenhithe, Baffin probably lived near, xxiii
Quinira, 158, 172

Ramel's Fiord, 23, 25, 26
Ras al Had, xliii
Red Beach, Spitzbergen, 90, 91, 92, 96, 97
Red Sea, the *London* sent to, xxxviii ; Captain Blithe ordered to, xliii ; Baffin's surveys in, xxxviii, xxxix
Refraction of the sun, Baffin's observation, xlviii, xlix, 51
Reindeer in Spitzbergen, account of chase of, 57, 58 ; food, 70, 71, 35, 47, 62
Resolution Island, position, 105, 113 ; sighted, 115 ; at anchor off, 116, 137 ; description of, 117 ; tide at, 116, 119

Resolution, Sir T. Button's ship, xxix, 157 (*n.*)
Richard and Barnard, ship of Spitzbergen fleet, 38, 41, 48, 55 ; homeward bound, 63
Richardson, Corsten, in second Danish Greenland voyage, xix ; commands third Danish voyage, xx
Roads, Cross, 85 ; Swalley, xxxviii, xl
Robinson, Peter, wounded in Portuguese action off Jáshak, xli
Rochelle, ship of, at Spitzbergen, 41, 43
Roe, Sir Thomas, draws up instructions for Captain Shilling in Red Sea, xxxviii
Roebuck. (*See* Ships.)
Ross, Sir John, on Baffin's accuracy, lii, lvii
Rosselgate. (*See* Ras al Had.)
Royal James. (*See* Ships.)
Rudston, Master, 127
Rundall, Mr., editor of MS. of Baffin's 1615 voyage, xxxi, 113 (*n.*)

Saccharissa (Lady Dorothy Sydney), x (*n.*)
Saddle Island, Spitzbergen, 87
St. Jean de Luz, ships from, at Spitzbergen, xxvi, 40, 63, 65
St. Lawrence Island. (*See* Madagascar.)
St. Margaret's (Westminster), name of Baffin in parish registers, xxii
St. Thomas (Apostle) Vintry Ward ; name of Baffin in parish register, xxiii
Salads for scurvy, 148
Salbank, Joseph, merchant in the *London*, xxxviii
Saldanha Bay, Captain Pring's fleet at, xxxvii, xl
Salisbury Island sighted, 127, 135
Sallowes, Allen, 40, 42
Salmon, 36, 71
Salmon peele, 148
Salmon trout, 18, 19
Salmon, Nathaniel, master of the *New Year's Gift*, xxxv
San Sebastian whale fishery, xxvi
Sanderson's Hope. (*See* Hope Sanderson.)
Savage, or Salvage Isles ; position, 105, 117, 120 ; tide at, 120
Scarborough, W. Huntriss a native of, xxi
Scout-nes, variation at, 39
Scurvy in East India ships, xxxv, xxxvi ; cures and preventives, xxxvi
—— on board *Discovery*, 148 ; cures for, 148

Scurvy grass, 148
Sea Horse Bay, Spitzbergen, 49
—————— Point ; position, 105, 135
Sea Horse, ship of Spitzbergen fleet, 38
Sea Parrots. (See Puffins.)
Sea Pigeons. (See Dovekeys.)
Sea Unicorns. (See Narwhals.)
Seals, 35, 36, 61, 71
Searle's Ephemeris, 124 (n.)
Shackleton Cape, lii
Sherin, Thomas, master of the Mathew, 45 ; of the Thomasine, 81, 89, 99
Shilling, Captain Andrew, commands the Anne Royal, xxxiv ; sent to the Red Sea, xxxviii ; obtains a firman for English to trade at Mocha, xxxviii ; appointed General of the fleet, xxxix ; fight with Portuguese, xli ; death and burial, xlii
Ships, foreign, fishing in Spitzbergen waters; treatment of, xxvii, 40, 41, 42, 43, 44, 48, 49, 60, 63; Dutch, 95 ; ship of St. Jean de Luz, with leave from the Company to fish, 40; Dunkirk ships; Claes, Martin, and Fopp, masters, 41 ; foreign ships in Pooppy Bay, 41 ; ship of Biscay, 42; Rocheller and Biscayner to depart, 42, 60 ; all depart, 43 ; a Holland ship resisted, and was seized, 44 ; two Biscayners agree to go, 46, 47 ; a great ship of Biscay, and two Dutch, 48, 63, 65 ; two Rochellers ducked at the yard-arm, 49
—— Arctic, Annula, 38, 51, 55
—————— Desire, 38, 41, 42, 45, 49, 67, 81, 82, 84
—————— Discovery, xxix, xxx, xxxii, 111, 138, 148, 149
—————— Gamaliel, 38, 41, 42, 45, 51, 55, 86, 88, 91
—————— Gilliflower, xix, xx
—————— Heart's Ease, xxiii, xxiv, 3, 22, 32, 93, 96, 99, 100
—————— Jacques, 60
—————— John and Francis, 38, 46, 51, 55, 84
—————— Kathen, xviii, xix, xx
—————— Loven, xviii, xix
—————— Mary and Sarah, 82
—————— Mary Margaret, 84
—————— Mathew, 35, 48, 55, 62, 63, 67
—————— Ornen, xix
—————— Patience, xxiii. 3, 23, 25, 26, 27, 33
—————— Prosperous, 81, 82, 85
—————— Richard and Barnard, 38, 41, 48, 55, 63
—————— Resolution, xx (n.), xxix

Ships, Arctic, Thomasine, xxviii, 80, 81
—————— Tiger, xxvii, 38, 48, 51, 55, 60
—————— Trost, xviii, xix
—— East Indian, Anne Royal, xxxiv, xxxviii
—————— Bee, xxxv.
—————— Bull, xxxv
—————— Dolphin, xliv
—————— Eagle, xxxix, xl
—————— Hart, xxxix, xl, xliii
—————— Jonas, xliv
—————— Lion, xliv
—————— London, xxxix, xl, xli, xlii, xliii, xliv
—————— New Year's Gift, xxxiv
—————— Roebuck, xxxix, xl, xliii
—————— Royal James, vxxiv
—————— Trade's Increase, iv
—————— Whale, xliv
Silvator, Pierce de, captain of the Jacques, 60
Spencer, master's mate of Mathew, 45
Sorrell, cure for scurvy, 148
Southampton Isle, west coast of, examined by Baffin, xxxi
Smith, Sir John, married a daughter of "Stella", ix
—— Simon, brother of Sir Thomas, ii
—— Sir Thomas, i ; his parentage, ii ; his brothers, ii ; his inheritance, iii ; director of the Muscovy Company, iii ; knighted and governor of the East India Company, iv ; embassy to Muscovy, iv ; advocacy of Arctic discovery, v ; retirement, vi ; death, vii ; epitaph, viii ; portrait, ix ; marriage and children, ix ; adventurer in Hall's Greenland voyage, xxi, 3 ; director of the North-west Company, xxix; Baffin's letter to, 103, xxxi ; not discouraged by failure of Captain Gibbons, 111 ; adventurer in 1616 expedition, xxxii, 138 ; his last descendants, x (n.) ; inspects East India fleets, xxxvii
—— Thomas, of Westenhanger, ii ;
—— Thomas, ancestor of Viscounts Strangford, ii. (See Smythe.)
Smith, Sir Thomas, Bay, 51, 56, 59, 60, 63, 85
—————— Inlet, xxviii, 94, 97, 100
—————— Sound, 145, 152 ; variation in, 145 ; whales in, 152
Smythes, Viscounts Strangford, ii
Smythe, Chief Baron, last descendant of Sir Thomas Smith, ix (n.)
Sophia Cape. (See Queen Sophia.)
Sounds, Bell, 49, 63 ; Cockin, 16, 20,

21, 22, 148, 149; Horn, 39, 43; Ice, 48, 60; Jones, 146, 152; Lancaster, 147; Low, 43; Maudlin, 83, 84; Red Cliff, 91, 96; Smith's, 145, 152; Wiche's, 92, 94; Wolstenholme, 144, 152

Spitzbergen, voyages to, sent by the Muscovy Company, xxv; fleet of 1613, 38; treatment of foreign ships at, 40, 41, 43, 44, 48, 49, 60, 95; glacier at, 66; position, 69; climate, 70; fleet of 1614, 81; discoveries along north shore, xxviii, xxxiii, 89, 90, 91, 92, 94

Stanmore Church, built by Sir J. Wolstenholme, xvii; burial place of his family, xvii

"Stella", Lady Rich, ix

Stints, 71

Stone, William, vi

Strangford, eighth Viscount, the eminent geographer descended from a brother of Sir T. Smith, ii

Strangford, Viscounts, ii

Súr, Port, on Omân coast, *London* anchored in, xliii; account of, xliii (*n*.)

Surat, Captain Pring's fleet arrives at, xxxvii

Surgeon's Mate, book dedicated to Sir T. Smith, i, x; account of, xxxvi (*n*.)

Sutton-at-Hone in Kent; residence of Sir T. Smith, iii; epitaph to, in the church, vii

Swally Roads, xxxviii, xl

Swan Island, 135

Swan, Richard, captain of the *Roebuck*, xxxix; his account of the fight with the Portuguese, xli; his journal, xl (*n*.); removed to the *Hart*, xlii

Sydney, Sir Philip, his "Stella's" daughters marry sons of Sir T. Smith, ix

—— Lady Dorothy ("Saccharissa") married a grandson of Sir T. Smith x (*n*.)

Symonds, Bartholomew, surgeon of the *London*, xl

Taylor, Thomas, master of the *Eagle*, xlii

Thomas Bonaventure, ship in the Spitzbergen fleet, 85

Thomasine, Baffin's ship in the Spitzbergen fleet of 1614, xxviii, 80, 81

Thompson, J. Atlas. Map of Baffin's Bay in, lvi

Throughgood, Island, 18

Tides, Parry's remarks on Baffin's observations on, xxxi; at Savage Isles, 120; at Resolution Isle, 116, 119; in Hudson's Strait, 130, 133, 156, 157; at Cape Comfort, 132; in Baffin's Bay, 139, 151

Tiger. Admiral, in Spitzbergen fleet of, 1613, xxvii, 38, 48, 55, 60; homebound, 51

Trades Increase, largest merchant ship ever built, iv

Trinity Harbour, Spitzbergen, 86

Trost, Danish ship, on board of which Hall was pilot in the Greenland voyages, xviii, xix

Unicorn. (*See* Narwhal.)

Van Keulen's map of Baffin's Bay, lv

Variation of compass in Spitzbergen, 69; in Cockin Sound, 32; Ramel's Fiord, 26, 29, 30, 52, 53; Scout-nes, 39; Horn Sound, 44; Green Harbour, 50; Maudlin Sound, 86; Smith Sound, l, 145, 154; Wolstenholme Sound, 154; Baffin's observations, xlviii, xlix

Vere, Lord, Henry Wolstenholme slain while serving under, xvii

Virginia, colony of, 169

Vischer, atlas, map of Baffin Bay in, lv

Vogelsang, li, same as Cape Barren (which see)

Walrus. (*See* Morse.)

Wayman, Richard, cook of *Discovery*, his death, 148

Wellsted, Lieut. I. N., his account of the port of Súr, xliii (*n*.)

Werner, on finding longitude by lunar distance, xlix

Westenhanger, estate of the Smythes in Kent, ii

Weymouth, Captain, expedition of, v

Whale, Biscayan, xxvi; right, 7; first killed in 1613, 40; man slain in attack on, 46, 47; killed in Ice Sound, 49; rule of the Basques, 49; killed by the Basques, 59; in Spitzbergen, 71; manner of killing, 72, 73, 74; flensing, 76; boiling down, 76; whalebone called fins, 77; in Fair Haven, 88, 91; raising a sunken whale, 99; flensing a dead whale, 139; in Baffin's Bay, report of Baffin, 151; prospect of a fishery in Baffin's Bay, 153

—— Sound, liii, 144, 152; whales in, 151

—— White, 71

Whale. (*See* Ships.)
Wiches Sound, xxviii, 92. (*See* Wyche.)
Wiide Bay, reached by Baffin, li
Wildmans, owners of Chilham, xv
Wilkinson, Mr., merchant of the venturers in Hall's Greenland voyage, 15 ; in conference as to returning home, 26
────── Thomas, master's mate of *Mathew*, 62
────── Islands, 12
Willocks (guillemots), 62, 71, 136
Wilmot, John, master's mate, on a shooting expedition with Fotherby, 57
Wilson, T., his account of the taking of Ormuz, in Purchas, xlv (*n.*)
Winestead, seat of Sir C. Hildyard, 1 (*n.*)
Wolstenholme, Sir John, i, xvi ; account of family, xvii ; burials of the family in Stanmore Church, xvii ; Baffin's letter to, v, xxxi, 103 ; not discouraged by failure of Captain Gibbons, 111 ; the younger Sir John goes on board the *Discovery*, xxxii, 111 ; set forth expedition of 1616, xxxii, 138 ; Baffin's letter to, xxxiii, 149 ; to negotiate with Mrs. Baffin as to her claim, xlvi
Wolstenholme Sound, lii, 144, 152 ; variation in, 154
Women Islands of Baffin, lii, liii, 141
Woodcock, Master, 46, 85 (*n.*)
Woolhouse, John, chaplain of the *London*, xl (*n.*)
Wright, Edward, lectures on navigation at Sir T. Smith's house, vii
Wyche, Richard, vi